Transforming Masculinities

Men, cultures, bodies, power, sex and love

Victor J. Seidler

Routledge
Taylor & Francis Group

LONDON AND NEW YORK

First published 2006
by Routledge
2 Park Square, Milton Park, Abingdon, Oxon, OX14 4RN

Simultaneously published in the USA and Canada
by Routledge
270 Madison Avenue, New York, NY 10016

Routledge is an imprint of the Taylor & Francis Group

Transferred to Digital Printing 2009

© 2006 Victor J. Seidler

Typeset in Sabon
by Keyword Group

British Library Cataloguing in Publication Data
A catalogue record for this book is available from the British Library

Library of Congress Cataloging in Publication Data
Seidler, Victor J., 1945–
   Transforming masculinities: men, cultures, bodies, power,
sex, and love/Victor J. Seidler.
      p.cm.
Includes bibliographical references and index.
1. Men – Social conditions. 2. Men – Psychology. 3. Men – Identity.
4. Masculinity. 5. Sex role. I. Title.
HQ1090.S444 2005
305.31–dc22   2005002733

ISBN10: 0-415-37073-6 (hbk)
ISBN10: 0-415-37074-4 (pbk)

ISBN13: 978-0-415-37073-8 (hbk)
ISBN13: 978-0-415-37074-5 (pbk)

Publisher's Note
The publisher has gone to great lengths to ensure the quality of this reprint
but points out that some imperfections in the original may be apparent.

For Anna, and for Daniel and Lily

Contents

'Choose Life!' is the great legacy of the Hebrew Bible....
However, life is not a thing, static and final. Life means living,
and in living you have to choose a road, direction, goals.
Pragmatists who believe that life itself can provide us with the
criteria for truth overlook the fact that forces of suicide and
destruction are also inherent in life.

The essence of living as a human being is being challenged,
being tempted, being called. We pray for wisdom, for laws of
knowing how to respond to our being challenged. Living is not
enough by itself. Just to be is a blessing. Just to live is holy. And
yet, being alive is no answer to the problems of living. To be or
not to be is *not* the question. The vital question is: how to be
and how not to be.

A.J. Heschel

Preface and acknowledgements

Naming

Can men change? Why has it taken so long for men to respond to the challenges of feminism for more equal and loving relationships? Traditionally feminism was concerned with claims for equal rights, for equal opportunities to compete for careers, jobs and professions as well as representations with the political sphere from which they had been excluded. This was not to challenge the masculinist terms of the public sphere that had been presented within modernity as a realm of reason which a dominant masculinity alone could take for granted. Women were positioned as having to constantly prove that they were rational, because they were deemed to be 'closer to nature' and thereby more influenced by their emotions, feelings and desires. Liberal feminism affirmed that women were equal in their rationality to men and so should be entitled to compete on equal terms.

But with second-wave feminism in the Anglophone world there was a crucial assertion that 'the personal was political', which meant that power had to be recognised within the personal sphere of intimate relations as well as within the public sphere of politics.[1] We could no longer think about the public sphere as a space of reason and power while the private sphere was a space of love, emotion and intimacy. This meant that if women were to be free to compete for jobs and careers, then men had to reconsider the masculinist terms that were taken for granted in the very ways workplaces had traditionally been organised. Women wanted to be able to compete on their own terms, rather than feel forced to deny their continuing responsibilities for childcare and domestic work.

This meant that men's support for feminism could no longer be a matter of supporting women in their own struggles for equality, but involved men learning to name their experience as 'masculine'. This was something that men had to learn to do for themselves, but was not easy within a generally homophobic culture in which male identities were largely defined in negative terms – in terms of not being 'soft', 'emotional', 'dependent', which meant 'not being a woman'. This could make it difficult for men to support each other in consciousness-raising groups because they learnt as boys that they needed to be 'independent' and 'self-sufficient' – they could not show 'weakness' in front of each other out of a fear that this could be used against them by other men in the competitive relations of masculinity. Often men can only feel good about themselves through knowing that they are 'doing better' than others.[2]

These patterns start early, and it has become necessary to reflect upon the ways in which boys learn their masculinities in school as well as in their families. Often they are left feeling they have to survive on their own and that, for instance if their parents are separating or a parent has died, they cannot talk to others or look for support. They feel shamed and learn to pretend that everything is OK. They learn to carry their inner emotional turmoil and confusion on their own, or else they can take it out on other children by bullying as a way of affirming a threatened male identity. There has been a recent focus in the West on bullying cultures as part of a discussion of 'boys' underachievement' in school, which relates to girls doing so much better in assessments, possibly because of the kind of encouragement and support they have received for their sense of self-worth as young women.

We should also reflect upon the kind of support that boys need in their transition to manhood when there are so many uncertainties about what it means to be a man in the contemporary world. In part this is a cultural issue and has to do with an ongoing dialogue between the generations. But with the decline of so many traditional industries in industrialised economies fathers are often no longer in a position to hand over a job to their sons. With the decline of apprenticeships in many countries there is less context for a dialogue between older and younger men as they transfer skills, and young working-class men can feel more dependent upon formal schooling, from which their parents feel alienated. Young men can feel more on their own, unable to reach out towards others.

With the decline of traditional work it can be harder for fathers to sustain a sense of their male identities as providers and bread-winners. This can create its own forms of depression that can uncon-sciously be passed on to the next generation. Boys may feel uncertain about their identities as young men. They may feel antagonistic towards a feminism that insists that men can only name themselves as figures of power who are somehow responsible for the subordination and oppression of women. Since this is not the way young men experience themselves, they can feel uneasy and confused.

If we are to engage with the ways young men feel about themselves, we have to be able to think about the tensions between the power they may be able to exert in different spheres of their lives in relation to young women and their own feelings of powerlessness. We also need to engage with the changes in gender relations, which means that in contemporary Western societies we have to think in new ways about how young men and women affirm their gender and sexual identities within postmodern cultures.

Power

If young men feel surrounded by confident young women who seem to have more sense of direction in their lives, they can withdraw into a sullen silence. Early feminist theory insisted on identifying masculinity as exclusively a relationship of power, as if there were no way of 'rediscovering masculinity', an early title I chose, since the task was to deconstruct masculinity. It was as if there were no ways that men could change, or no way that masculinity could be redeemed; rather they had to accept that masculinity was the problem and could be no part of a solution. This is still a weakness in certain forms of anti-sexist men's politics that assumes that men name their experience through coming to recognise their power in the subordination of women.

Moved by its engagement with the terrible violence that men so often perpetrate against women, this form of men's politics is clearer about what it is against. It insists that men take responsibility for what has long been denied. But the focus tends to stay on women's suffering and has relatively little to say about the experience of men. As I explored in *Man Enough*, we need to engage with the abuse of men's power in the violence that is done towards women. We need to break with the collusion in domestic violence and sexual harassment at work: it is through trivialising these experiences that we unwittingly collude, or we insist that this is a private matter that has to do with the individuals concerned. I know from working in Mexico how the presentation of 'good behaviour' in public often hides the violence that is taking place behind closed doors. Women are too terrified to speak about it, or else they learn to blame themselves.[3]

But we need to be able to acknowledge both the social power that men continue to assume within a patriarchal society that is largely shaped according to their own image, and the feelings of confusion and powerlessness that individual men can feel. These are both aspects of a complex social reality in which we have to rethink the relations between power and emotional life and the different spheres in which power is also exercised within heterosexual and gay relationships. In part this opens up issues of gender difference and the ways, for instance, in which women can exercise power in specific areas of life while men do so in others. Women often complain that their male partners are like children, unsure of what they feel emotionally.

Traditionally the father has been the source of authority within the family. His word has been law and he has expected to be obeyed. Fathers felt they would compromise their authority if they allowed themselves to be emotionally involved with their children. They expected to legislate 'what is best' for their children, without really having to communicate with them. It was their duty to punish their children if they disobeyed. This often meant that the patriarchal father was strangely distant in the family, organised around mothers and children. If the father felt lonely and excluded, he had his own company of men at work, or he engaged in affairs where secrecy gave his life the intensity it lacked. Often it was difficult for sons to articulate that they missed the contact in their relationships with their fathers, though recently they have begun to express that they want more emotional contact with their own children.

In Britain it was often the increased presence of fathers supporting their partners through pregnancy and later at the birth of their children that proved transformative. Young fathers wanted to be more involved, only to feel uneasy when they were forced to return to work after limited paternity leave. This sometimes proved devastating for women, who were literally left 'holding the baby' when they had formerly lived in more equal gender relations in which both partners worked and felt responsible for the upkeep of their living space. Visions of gender equality that seemed to work when both partners were working could not be revisioned to allow for children. Often the solution was to hire poorer women to look after the children, and so pass on the burden of care, but mothers often feel uneasy about this. The early months are often a period of mere survival, so that couples cannot deal with the emotional issues that have emerged. Sadly, within the United States and Western Europe, after 16 months, when things are a little easier with the new baby, there is often a divorce.

With the intensification of work, parents find it difficult to have the kind of time with their children that their children might want. Sometimes women are as relieved as men to go to work, to escape the endless demands and emotional chaos of family life. We could say that in the Anglophone world there was considerable pressure for women to conform to a gender-neutral identity, which in reality was set within masculinist terms. Once they had been accepted into the workplace they were expected to 'take the pressure', 'like everyone else'. Recent work has shown that some women at work resent women who have children for somehow 'letting the side down' and making special demands for themselves when they should not.[4]

Difference/s

As we reflect upon the experience of men, so we can appreciate the tensions that men also feel between family life and work. It is not simply a matter of having 'quality time' with children over the weekend. It is also a matter of listening to what children want and need for themselves and revisioning gender equality to include children. This means recognising how important it is for men as well as children for fathers to be more involved on a day-to-day basis. We need to rethink the nature of postindustrial work and the balance for both men and women between work time and family time. In part this involves men recognising just how much 'emotional work' goes into sustaining a long-term sexual relationship.[5]

Men in the West have tended to think about relationships as a background they could take for granted. Even though men say they are 'working for their families', male identities are still organised around work, so that men rarely learn how much time, attention and effort goes into sustaining a long-term relationship. This is work that women are expected to perform within heterosexual relationships, a kind of invisible labour which women are now less keen to do, wanting more for themselves emotionally within relationships than their parents' generation. Of course it is important not to generalise, but to examine these issues in particular cultural and historical contexts. For example, the ancient laws of the Basque lands have allowed women to inherit, and so have sustained sources of women's power within the community. Again we can only learn from each other's experience through reflecting upon these issues in specific cultural settings.[6]

When we think about power and difference, we are not only thinking about relationships between men and women; we also have to think about different sexualities and the complex relationships that separate diverse masculinities. We cannot forget about issues of class, culture, 'race' and ethnicities and how these set up relationships of power and entitlement between different masculinities. In recent discussions of class it has been made clear that some men from working-class backgrounds could not imagine themselves going to university. This was not a possibility that entered the social world they lived in, where the future was shaped through a choice of which trade they might enter.

As we have learnt to think about differences of culture, 'race', ethnicity and sexualities between women, so we have also learnt to think about different masculinities. In the same way that women discovered a freedom to explore what they wanted and needed for themselves, separating themselves from the judgements and evaluations of a dominant masculinity, so men also need to take time and space to explore their inherited forms of masculinity. This is part of men learning to name particular classed and sexed masculinities they have grown up to take for granted. It can be difficult to do in a period of uncertainty, when traditional models of masculinity organised around notions of men as 'breadwinners' and 'providers' have broken down. Men may feel they should be 'in control' of their experience, so admitting that uncertainty can threaten their male identities. Rather, men learn to keep their anxieties and fears to themselves as they project a certain public image. Inner distress can build as men are haunted by a fear that if they show what they are feeling to others, they will surely be rejected. Anger can be turned in against the self, and this is reflected in the high rates of young male suicide as a global phenomenon. It can feel easier to kill yourself than to show your despair to others.

Technologies

Globalisation and new technologies have produced a break between the generations which makes young people feel they are growing up in a world that their parents cannot understand. New software and telecommunications technology compresses time, which makes young people overstimulated and anxious to be 'in contact' in a web of ever-accelerating connections. In Western industrialised societies we live increasingly in nanosecond cultures that are redefining the relations between the urban and the rural, as place no longer has the same relevance. Within a non-stop 24-hour, 7-day culture, although we have created every kind of labour- and time-saving device, it is easy to feel we have less time available to us and our relationships than any other human beings in history. Email can be a great convenience until we find ourselves frantically responding to a never-ending stream. The cell phone is a time-saver, except that we are always now potentially in reach of someone who wants our attention. We switch off the computer and leave the phone off to find space for ourselves, only to feel anxious about what we might be missing.

New technologies have brought about the circulation of images of global masculinities that young people learn to identify with. They adopt a particular look but at the same time can find it difficult to express what is going on for them since this might compromise the image they are trying to project. We should not be surprised that stress-related illnesses are rising dramatically all over the world, many of them attributable to information overload and burnout as more people find themselves unable to cope with the pace, flow and density of human activities. In the UK, three in ten employees suffer mental problems each year from stress-related behaviours. As Jeremy Rifkin, author of *The Age of Access*, has written recently, 'if a child grows up surrounded by video games and computers, and comes to expect instant gratification, is it any wonder that he develops a short attention span? Quicken the pace, and we risk increasing the impatience of a generation' (*The Guardian*, Saturday 26 May 2001, p. 22). Rifkin suggests that the hyper-speed culture is making us all less patient, and that these new stress-related patterns emerging as 'road rage' or 'domestic violence' demonstrate how more people are acting out their stress in violent outbursts.

Rifkin makes a significant point when he says that 'If this new technology revolution is only about speed and hyper efficiency, then we might lose something even more precious than time – our sense of what it means to be a caring human being' (p. 22). This issue can touch both men and women: it helps us to see how we can blame ourselves for not being able to 'keep up' with these new patterns, for instance by reducing the amount of sleep we need. But rather than judge ourselves according to these external standards, we need to recognise that there is more than just the question of how best to integrate our lives into the new technology revolution or adjust to globalisation. We need to ask deeper questions about how we create a social vision that makes use of technologies without allowing them to take over our lives.

Deeper questions

It is only when men get ill that they ask some of these deeper questions. Then they can feel angry at their bodies that have somehow let them down. Sometimes the stresses of sustaining traditional masculinities have made men ill, because they have found it difficult to listen to their bodies, which have within modernity been regarded as machines at their disposal. Men may find it difficult to seek support when they are ill, say with prostate cancer. They would prefer not to talk about it, in the hope that if the cancer has grown from nowhere, it might as easily disappear. They do not want to reflect upon how the tensions and stresses of holding everything together have helped to make them ill. They want the medical profession to fix their condition so they can get back to work and so back to 'normal life'. They do not want to hear the doctor's uncertainties about appropriate treatments. This has meant that insufficient attention has been given to men's health. Rather men have tended to judge themselves in terms of living up to external standards, feeling inadequate if they somehow failed to do so. It can be difficult to express your fears to the doctor or nurse who is examining you, even if this would be helpful to them, because it is easy to feel that you are being 'weak' and so not 'man enough'.

Generations of men have learnt to keep their own silence, coming back from war or conflict. Often they have not told their partners or children what they have lived through, the fears and terrors of war. They have wanted to protect the next generation, but in the process they have not received the support they could have used for themselves. The pain of war is still felt in many societies across the globe, from Latin American cultures still dealing with the silences that have followed on military dictatorships, to the echoes of the civil war in Spain and the Basque lands and to the silences in Japan in the wake of the bombings of Hiroshima and Nagasaki. Societies have learnt to turn their back on their traumatic pasts, but these historical memories need to be shared, so that grandchildren can know what their grandparents have lived through. This memory work helps the new generation explore their own ground and gives them a sense of what matters in life. Courage and determination need to be revisioned as we learn from the experiences of the past in opening up a dialogue between fathers and sons, and fathers and daughters. Often it is the children who carry the unresolved conflicts of their parents, so that it is crucial for men and women to learn how to speak to each other across differences of power and vulnerability.

As men learn to show more of their own vulnerability, they will learn to recognise this not as a sign of weakness, but as a source of courage. As young men learn how to be caring and intimate in their relationships with whatever sex, they will learn what matters to them. They will learn to cherish love as they struggle to realise greater justice in the relationship between the genders in a more democratic and egalitarian society. We need to reflect upon the new orders of gender and sexual relationships that are emerging within different societies in a globalised world. This means challenging theories that have tended to identify men with prevailing masculinities and are thus unable to explore the tensions that have emerged for many young men in relation to the masculinities they inherit. We need to move beyond the terms of a hegemonic masculinity that tends to offer a universalised and top–down vision that orders the relationships between diverse masculinities only in terms of power and subordination.

While being aware of the structural relations of power and violence that can characterise the relationships between societies as well as between individuals, we need to be able to imagine new forms of gender and sexual relationships. We need to question theories that might suggest that men cannot change, and that masculinities need to be deconstructed because they are always part of the problem and so can never be part of the solution. Rather than defining masculinities exclusively as relationships of power, we need to be able to imagine complex relationships of power and vulnerability, authority and love, equality and recognition. I want to question traditions that have settled for the terms of an earlier anti-sexist men's politics that have been unable to illuminate transformations that have taken place both in men's lives and relationships, but also in the order of gender and sexual relationships since the early days of the women's movement and sexual politics in the 1970s.

We must learn from the past if we are to be able to engage creatively with the present, rather than assume that an earlier period can be dismissed for supposedly attempting to reduce the 'political' to the 'personal'. We need to appreciate the fears that still haunt the present in relation to the 'personal' and the 'emotional' so that we can move beyond the terms of post-structuralist traditions to new ways of thinking about relationships between the 'psyche' and the 'social' that can both honour the insight that 'the personal is political' as well as engage critically with very different social realities within a risky and uncertain globalised world.

I have benefited from discussions with many people, engaged both theoretically and politically, in different parts of the world who have helped me appreciate the need to question universalist theories in relation to men and masculinities. Such theories can support rationalist traditions that reproduce and sustain existing relations of global and local power while attempting to question them. I gradually became aware of the hold on the patterns of my own thinking and feeling of cultural assumptions that a secularised Protestant culture had shaped in me. This helped me to raise questions about my own work as I attempted to translate it into different cultural settings, and made me think about other theoretical paradigms that had developed within the Anglophone world. Visiting Italy, Spain and the Basque lands made me aware that Catholic traditions, even if disavowed within secular cultures, needed to be acknowledged if we are to be able to engage critically with diverse cultural masculinities. It was tempting to generalise from theoretical models developed in Northern Europe and the United States, especially when they spoke in the seemingly neutral and universal discourse of power.

So often these models have emerged from secularised Protestant cultures and have thus been tied to a rationalist tradition that works to discount emotions and feelings as sources of knowledge, as well as to reproduce disembodied forms of identity and experience. Framed within the terms of Kant's rationalism, they fail to appreciate that reason cannot be identified with morality, and that emotions and feelings can help shape moral experience and gendered identities. We learn from Freud about the dangers of intellectualising or rationalising experience, and so recognise that a commitment to reason and rational argument does not have to involve sustaining a rationalist tradition.

A developing awareness of the difficulties of translation across diverse cultural spaces, and of the diverse cultures of masculinities helped me appreciate some of the Protestant cultural assumptions that had underpinned some of my own early work in *Rediscovering Masculinity* and more generally the weaknesses of universalist theories of hegemonic masculinities that, despite their analytical reach, have also made it difficult to engage creatively with issues of culture and difference and tended to minimise issues of cultural translation. This has made it important to share the reflections in relation to men and masculinities that have emerged in Scandinavia, the United States, Spain and Latin America, in order to learn about the workings of difference/s as well as the need to engage with diverse histories and memories. This is a process that I can only begin in this work.

Differences of culture and tradition easily get forgotten within an Enlightenment vision of modernity that tends to frame reason in universalist terms. As we become aware of the need for dialogue between discrete cultural traditions, so an awareness of women's oppression makes us wary of traditions of cultural relativism that can be used to legitimate and normalise violence against women and homophobic violence against gay men and lesbians. As we learn to 'queer' these categories and allow for more fluid identities, we also need to explore relations between morality and power. We need to make judgements about forms of gender and sexual oppression and so be ready to question prevailing cultural traditions while recognising the emotional and cultural force they carry.

As we open up dialogues between North and South, but also between East and West, so we need to explore the generational experiences of young people growing up in very different technological worlds. We need to appreciate the circulation of global images as well as the production of virtual spaces that allow for experimentation and contact that might not be available in local traditional communities. But at the same time we need to recognise that transnational identities carry their own joys as well as fears, as people contend with various influences and pressures in their lives. As young people seek to escape from traditional patriarchal definitions, so they are also exploring new ethical visions of identity, not simply finding themselves positioned in relation to available discourses. Rather than dispensing with conceptions of self, we need to explore new ethical visions of self-identity that can help people to recognise the different sources of power they might be up against. The dangers of global warming and ecological devastation have made it necessary for us to explore new ways of relating ethics and politics in ways that recognise the constraints of nature, rather than assume that, with technological change, 'nature' has somehow become 'artificial'.

Aims of the book

Drawing upon the experience of diverse masculinities and the struggles of researchers and activists in different countries to get to grips with the cultural masculinities they live with, I have tried to frame new questions as I engage critically with some of the traditions we have inherited. The tendency to assume a pervasive distinction between modernity and tradition, and to think that because urban elites often occupy secular worlds religious and spiritual traditions can be dismissed as 'backward' forces that will inevitably give way with the advances of science, reason and progress, has proved a dangerous assumption post 9/11. We need to rethink the ways we have imagined secularisation within industrial societies if we are to be able to engage critically, for instance, with religious movements in the United States and the developing Protestant presence in Latin America.

Blindness to movements in the Islamic world and the difficulties we have in developing dialogues across diverse intellectual and spiritual traditions have made it difficult to understand some of the cultural transformations that have accompanied globalisation in a postmodern world. Held within the grip of a pervasive rationalist modernity, it has been difficult to appreciate what are too easily defined as 'non-rational' aspects of thinking, feeling and behaviour. Tendencies towards deconstruction have often unwittingly undermined the moral resources we need to imagine forms of post-humanism that can question rationalist forms of modernity.

This also involves questioning a rationalist vision of discourse that often disdains the emotional and the personal and assumes that an analysis of discourses could uncover the implicit values and assumptions people live with in their social practices. Rather than assuming that emotions, feelings and desires are 'non-rational' and so threats to objective thinking, we need to question rationalist humanist traditions that have failed to recognise how we hurt and undermine others and so show them a lack of respect through failing to validate their emotions and desires as much as their ideas, thoughts and opinions. Treating religious belief as 'irrational', we have tended to take for granted disembodied visions of identity that assume that moral actions are guided, in Kantian terms, through reason alone. But we can learn from Freud and traditions of psychoanalysis that there is a crucial difference between a commitment to reason and rational dialogue, and a rationalist tradition that would treat emotions, feelings and desires as forms of unreason. In this way feminisms have remained critical of Enlightenment visions of modernity, though aspects of this challenge to a rationalist modernity could also be lost in its translations through post-structuralist traditions.

A critical analysis of men and masculinities can provide a reminder of embodied identities and emotional lives since in the West a dominant white European masculinity has not only taken its own reason for granted, thus being able to legislate what is good for others, but it has often worked to police and regulate a dominant rationalist tradition. But a wariness in relation to the 'personal' and 'emotional', and so to embodied forms of existence, has not only characterised conceptions of hegemonic masculinities, largely cast within rationalist terms. Within post-feminist cultures both men and women increasingly learn to identify with emotions as a sign of weakness and dependence, and so as a threat to their identity as autonomous selves. These fears have been encoded with post-structuralist traditions that, until recently, have reinforced distinctions between 'nature' and 'culture' and the notion that identities are articulated within the discursive realm of culture alone.

Opening up new questions about contemporary relations between 'secular' and 'religious' identities within a post-9/11 world involves rethinking cultural, religious and spiritual traditions and the ways they still shape global and regional differences in relation to men and masculinities. These differences unknowingly shape men and women's relationships with bodies, emotions and sexualities, and their expectations within gendered and sexed relationships. Frustrations produced through mass unemployment of young men can turn people towards religious traditions that seem to have an explanation for their plight. This questioning involves both a recognition of the difficulties of translation across cultural worlds as well as a personal and theoretical exploration that can open up issues of bodies, desires and sexualities.

Sometimes this means returning to discussions of the past to remind ourselves of what we have learnt from our own personal histories and transformations and what we need to value and remember in the present. But it also means listening to men as they have been struggling to question the masculinities they have inherited, and thus questioning a notion that men can be identified with prevailing masculinities and so positioned within relationships of power. This involves recognising the presence and workings of power in different spheres of social life. As Foucault appreciated, power cannot be centralised within the institutions of state but has to be investigated through its workings across institutions and relationships. But Foucault only questions a rationalist tradition in his later writings, where he seeks to uncover and explore Christian and Greek cultural traditions that have long been disavowed in the shaping of contemporary subjectivities. Aware of the ways gendered and sexed bodies are inhabited through a dominant Christian culture that has shamed sexualities and desires in quite different ways, he knows to listen to silenced histories.

Foucault himself acknowledged his difficulties in shifting from an analysis of knowledge/power to finding his way to an analysis of subjectivities and ethics. He felt the need to make the break in his own work but could not trace the connections. This is partly because he could never really appreciate how power reduces people to silence and works to undermine a person's sense of self-worth, so we need a language of power that can relate to ethics. This was a transition Foucault wanted to make and eventually he might have explored, as Simone Weil does in radically different ways, as the relationship between power and ethics. This involves appreciating the emotional life of bodies and so thinking against a rationalist tradition that might want to think of the materiality of bodies and affect without having to deal with the uncertainties and disappointments of personal and emotional lives.

A concern with the relationship between a dominant white European masculinity that can take its reason for granted and the visions of modernity we have inherited within different traditions of social theory opens up this space between power and ethics, subjectivity and emotional life. This is partly because the identification of a dominant masculinity with reason already involved a reason radically separated from nature. Rather than questioning a modernity that was framed by a disenchantment with nature, a post-structuralist tradition has assumed a radical split between nature and culture and taken it that identities are framed within the linguistic realm of culture alone. It is hoped that, by drawing upon both theoretical and more personal concerns, these connections will be made clearer as we grasp what is at stake in these different positions in relation to men and masculinities. This means that as we transform theoretical traditions, we will also appreciate the space in which both men and women can explore what they want and dream for themselves within more equal gender and sexual relationships.

Acknowledgements

Over the long years of writing this book I have had consistent support from my men's group and from discussions with many men and women concerned both intellectually and politically with issues around men and masculinities, including Michael Kimmel, Jeff Hearn, Bob Connell, Michael Kaufman, Terry Cooper, Paul Morrison, Tony Dowmunt, Mathew Gutmann, Ana Amuchástegui

Herrera, José Olavarria, Terésa Valdez and Mara Viveros Vigoya, who in different ways have been supportive and helped to shape my thinking. The dialogues, spoken and unspoken, seem to carry forward. Claes Ekenstam organised an important gathering in Gotenberg, Sweden, bringing together researchers from different Scandinavian countries. Jørgen Lorentzen organised a seminar on 'Masculinities, Bodies and Emotions' at the University of Oslo in October 2003 that helped focus issues around bodies, sexualities and emotional life. José Olavarria and Terésa Valdez were responsible for organising a conference on 'Variones adolescentes: genero, identidades y sexualidades en América Latina' in Santiago, Chile, November 2002 that helped focus my dissatisfaction with theories about hegemonic masculinities.

Over many years, working with researchers and activists in Mexico, including Ana Amuchástegui Herrera, Juan Figueroa Guillermo and Benno de Keijzer, and participating in the development of research and practice have proved invaluable in questioning the idea that theoretical frameworks could be imported and that researchers needed to perfect their frameworks before engaging effectively in the field. It made me aware of the importance as well as the challenges of bringing activists into the research process. Most recently, the first national conference on Men and Masculinities organised at the University of Puebla, Mexico, June 2004 established a network of Latin American researchers and activists. It created a stimulating environment in which to think across cultural differences.

Ulla-Britt Lilleaas from the University of Oslo has been a reassuring presence as a visiting research fellow at Goldsmiths while I have been struggling to pull different strands together. Duncan Branley helped at a vital time with computer skills to get the typescript in order. Many people will recognise some of the arguments and exchanges we have had over several years and I hope they will forgive me where they feel they have been misinterpreted. The Department of Sociology at Goldsmiths has also provided an open and stimulating environment in which we could think across disciplinary boundaries and create spaces for daring to think differently. Most recently, with Joanna Ryan we have set up a research group on Embodied Psyches/Life Politics to explore new ways of thinking about the relation between 'psyche' and 'social'. Though not explicitly concerned with issues of gender and sexuality, these categories have been constantly present in our deliberations on the relations between psychoanalysis and social theory.

Over the years many postgraduate students have challenged me to question some of the generational assumptions and forms of social theory I was accustomed to. Working with Luis Jimenez on his work on Entendidos – young gay men in Barcelona – Danny Kelly on prostate cancer, and Dean Whittington on his study of drugs, violence and white working-class masculinities in Deptford has helped to identify questions and concerns that have inevitably found their way into the arguments here. They have provided rich empirical spaces in which to explore theoretical issues. I am learning as much from a new generation of students who have followed in their wake and are working in different areas.

This has been both a theoretical and personal exploration in which I have been trying to make clear a developing sense of unease in relation to theorisations that seem to be caught within a particular historical moment when men were first reacting to the challenges of feminism. I was feeling that in order to relate to different generations and cultural experiences of masculinities, we needed to break with some of the inherited frameworks and attempt to ask new kinds of questions. I have been less concerned to engage critically with particular texts than to follow through some of the implications of more general ways of thinking about relationships between men and masculinities. This is particularly so in relation to discussions of hegemonic masculinities that have sometimes acquired a general theoretical currency that seemed to bear little relationship to the empirical studies they were supposedly meant to illuminate. I hope that the questions I explore through different realms of gendered and sexed experience will help to establish broader terms of discussion that can escape from rationalist traditions that unwittingly echo terms of a dominant white European masculinity.

This has been a discussion that has stretched across generations but it is hoped has been open and inclusive. My partner Anna has given her love and support and her critical awareness and sensitivity for more years that I would wish to record. Our children are now adults themselves and they still teach us about both the difficulties and rewards of parenting and the importance of knowing how to let go. Daniel has found his own way in the world through music and Lily is finding her own way into sociology. Through the years they have both taught me a great deal. I hope that they will play their own part in making this a more just and loving world than my generation has been able to achieve. As we learn for ourselves, we are also learning for the generations to come. It is difficult to tell what the future will bring, but with vision and understanding we can at least learn from the pasts we have inherited and the attempts we have made to transform the present.

1   Introduction: Cultures, power and sexualities

Crossing borders

The discourses around men and masculinities have emerged in different national contexts in Europe and the United States since the early responses to the women's movement and feminisms in the 1970s, with initiatives in Europe initially being taken in England, Holland, Germany and the Scandinavian countries. Sometimes we have been able to share diverse experiences across European borders, but it has been striking how this work has been interrupted at different historical moments and how it has fallen away in particular settings. The work in Scandinavia has been unique in being supported by national governments and also by governments working in cooperation. Even where the work has flourished it has taken time to organise gatherings in which diverse experiences can be shared and researchers and activists open up new areas of discussion. As work consolidated in the Protestant cultures of Northern Europe, the 1990s has seen significant developments in Southern Europe, particularly in Spain, Italy and Greece, but also notably in Central and South America, particularly in Mexico, Chile, Brazil and Colombia. It is these developments that encourage us to think about diverse masculine cultures that have been shaped within different religious traditions within Europe, the Middle East and Asia, and it is hoped that they will open up future dialogues between North and South.

Bringing together men and women involved in doing critical research on men and masculinities also allows us to rethink theoretical traditions that have informed our thinking as well as traditional positivist and interpretative methodologies in the research practices being developed. In different settings we have been able to sustain dialogues that were valuable in encouraging people to voice concerns that might otherwise remain unspoken. When I could not understand the languages spoken I could appreciate the thinking as well as the laughter and the love that was being communicated; this made me aware that not everything that is communicated is communicated in language. This is particularly significant when we are reflecting upon issues of intimacy, relationship and power.

We have been living through dangerous times in the aftershock of 9/11, when the United States and Britain took a critical position in relation to a war with Iraq that despite the widespread protests in different parts of Europe we were unable to prevent. This was a struggle that involved diverse global masculinities being locked into terrifying relationships with each other. Bush had won the support of Blair in his 'war against terror' where careful consideration of the new global realities were blocked by a simple warning that 'you are either with us or against us'. That is, you will either take the side of the United States as the representative of 'freedom' and 'good' on earth or else you will be castigated as 'soft on terrorism' and 'anti-American', and treated as somehow identified with an enemy.

This was a discourse of global male power that largely worked in the war in Afghanistan but failed to mobilise when it came to the fight against the weapons of mass destruction in Iraq. There was a refusal, particularly on the part of France and Germany, to identify the war against Iraq with the 'war against terror', and there was a widespread feeling that the world would be made a more dangerous place if the war against Iraq took place. There was a fear that the occupation of Iraq, even if it brought the downfall of Saddam Hussein, could end up encouraging terrorist activities against the perceived occupying powers of the West. Many of these fears were realised. For a time it was unclear whether the war would go ahead immediately or whether it would be postponed as attempts were made to win the support of the United Nations. The global conflicts that can feel so threatening and immediate reflect the urgency of the moment and an awareness that issues in relation to men and masculinities have assumed a particular global significance in these dangerous times.

Such a situation gives urgency to our theoretical reflections but also forces us to engage with diverse cultural and ethnic masculinities and the danger that universalist discourses that have emerged in the West will too easily be applied to very different global settings. If we are to understand the sources of terror, then we have to listen to what non-Western young men are saying about what attracts them into religious fundamentalist organisations. We need to appreciate the instabilities in traditional male identities that have been wrought through globalisation and high levels of young male unemployment, and the appeal of religious movements that can promise renewed male pride and power. We need to think about different 'racial', ethnic and cultural masculinities in order to understand the continuing appeal of religious traditions too often ignored within the secular traditions of a Western modernity.

Generations

As we appreciate the significance of a particular historical moment in which we reflect how our identities as men and women have themselves been shaped through particular historical contingent circumstances, we can recognise the significance of generation in opening up dialogues across different masculinities. We need to listen to young men and women in their late teenage years and early twenties, with their willingness to question the theoretical frameworks and methodologies developed in the 1970s and 1980s. Rather than assume the viability of these traditions that largely emerged in relation to feminism, we need to be aware of how gender relations have been transformed within patriarchal cultures, at least in the West over the last twenty years.

This does not imply that patriarchal relationships have disappeared or that violence against women and gays has lessened, but such relationships do not carry the same legitimacy for young people who have often grown up within very different gender and sexual orders. They do not have the same concerns as a previous generation; nor do young women and men identify the centrality of their relationships with feminism. Young men have to be reminded of the power they can still assume within patriarchal cultures and their silent collusion in the suffering, devaluation and violence so often endured by women. But when young women and men say they can no longer recognise themselves within the language of sexual politics, we have to take these insights seriously. Different generations have different concerns, and even though it might be misleading to think that issues of gender equality have been solved or that we have moved 'beyond gender', we need to recognise the resistance young people can feel to being 'fixed' in relation to their gender and sexual identities. Sometimes they are expressing a feeling that the difficulties they face in relationships and work can no longer be illuminated in these strict gender terms.

In *Gender and Power* and his later *Masculinities* Bob Connell remains caught within a framework of gender and power that insists that men can still take for granted privileges and opportunities that women are denied.[1] This can be helpful in reminding us of the continuity of patriarchal relations but it tends to render invisible the differences between generations and also the difficulties that boys can face in their own lives. Connell has continually resisted the idea that we can talk about men being 'oppressed' even if not in the same terms as we think about the oppression of women. But we have to be careful about assuming a duality that haunts his work, namely, that the oppression of women is 'structural' and so grounded in material relations of power while the 'sufferings' of men can only be considered as 'personal'. Such 'sufferings' do not relate to their positions as men within a patriarchal society, but to emotional issues in their individual personal lives.

Not only does Connell's work implicitly echo a radical feminist conception of men as the bearers of power, but it reinforces a radical duality in the ways we think of men and women and so frames the relation between men and masculinities reductively. We are encouraged to think of men as instances of particular masculinities that are related to each other through relations of power. This tends to reinforce the notion that masculinities can be thought of exclusively as relationships of power. It also frames masculinities as the problem that needs to be solved, as if we could do without the term at all. Having little sense that men can change, Connell is trapped into seeing masculinities as not part of a solution. At the same time a notion of 'hegemonic masculinities' works to silence the tension between men and their ambivalent feelings towards inherited masculinities.[2] This is something gay men have long explored as they have distanced themselves from established masculinities. They learn to treat diverse masculinities as performances they might choose to assume.

As we think about dislocated masculinities we are aware that we can no longer speak with the same assurance about the ways men and masculinities are positioned within patriarchal cultures. As we learn to think about different generational masculinities, so we have to face greater complexities in the ways we think about gender relations. We also recognise that ruling notions of 'hegemonic masculinities' have worked to make it more difficult to think about the relation between bodies, fears and emotional life. Rather than open up these concerns, we can find ourselves trapped into thinking about masculinities in ways that are strangely dislocated because they fail to interrogate positions from which men are speaking. Rather, we can find ourselves echoing the very universality that has been associated with dominant white European masculinities in their colonial relationships with non-European 'others'. Rather than a diversity of male voices that can recognise diverse 'racial', ethnic and cultural masculinities, an implicit rationalism shapes how we conceive male power in universal terms within patriarchal cultures.

Threat

Anyone who grew up during what was called the Cold War supposedly knew where the threats were coming from; post 9/11 we no longer know this. We are living in a new global climate in which questions of masculinity need to be refigured. The world was traditionally divided into separate spaces, and Bush still insists on talking about the 'free world' as if it were a space of 'the good'. This was set against the communist world that Reagan famously called the 'Empire of Evil' and Bush refigured in a post-communist period as an 'Axis of Evil' that was deemed to be a threat to the civilised values of the West.

Supposedly the West alone could take its 'civilisation' for granted, and it has long been seen as the moral duty of a European white masculinity to engage in a civilising mission to those who would otherwise remain uncivilised. Colonial projects framed within the terms of a European modernity deemed that colonised 'others' could only develop freedom and democracy if they accepted subordination to their Western superiors. The uncivilised remained a threat that needed to be contained. Paradoxically it was supposedly only through accepting subordination that they could gradually learn to accept the practices of freedom. Since the uncivilised could not be 'reasoned with', the only language they could understand was the language of force and violence.

Within a patriarchal culture where women are paradoxically positioned as a 'civilising force' in men's lives, we often find a similar rhetoric invoked in relation to women and children when they dare to question patriarchal authority. If a woman dared to question her husband in public, she showed disobedience and proved deserving of punishment. Children were also expected to show obedience to their father's word as law, for he represented authority within the family. Identified with their 'animal natures', children were deemed a threat to civilised family life. Within an Enlightenment vision of modernity 'culture' was to dominate 'nature' and human reason was to control bodily nature. A dominant white European masculinity alone could take its reason for granted and so could legislate what was good for others without having to listen to what they had to say for themselves.[3]

As Caroline Merchant has framed it, with the seventeenth-century Scientific Revolution came the 'death of nature', as 'living nature' came to be represented through the scientific gaze as 'dead matter', governed according to scientific laws.[4] This echoed an older Christian tradition of the sinful body that came to be regarded as the dead body, and then became the object of the medical gaze. This encouraged a dominant masculinity to assume an instrumental relationship to the body that within a Cartesian tradition was not 'part of' an identity as a human being but rather part of a disenchanted nature. As reason was regarded as an independent faculty radically separated from nature, so with Kant the notion of 'human nature' was fragmented, where the 'human' was identified with 'reason' and 'nature' came to be disdained as 'animal'. By echoing a fundamental Greek/Christian distinction between the 'human' and the 'animal', reason came to be marked as a sign of superiority that allowed a dominant masculinity to disdain emotions, feelings and desires located in a body itself regarded as 'animal'. As women were deemed 'closer to nature', they were more likely to allow their behaviours to be influenced by their emotions, which came to be regarded as 'feminine' and a sign of irrationality.

Reason was deemed to be a divine faculty, for it was through reason alone that a dominant masculinity could discern God's plan for the natural world. Through reason the mind of God could be revealed. But this also established the authority of fatherhood, since it was as fathers that men were supposedly to exercise legitimate authority over women and children within the family. Within a secularised culture, scientific rationality assumed power in relation to nature and progress came to be identified with the control and domination of nature. This was something that men could exercise also in relation to their inner natures, where they learnt to identify masculinity with self-control.

Francis Bacon saw the reordering of gender relations of power with the Scientific Revolution as critical to a new 'masculinist philosophy'.[5] As well as occupying a central position in the scientific and political establishment, he served as a judge on witch trials. As Ehrenreich and English showed in *For Her Own Good*, women who had been healers were to be castigated as witches and brutally murdered in witch burnings in Europe and North America. When we think of the Enlightenment as marking a victory of reason over faith, we tend to forget the tragic histories that accompanied it. Within cultures with strong positivist traditions we often fail to appreciate links between masculinities and methodologies.

Bodies

This new vision of scientific progress was expressed in masculinist terms. A certain tradition of scientific rationality in research methods silently echoes this form of 'masculinist' philosophy. Even though space has been won for 'feminist methodologies' as a distinct paradigm for research, we have been less able to break the silences that accompany positivist methodologies so often assumed to be impartial instruments of science that have worked to eradicate forms of bias. Nature was no longer to be 'listened' to and human beings were no longer to understand themselves through a relationship with nature. With its death, nature had become mute and creation came to be revisioned within the image of the dominant masculinity that had learnt to think of nature as a threat. Femininity itself came to be experienced as 'threat' to a dominant heterosexual masculinity though its identification with emotion and irrationality.

As Bacon makes clear, nature would not give up her secrets easily; she had to be forced. So we discover that images of sexual violence inform relationships between scientific knowledge and nature. Metaphors of rape and exploitation in relation to nature came to frame scientific discourses as nature was no longer seen as a source of meaning and value. Inner nature was also framed as a 'threat', giving a secular form to a Christian disdain for the body. The body comes to be identified with sexuality and the 'sins of the flesh'. Supposedly it was only through the punishment of the body that the soul could be purified. This helped shape an idea that men need to prove their masculinities by showing that they can endure pain.

We find this reproduced in a postmodern gym culture where the male body has to be constantly disciplined against the threat of 'fat'. There is a disdain for the flabby body that reveals a lack of morality in the form of self-control. The gym becomes the new cathedral of body cultures – a space where men can prove themselves able to endure pain and so show themselves worthy of salvation and also of 'winning' admiring sexual partners. This becomes a way of affirming male identities in the present and confirming particular forms of superiority in relation to other men.

Even within secular cultures that have lost touch with their religious sources it remains important to identify how these religious traditions help shape contemporary subjectivities, in ways otherwise difficult to recognise. Within Protestant cultures there is often a hidden sense that people have to prove themselves worthy, a feeling that has become more equally shared with women in post-feminist times. Women can equally fear dependency as a sign of weakness, and this can make it difficult to negotiate emotions and feelings within relationships. Where it is difficult to express anger we find indirect ways of showing resentment. Sometimes little is said but emotional distance is created within the relationship, and people suddenly realise that their partner has become a stranger to them. This can come as a shock where both parties are so identified with their independent work lives that they have had little time and emotional energy for the relationship.

Even though we see ourselves as secular and learn to disown religious cultures as having little significance in the present, as Foucault was exploring in his later writings, they continue to influence and shape subjectivities. Unless we are prepared to explore connections between secular cultures and diverse religious traditions that can still unconsciously help to form them, we can be bereft of terms to illuminate predicaments we face in contemporary life. These latent structures can still be shaping our gender identities without our being able any longer to recognise their influence in the ways we learn to relate to our bodies, emotions and desires. As we explore the shifting forms of gender identity across different generations, we need to investigate the very different gender worlds in which young people are growing up. At the same time a sense that our natures are evil and cannot be trusted – so powerfully expressed in Luther and Calvin – can help shape the compulsive activity so many men can feel prone to. Hesitant to identify themselves as 'workaholic', they resist acknowledging their addictive behaviours. As a postmodern culture thrives on speed and constant activity, it can be difficult to 'slow down' enough to feel more of what is going on emotionally.

The traditional framing of gender relations that Aristotle originally terms an 'active' masculinity and a 'passive' femininity no longer resonates within a post-feminist culture, however we think of it. Both men and women, particularly in Scandinavian countries, participate more equally in the labour market, and they can easily identify with a tradition of rationalism that might historically have been identified with a dominant masculinity. Younger people tend to think beyond gender categories because they no longer seem to make sense of their lived experience. Often young men in their early and late twenties fail to find a sense of direction in their lives, and experience difficulty in leaving the parental home to which they have retreated. Sometimes they feel uneasy about the meaning of their masculinities, though they do not relate their uncertainties to feminism as a previous generation might have done. Rather, they can be concerned with existential issues in relation to their male identities that cannot simply be reduced to those of power. The ways we have learnt to theorise men and masculinities somehow fails to speak to their situation.

As we learn to think across different emotional cultures between, say, different Scandinavian countries, the United States and Britain, we might think about whether anger is expressed easily or not. If, for example, anger is not easily communicable either for men or women, what does this mean about how difficulties in relationships are handled? If anger is an emotion that needs to be curbed and controlled, what does this mean about the ways emotions are 'passed on' between different generations? This can mean that the body needs to be silenced as anger needs to be controlled. Men might feel it difficult to share their emotions and dreams if they are already designated as 'negative'. To share these emotions might only serve to devalue them in their own eyes and in the eyes of others. They might be anxious to be able to 'present themselves' in socially acceptable ways, so they learn to suppress their 'negative' emotions. This is the way they civilise their bodies through processes of discipline and regulation. But these practices are only intelligible against a background understanding of the ways secular cultures have been shaped through past religious traditions.

So, for example, anger needs to be controlled because it indicates an uncivilised body that is already unconsciously identified with the 'sins of the flesh'. If the body is to remain pure and uncontaminated, then it must allow for a 'pure love', traditionally untainted by sexuality, which is identified with lust and carnality. As the body comes to be disowned as a site of temptations that need to be disavowed, so fears are projected onto 'others' who are made to carry features that the dominant culture is unable to recognise in itself. Traditionally, sexuality was not recognised as an expression of human love but as a weakness that was necessary for procreation, not for pleasure. The body's desires come to be disavowed and so carried by the disowned other. Traditionally, too, within discourses of Christian anti-Semitism the body was identified with 'carnal Israel', and the figure of the Jew was made threatening to the 'health' of the body politic. We only have to think back to the pervasive character of eugenic discourses not only in Scandinavia, but in the West more generally, to appreciate the ease with which Jewish neighbours in the Holocaust were often denied the protection of the state.[6]

As sexuality comes to be displaced within a dominant Christian tradition it also comes to be gendered. Eve becomes the figure who supposedly could not resist temptation and so is blamed for bringing evil into the world. This has meant within the Catholic tradition, but not only there, that women cannot be trusted. Reflecting on masculinities in Italy, Spain and Portugal, the notion of trust in intimate relations often echoes this background. It could become dangerous for men to listen to women, for women needed to be controlled and traditionally were seen as subject to the possession and authority of the father. So within modernity, as Rousseau framed it, women who were deemed to be 'closer to nature' were identified with their bodies.[7] This was reflected in second-wave feminism, which challenged the ease with which women in diverse cultures could be treated as sexual objects. To be treated as a sexual object is not to be recognised as a human being. Within postmodern theories we easily forget these critical insights into objectification. Even where we acknowledge these insights, we can find it difficult to think through their implications for our research practices.

Part of the feminist critique of modernity has been the reclaiming of the body and sexuality, which had been disavowed as 'part of' our identities as human beings. This was a reframing of the 'human' that had been traditionally constructed through a disavowal of the body and sexuality that had been deemed 'animal'. Sometimes it has been difficult to sustain these insights within post-structuralist feminisms that can recreate an abiding distinction between nature and culture and would want to treat identity as discursive. Rather than identifying modernity with a Cartesian vision of the unified self that a postmodern tradition could break with in its recognition of identities as fragmented and fluid, we need to appreciate the ways in which a Cartesian vision of the rational self was already gendered and racialised. If emotions were radically separated from thoughts and sited in the body whereas thoughts were located in the mind, they were discounted as 'feminine' while bodies were deemed to be 'animal' and so identified with a carnality that was identified in different ways with the figure of 'the other' as Jew within or uncivilised, colonised Black without.[8]

Dislocations

Within a restless postmodern culture it can be difficult to identify the tension around reclaiming the body and sexuality as part of the expression of human love and inherited religious cultures. As Susan Griffin explored it in *Pornography and Silence*, a dominant masculinity in modernity identified itself with culture, reason and language and disavowed its relationship with nature, the body, sexuality and emotional life.[9] Unable to ground embodied experience, it becomes dislocated and projected onto others in a way that has become even more confusing and difficult to identify within a culture of gender equality. Younger people brought up to imagine their experience within a culture of gender equality can find these processes even harder to identify. Women can still feel obliged to carry emotions that men cannot acknowledge in themselves. In traditional heterosexual relationships she is to be blamed for his desire and even his unhappiness.

Rather than question these complex inheritances, which is necessary to understand different cultures of masculinity, the ways we have often theorised masculinities have made it difficult to think about diverse masculine cultures. Connell's theorisations of 'hegemonic masculinities' have often also made it difficult to understand the relationship of diverse masculinities within particular cultures. Cultures have been reduced to relationships of power and therefore we have been unable to theorise about the ways culture relates to power and emotional life. Power remains crucial in analysing gender relations, but we have to be aware of how it is lived in the ways that it is theorised. A recognition of the gender relations of power and the different ways they are encoded is the beginning of an analysis, not the end.

As male researchers we may find ourselves in an externalised relationship both with ourselves and with the particular relationships we are seeking to explore. This leads us to assume that positivist and interpretative methodologies are in some way gender-neutral and that in cultures with particularly strong traditions of positivist research we can find ourselves in this externalised relationship. But rather than guaranteeing a lack of bias, this makes it difficult for us to identify the issues that need to be opened up in research. This means that too easily men and masculinities becomes a new research object but the methodologies remain unquestioned.

The feminist notion that 'the personal is political' brought into question the relation between power and emotions, but often within post-structuralist feminisms questions in relation to emotional life have tended to be lost around notions of essentialism. To refer to emotions, feelings and desires is often deemed to be a form of 'essentialism', which means that though the body has been a central area of concern, it has often been treated simply as a space of discourse. The body becomes a space in which culture plays out its diverse meanings. If feminisms questioned the rationalist terms of a patriarchal modernity, they were re-encoded within post-structuralism and its categorical distinction between nature and culture. As we have learnt to recognise the problematic character of these distinctions and acknowledged that post-structuralist theories often see gender identities as being worked out within the sphere of culture and language alone, we have identified weaknesses in post-structuralist traditions that have been hard to identify for those who have been introduced to social theory in its terms.

Gendered identities came to be seen as the articulation of particular discourses, kinds of languages. So, in a sense, we did not have to listen to ourselves or to others because we could safely manage an externalised relationship both within a post-structuralist theory and within the structural theory of hegemonic masculinities. We were left not really having to explore the connections between our own masculinities and the men and women we were trying to understand. This paradoxically reframed a dominant masculinity that could take its reason for granted and thus legislate what was good for others. So the theory of hegemonic masculinity had become hegemonic. It became a universalist theory that could be imported into different regional contexts. According to such a theory you simply have to 'fill in' the cultural differences and rethink the relations of gender power within a specific culture. This renders cultural differences less significant and threatens to make them invisible as masculinities are identified exclusively as relationships of power and as the tensions between men's lived experience and prevailing masculinities are dislocated. Rather, it is easy for men's experience to be reduced to exemplars of particular masculinities.

The dangers of a globalised theory of hegemonic masculinities is that it allows the West to legislate what is good for others without ever having to learn to listen to young men and young women in different cultural settings who might question the terms in which they are being theorised. It is the marker of a rationalist theory that it can invoke reason to legislate what others need, as traditionally fathers could say what was good for their wives and children without having to listen to what they had to say. Rather, for them to question was a sign of disobedience that showed they were deserving of punishment. Connell's theory remains part of a rationalist tradition in that it cannot deconstruct the terms of masculinity that are paradoxically affirmed through being identified exclusively as relationships of power. A rationalist tradition does not have to learn to listen, and often in research methodologies we do not have to listen to ourselves in order to be able to listen to others. The theory already takes an externalised relationship to its object of study and so does not have to question the masculinist assumptions within traditional research practices. We are therefore in danger of treating men and masculinities as a new object of social research without having to explore new methodologies.

As Connell tempts us into shifting attention from men to masculinities, with 'men' taken almost as an essentialist category so that we shift to masculinities, which are taken to be 'structural', we think about the relationship between different masculinities as relationships of power. It therefore becomes difficult to explore the tensions that men often feel in living out different masculinities, and have no way of exploring the often unspoken issues that men learn to 'keep to themselves', thinking that they somehow 'should be' in control of their emotional lives. This is a suppression that a theory of 'hegemonic masculinities' tends to sustain. It is invoked as a theoretical framework that has little connection with the empirical studies into men's lives that often follow. It is as if the theory stands alone in its own space and is not open to critical reframing through an engagement with the lived experience of diverse masculinities.

Sometimes this means that researchers have had to rediscover the category of 'men' in order to be able to listen to the men they are working with, who would otherwise have been too easily reduced to exemplars of particular kinds of masculinities. Even within ethnographies it becomes tempting to take at face value what men say as revealing particular masculinities. In Connell's *Masculinities* there are abiding tensions between the ethnographic studies and the theoretical framings. It becomes difficult in the ethnographies to understand how these men have become who they are because they tend to be read through particular masculinities.

Often we do not know how men have come to feel and think about themselves in these ways. The neglect, abuse and violence they might have suffered as children and the powerlessness they have experienced tend to be rendered invisible if masculinities are identified as relationships of power. We tend to think of every young men in terms of power, and we find ourselves unable to think about the powerlessness of men in specific situations. This can distance a younger generation of men who feel the complex shift in generations where the younger women they know can often be more self-confident and self-assured. They might still face discrimination when they enter the world of work, but at least they have a sense of direction and what they want to achieve for themselves.

Jacqueline Wilson, who writes books for children and who has a gift for presenting complex issues to young people, says, 'the worst thing for children who have had to grow up too quickly is that they cannot be relaxed. They cannot just glide through things or be ordinarily silly'. Boys often grow up too quickly, particularly because emotions and feelings are seen as 'feminine' and so have to be disavowed. Again this might have changed, but many young men in diverse cultural settings can find it difficult to share their emotions because they feel it is a sign of weakness that still threatens their male identities even if they have sometimes learnt to think otherwise. This happened in a sense to Tony Blair, whose mother died when he was quite young and who is constantly modelling himself on Margaret Thatcher. He was born into a generation that never knew war, so his masculinity was never proved beyond doubt. In England, where an older generation of men had fought in the war, they felt assured of their masculinity, so that they could sometimes be open to change.

My generation also never knew war, while in relation to the children's books we read war was still the paradigmatic experience through which male identities were affirmed. Blair's generation did not know war but Blair is the leader who led Britain into four wars as if somehow to affirm a masculinity that can never be affirmed unless one has fought oneself. So there is an uncertainty about being 'man enough' in post-military cultures, and the decline of the breadwinner role leaves fewer ways to affirm male identities.[10]

Connell returns us to a structural rationalism and to an externalised analysis through the distinction that he makes between the 'therapeutic' and the 'political' in the framing of both *Gender and Power* and his later *Masculinities*. He regards the sexual politics of the 1970s as basically to do with consciousness-raising and emotions and thus with individual personal lives, but not with politics and power. He tries to draw a firm line between the 1970s notions, and thus the relations with early feminist work, and 'real politics' that supposedly had to do with issues of power and presumably developed in the 1980s. So the relationships between emotions and power cannot be thought about within that framework because they become delegitimated as 'therapeutic'. Rather than respecting the history of men's relationships to feminism within Achilles Heel and other movements and learning critically from our own histories, they were silenced and disavowed.[11] Of course there were related shifts within feminism with post-structuralist theory, but somehow they still wanted to sustain the insight that the 'personal is political'. If someone had sought to dismiss second-wave feminism as 'therapeutic', people would have immediately recognised a failure of historical imagination.

We need to interrogate Connell's structural analysis of power, which has been valuable in opening up relations between diverse masculinities but at the same time has narrowed the terms in which they could be understood. Left with a disembodied vision of power, we are unable to illuminate relations between bodies, power and emotional life. By identifying masculinities exclusively in terms of power, Connell's socialist feminism vision tends to share with radical feminisms a limited sense of male transformation, of how men can change. It also fails to engage critically with feminist discourses around men when necessary. In treating men as always having the power and privileges that are denied to women, it has no sense that men also have hurts, insecurities and sufferings that need to be listened too. We have to recognise diverse pro-feminist positions in relation to men and masculinities, rather than assume that anti-sexist positions that think of masculinity as power remain the only pro-feminist positions. In *Man Enough*, I sought to set out the differences between anti-sexism, mythopoetic and critical positions. We need to open up a dialogue between diverse theoretical positions if we are also to speak meaningfully across different generations.[12]

Young men who do not relate to the discussions around feminism can feel outside the paradigm that defines the critical work in relation to men and masculinities. They can feel that this work sustains feelings of guilt that no longer speak to their situation and that it is only through listening to a diversity of masculinities that we can open up theoretical frameworks that otherwise can seem fixed and unable to illuminate different generational identities.

Listening

If we choose to maintain Connell's distinction between the 'therapeutic' and the 'political', we are in danger of losing connections between how reflections on the personal and the emotional can open up to an appreciation of the structural and the political. The tensions between language and experience get lost within a focus with post-structuralist theory on discourse that too easily assumes that discourse articulates experience. The prevailing mantra becomes that there is no experience without discourse, and we only know experience through what people say, but this threatens to lose some critical insights of sexual politics. But discourse theory, narrowly conceived, can make it difficult to break men's silences because often men do not say very much. This does not mean that it is not 'real' and that there is not a lot going on, but it means that we cannot take what men say initially as 'reality', but must be prepared to build a relationship. It might mean that we have to take time to establish trust and be ready to share some of our ambivalent feelings, if they are to risk opening up to discussion. It might mean that we cannot rely upon single interviews but need to develop different methods to interview men about more personal issues.

If we recognise the ways that language is gendered and that men often learn an instrumental relationship to language as a form of self-defence, we will realise that it can take time for men to share more of their experience. Men often learn a modernist disdain for the 'personal' and the 'emotional' and paradoxically this disdain is sustained through the distinction between the 'therapeutic' and the 'political'. Rather than questioning dominant male rationalism, we sustain it by the ways we think of 'hegemonic masculinities'. This disdain is also echoed in post-structuralist theories that have helped us think about the fragmentation of identities but often at the cost of understanding how people might develop and grow into a deeper relationship with themselves. On the other hand, in theoretical developments in relation to race and ethnicities around notions of identity and identification, especially in the recent writings of Stuart Hall, there seems to be a turn towards recognising the importance of writing out the personal in relation to a political context.[13] Insights that were alive in issues of gender have been translated into other areas at the moment when a post-structuralist paradigm is being more widely questioned.

Within a Cartesian tradition we learn to have an inner relationship with our minds and an external relationship with our bodies. This reflects itself as a rationalist split between thoughts positioned in the mind and emotions and desires that are framed as forms of unfreedom and determination in the body. In the split we live in a schizoid culture that makes it easy for us to disdain emotions because thoughts and opinions, defining who we are, are framed as mental categories while emotions are already separated as part of our bodies. It was part of the project of psychoanalysis to think of ways in which we could bring thoughts and emotions into relationship with each other. In some way feminist work discovered how to do it through a practice of consciousness-raising. Issues to do with the 'psyche' and the 'social' also remain alive in forms of alternative psychotherapy which have explored 'emotional bodies'.

This means that emotions such as sadness, fear and vulnerability cannot be acknowledged within a dominant male culture that still defines emotions as 'feminine', as impurities or contaminations within a racialised discourse. Bodies here have been identified within a discourse where whiteness is associated within European modernity with 'purity' and 'goodness'. These identifications are present within European cultures even if they are not made visible or questioned by racial and ethnic groups.

In a post-9/11 world the powerful in the West who have so long taken their control for granted feel disturbed and unsettled because they do not know where the new threats are coming from. They do not know who the enemy is and where they might strike. They were shocked at the intensity of the hatred towards the United States and the destruction that was perpetrated against a country that sees itself as the bringer of freedom and democracy to a world that would otherwise be denied it. This is part of an arrogance of modernity that long sustained colonial projects of empire. Colonial powers could know what others supposedly wanted without having had to listen. So, speaking with the authority of power and civilisation, the West has not felt a need to learn about other religious traditions or about the diverse masculine cultures they sustain. Too often we have lumped them together as patriarchal expressions of male power without feeling a need to investigate critical differences.

Unsure of where threats are coming from, the United States and Britain preferred to deal with Iraq as a rogue state whose weapons of mass destruction might fall into dangerous hands. Fears could be projected onto the figure of Saddam Hussein even though they knew how the country had been weakened since 1991. But if fears can be focused on a 'war against terror' where the targets can be specified, then there is no need to reflect upon other global threats and dangers, and the complex sources producing these threats. Believing in their own rhetoric, the United States and Britain imagined that the weapons of mass destruction must have been hidden, because they already knew that the threat was real. They did not want to face the question of whether a war with Iraq would actually make the world less safe because it might encourage a new generation of terror in response to the occupation of a Muslim country. Out of control, a particular masculine mind often imagines the worst and organises itself for war as a way of proving itself against a target it can identify. We can hear the echoes of a liberal imperialism that believes that the uncivilised will eventually appreciate the gifts of freedom and democracy that are being offered even if they have not been consulted about the forms they want this post-Saddam regime to take.

According to some spiritual traditions, the world began with sound and people had to listen for creation. The first words of Genesis, interpreted differently within Jewish, Christian and Islamic traditions, declare that God spoke and said 'Let there be light'. Creation comes out of sound and God's words are to be listened to. Sound is creative: the world emerges out of it. In Hindu tradition this divine generative speaking – *shabed* – is the subtle holy sound for which yogis spend years quietening their minds to be able to hear, believing that it will bring enlightenment. Taoists say 'Be quiet' and listen properly, and all will be revealed. According to Taoist medical wisdom the ears are the so-called flower or expression of the kidneys. Hearing ability is directly influenced by the amount of energy in the kidneys, hence hearing diminishes with age as the kidneys grow weaker.

But if, say, a child does not want to hear its parents arguing or does not want to listen to its father's commands, knowing that it is powerless to question them, its kidney region contracts, thus reducing energy flow. This triggers a subtle 'closing down' that can help us understand how men learn to 'close down' on themselves. Sometimes men do not 'hear' what their partners have to say and, as a form of self-protection, they learn to listen in a way that does not 'take in' what is said. In the same way people generally 'close down' in the face of threat or possible challenge on an energetic and emotional level; they consciously choose to block it out, in effect saying 'I don't want to hear'. The message might be 'I don't want to listen because I already know' or 'There is nothing you can tell me that I don't already know.' In his later years, according to Ferenzi who had been a close colleague, Freud found it difficult to listen to what his patients had to say. This reflected a weakness in the authority relations of psychoanalysis otherwise justified in relation to encouraging transference, where Freud 'already knew' what the unconscious could reveal.[14] As the doctor, he had authority in relation to the unconscious that was supposedly denied the patients themselves. This reflected the authority that modernity granted to a dominant masculinity that could alone take its reason for granted.

Often we do not want to hear what is going on in ourselves, let alone in others, and in the wider political world on the edge of war we learn to displace fear and anxiety onto those who are made to carry our unresolved feelings. Rather than dismiss as 'therapeutic' what we also need to be able to engage with, we should listen to the voices of the dispossessed who feel threatened by processes of economic globalisation that destroy traditional sources of work. In some regions work is much more available for young women, which undermines the status of men within relationships and families, and draws young men towards fundamentalist movements where they can sustain their threatened masculinities with a radical Islam. Hatred often has its source in fear, but unless we in the West understand this, it is difficult to hear the pain and sufferings that motivate the hatred of others.

This also involves questioning secular modernist traditions within the human sciences that have treated religion as irrational and a sign of 'backwardness' that would give way in the face of progress. And it also means opening up spaces in the complex relation between men and masculinities to allow us to question a rationalist universalism that has made it difficult to reflect upon the emotional lives of men.

2   Masculinities, culture and difference/s

'Civilisation/s'

How are we to think masculinities across different cultures? How have we learnt in the West to be hospitable to cultural differences? We can still recognise traces of a Eurocentric vision expressing an imperial past that assumed the superiority of the West as the bearer of freedom, modernity and science. The different colonialisms that were shaped by particular European national histories allowed for diverse relationships between the 'mother countries' and their colonised others. The relationship was often conceived in familial and patriarchal terms, which positioned colonised others as children who were to be grateful for the guidance and mastery of the coloniser. The coloniser was bringing the benefits of modernity, 'civilisation' and progress to those who were deemed to be in need of these gifts. It was a particular colonial masculinity that was to carry the responsibility of 'the white man's burden'.[1]

These inheritances and the superiorities that go along with them are still with us, and we need to explore their continuing traces. Even if we have come to question a colonial inheritance intellectually, it can be difficult to undo the workings of white supremacy. Within an Enlightenment vision of modernity, hospitality was offered to the colonised other on the basis that reason, progress and modernity belonged to the West, which had everything to teach but little to learn. The process of decolonisation was an intellectual move away from a belief in absolute values which could be discerned through reason alone and which set a universal standard against which 'others' were to judge and evaluate their own 'backward'/'primitive' values. As Simone Weil recognised, an uneducated white working-class man could automatically feel superior to any of the Polynesians he met, knowing that he was the bearer of science and hence progress while 'they' were trapped within traditional beliefs.[2]

If a belief in moral universalism has given way to a different 'common sense' of moral relativism within the human sciences, we have to be careful about the kind of hospitality towards other cultures that this moral relativism allows. Often it does not mean learning from others about how we might live our own lives, but rather keeping a distance from 'other cultures' which have their own beliefs and values, their own inherited cultural conceptions of masculinity and femininity and so of gender and sexual relations. Within an Enlightenment modernity 'others' could only be seen or given hospitality as 'less than' ourselves, though 'the other', as Levinas frames it, could become/aspire to be 'like us'/'the same'.[3]

The project of emancipation was framed in relation to Jews as 'the other' within the Christian West. Jews could be recognised as being 'like us' and so offered hospitality as citizens with legal and political rights as long as they were prepared to deny hospitality to their own Jewishness, as Sartre explores in *Anti-Semite and Jew*. They were to learn to 'pay the price' of acceptance as 'free and equal citizens' as long as their Jewish differences were privatised and so made a matter of individual religious beliefs.[4] So Jews were to be rendered 'invisible' – they were to cease to exist as Jews within the public sphere, the sphere of masculine reason, while women were to be confined to the private sphere of love and emotion. Within Christian Europe, Jews had no longer been feminised in their difference – it had been thought that Jewish men were more influenced by their emotional natures and so had been deemed to be 'less masculine'. In some discourses in early modern Europe it was even said that Jewish men menstruated.[5]

These historical echoes remain significant because it was often in relation to the Jews that colonised 'others' came to be conceptualised as 'feminised' – as Asian men can still be 'feminised' within contemporary Britain. The Reconquista in Spain, which imagined the project of nation-building as the project of constructing the 'purity' of a Christian Spain that would no longer be 'polluted' by the presence of Jews and Muslims, the other who prepared the ground for the Inquisition. There was a fear of 'the other', especially when presented as 'like us'.

Thus the Inquisition was often focused upon 'New Christians' – *conversos*; Jews who had converted to Christianity were 'suspect', especially in a culture that still thought of spiritual inheritance as a matter of blood, tracing back to ten generations. Could Jews ever genuinely convert and could they really change their beliefs and values? Since the truths of Christianity could be assumed, the 'blindness' of the Jews and their inability 'to see' the truths of Christianity was proof of divine punishment. This explains the image in Strasbourg Cathedral of the synagogue as a blindfolded woman with a broken stick trying to feel her way.

When we think about how we conceptualise gender differences within different cultures, we have to remember the centrality of Christianity in the shaping of European cultures, and likewise for the complex relationships between Europe and colonised 'others'. This suggests that in crucial respects we have to think about how modernity is to be understood as the project of a secularised Christianity and how this helped shape the gendering of relationships with others. In the case of Spain, it was often the treatment of Jews as others that raised questions about whether the colonised others had souls, and thus how they were to be treated. The Inquisition was a transnational institution of terror that helped shape relationships with those deemed to be 'uncivilised'.[6]

In addition, there was the notion that Judaism had somehow been 'superseded' by Christianity; the 'new' testament could be seen as replacing the 'old', and framing visions of progress and development. If there were any truths to be learnt from the Jewish Bible, then these were expressed to a higher/'purer' level within the Gospels. It was because Judaism was conceived of as 'Carnal Israel', as Daniel Boyarin has explored it, that it was identified with bodies and sexualities – and so with the 'sins of the flesh'. Since sexuality was interpreted as a threat to spirituality and since the body and sexuality were deemed to be 'Jewish' – later being identified with 'black'/ 'oriental' – the 'purity' of Christian spirituality was to be measured through its distance from the body and sexualities.[7]

The very project of 'civilisation' was marked by a dominant Christianity and the way it related to bodies and sexualities as uncivilised. The sense that the West presented a 'higher' form of civilisation was expressed through a Christian disdain for these aspects. Thus, as the 'human' came to be defined through a radical contrast with the 'animal', so people could only aspire to being moral/ spiritual beings through 'rising above', in Kant's terms, their 'animal' natures. In this way Jews came to be positioned as 'less than human' because of their relationship with the bodily and the 'material'. Because Christianity was able to 'supersede'/'rise above' its Jewish sources, so it denied the Jewishness of Jesus, as it denigrated a Jewish tradition from which it supposedly had nothing to learn. At some level this vision of 'superseding' shaped the relationship between the coloniser and the uncivilised, trapped in an earlier – more primitive – stage.

Universalism/s

It was a mark of the moral superiority of Christianity in relation to other traditions and cultures that it could present itself as universal. Against the particularisms of Judaism, whose universal visions of love and justice came to be disavowed, Christianity came to present itself as universal. This universalism was also connected to a sense that it had captured a truth that others would need if they were to be saved – to find salvation. There were not different paths that could be followed towards God, but a singular vision that came to be expressed in universal terms. Again this gave rise to the view that Christianity had little to learn but everything to teach, and this shaped the urgency of the colonial projects. It was the 'nakedness' of the 'natives' that proved they felt no shame and so could have no moral sense. Christianity was to teach the uncivilised to cover themselves and so feel shame for their bodies/sexualities.

Jews came to be positioned within the confines of ghettos within Christian Europe. They were not offered hospitality within the larger community, but often existed as a community apart. But with emancipation they were offered a different form of hospitality, though this produced its own forms of self-rejection. It was only through a denial of their Jewishness that they could be accepted as free and equal citizens. But this was a universalism that proved fragile, since 'humanity' was refigured in relation to a discourse of rights. Humanism came to be redefined within the terms of a Kantian rationalism and its disdain for bodies, sexualities and emotional life. It was only a dominant white, heterosexual masculinity that could take its reason for granted. Traditionally it was only men who could speak and so be listened too within the public sphere. Women were often reduced to silence and their language devalued as 'emotional'. Kant made clear that it was only through the institution of marriage that women could secure an inner relationship with reason, which meant that women needed men in a way that men supposedly did not need women.[8] Men's dependencies were rendered invisible. Again it meant that men did not have to listen to women, for they had little to learn and everything to teach.

A dominant masculinity did not have to learn to listen to the voices of others. The coloniser did not have to listen to the colonised, who were thereby positioned with the feminine. But it also meant that a dominant white, European masculinity did not have to listen to its own emotions, feelings and desires, which for Kant were to be subjugated as 'inclinations' – forms of unfreedom and determination which were a threat to reason and so to morality. Rather, men learnt to experience their emotions as a sign of weakness and thereby as a threat to their male identities. It became a mark of their superiority as men that they could 'control' their emotions and deal on their own with whatever tribulations life offered. As Susan Griffin proposes, men unknowingly projected onto women the emotions and desires they could not accept in themselves. They were unable to accept their own natures, having learnt to identify masculinity with culture alone.[9] This means that men fail to learn to take responsibility for their emotional lives and is inflected differently within gay and straight relationships.

Reacting to a colonial past, it can seem easier to assume that gender relations are shaped according to particular cultures and traditions. But not only can forms of cultural and moral relativism serve to legitimate patriarchal relations of power and violence; again they can make us feel that we have little to learn from cultural difference/s. We can find ourselves locked into a space apart even if it is no longer framed as superiority, with little to learn. We pay deference and offer hospitality but we refuse to really learn. This is partly because we can be locked into the assumptions of a secular rationalism that still has difficulty in learning from religious and spiritual traditions. We need to think differently about secularism in relation to ethics and spiritualities.

But universalisms can remain implicit in theoretical framings of masculinities that encourage us, say in Connell's work, to think in abstract terms of hegemonic and subordinated masculinities. This becomes a theorisation of masculinity as power that is set within an uncritical relationship to a rationalist tradition. Connell's *Masculinities* already carries a disdain for the emotional in men's lives which is defined as 'therapeutic' and so contrasted with 'politics', which has to do with power.[10] This makes it difficult to engage with the complexities of men's experience in different cultures and to think radically about different forms of masculinities. Rather, we assume the universal framework of masculinity theorised more or less exclusively as a relationship of power. In some ways this echoes a radical feminist analysis of masculinities that makes it difficult to explore complex relations between growing up as men and the available masculinities within diverse cultures.

Language

As I explored in *Rediscovering Masculinity*, men from diverse backgrounds grow up to use language as a means of self-assertion, to project a particular image of themselves as men.[11] They learn that what they say can easily be used as evidence against them, so they hesitate about what they will share emotionally about themselves. Since within an Enlightenment vision of modernity it is a dominant European white heterosexual masculinity that takes its reason for granted, men often learn to talk for others rather than exploring the complexities of talking more openly and directly for themselves. This is partly because emotions are interpreted as 'feminine' and so as a threat to male identities, and partly because masculinities are identified with self-control as a mode of dominance in which reason supposedly silences inner emotions, feelings and desires.

This means that men within secularized Protestant cultures use language as a means of controlling their inner experience rather than a way of sharing what is happening for them. It is difficult to reach out for the support of others, if when you feel depressed or lack direction, if you have grown up feeling that you 'should' be able to control your own life and that needing help is just a further sign of weakness. Of course there are different registers in the ways men talk about themselves, but middle-class heterosexual men can feel trapped in an impersonalised and distant relationship with themselves. It is not just that they are refusing to share what is going on for them; they feel estranged from and locked out of their inner emotional lives. Sometimes through reading or movies men discover a language in which to express what seems to be going on for them. But then it can be difficult for men to make this language their own.

Thus men can feel locked into a position of being somehow observers of their own experience. They can feel that life is happening *to* them, and that they are always trying to catch up with what they are feeling. Within a rationalist culture men feel easier dealing with problems that have solutions, so that if they are depressed they think there must be something they can do to get rid of these 'negative' emotions. There is a desire for the quick fix and a fear of engaging in an inner exploration of emotional histories. It is not that men do not talk about their personal lives, but they often fear that they will compromise their heterosexual male identities and be found somehow lacking. Emotional life needs to be firmly in control, even if this control takes different forms within diverse cultural and historical settings.

It is as if men learn to fear knowing 'too much' of what is going on for themselves emotionally, partly because they fear the emotions they might discover. For them, emotions indicate a lack of self-control and thereby a threat to male identities, though the ways 'inner' and 'outer' are shaped depend very much on cultural settings. Within the Catholic cultures of the Mediterranean there might be more emotional expression, partly through the continuing relation with the mother, but at the same time an intense homophobic fear that can make it difficult for men to be close with each other. The ways men come together are ritualized; humour tends to maintain appropriate distances. In some ways this means less isolation and loneliness than men feel in the Protestant cultures of Northern Europe, where they feel more controlled and so less emotionally expressive. It is often only with alcohol that they can allow themselves more spontaneity.[12]

The ways that men learn culturally to relate to their emotional lives are also reflected in how they learn to theorise about masculinities. There is a tendency to escape from the more delicate exploring of men's personal experiences into more abstract discourses of straight and gay masculinities. We can be left with theories relating to masculinities that do not develop out of explorations in different cultural settings. Rather than exploring the contradictions in male experiences, we become trapped in homogenised visions of masculinity as if it were a single thing, even if modulated differently within diverse historical and cultural settings. But this becomes an easy temptation because what we hear about patriarchal or traditional masculinities can suggest that masculinity is an 'inner thing' or 'essence' we have in which an old model can somehow be replaced with a new less hierarchical model that is more open to gender equality.

There is a danger in talking about 'new masculinities' as if to suggest that a 'new model' can somehow be theoretically elaborated as a 'good' alternative to replace the 'old model' which no longer works. This implies that men do not have to engage with the tensions between their own experience as men and the diverse masculinities they have grown up with. These contradictions can be erased as the personal lives of men are replaced by an abstract discourse of masculinities.

Somehow the theoretical discourse introduced for instance by Bob Connell as hegemonic and subordinate masculinities comes to exist in a sphere of its own. Rather than question a tradition of Enlightenment rationalism that polices a distinction between reason and emotion, culture and nature, mind and body, we escape from the difficult task of exploring diverse cultures of masculinities. The contradictions men live between their inner emotional lives as men and the cultures of straight and gay masculinities are disavowed as men learn to think in the universalised and abstract discourse of patriarchal masculinities. Differences of culture, religion and nation become invisible as the relations between diverse masculinities are theorised exclusively as relationships of power.

So we can forget about our difficult personal experiences as straight men 'living up' to idealised images of masculinity and feeling that we are constantly failing, or as young gay men feeling estranged from prevailing notions of masculinity. Within a Protestant culture this means that men are haunted by feelings of inadequacy that they learn to hide, as if whatever they achieve they could have done more. There is a fear of pleasure often more intensified than within Catholic cultures that have a space for confession. This offers a chance to begin anew, which Protestantism does not allow to 'evil' natures. Different cultural traditions have different relationships of power between diverse masculinities, but this means refusing to think of power in abstract and universal terms. We need to acknowledge the power men inherit within a patriarchal culture, but we also need to be able to acknowledge the sources of women's power.

This is not to suggest, even implicitly, that heterosexual men do not continue to have considerable power to silence within patriarchal and homophobic cultures, but it recognises the dangers of a patriarchal analysis that is fixed within the terms of a 1970s anti-sexist men's politics. We need to be clear about the diversity of straight and gay masculinities and how they are being shaped within cultural and historical settings regionally, nationally and globally. We have to engage with the very significant shifts in gender and sexual relations that have taken place within a globalised world transformed at least in urban spaces through networks of mass communication and be ready to think about specific cultures of masculinity.

Modernities

We need to think critically about the relationship between universalist forms of social theory and dominant masculinities in the West. It has been easier within Western conceptions of modernity, which have often encoded secular Protestant Christian traditions, to assume the superiority of universalist theories. As Christianity represented itself as superseding Judaism, so a mark of its supposed superiority was the universalism it represented in contrast to the particularism of Judaism, which was taken to be tribal. This vision has helped shape the universalist claims of reason, science and objectivity which have marked the West's superiority in relation to its conquered and colonised others.[13]

In crucial ways feminism challenged the terms of a rationalist modernity in its critique of the distinction between reason and emotion and its insistence that emotions and feelings could be sources of knowledge. This questioned a scientific positivism that assumed that emotions were signs of bias that needed to be eradicated. Feminism was also challenging modernity in its idea that the 'personal is political', when this is understood not as a plea for reductionism but as part of a questioning of the distinction between private and public spheres. This distinction had been set in masculinist terms through the idea that the public sphere was the realm of reason, power and justice. This means we need to review how feminisms can work to provide critiques of modernity, so challenging the idea that it is another discourse of modernity organised around the emancipation of 'woman' as a shared category.

Although Bob Connell recognises the workings of power within the private sphere, he undermines this insight by his conception of power relations. His theory has proved appealing not only because it reminds us of a diversity of masculinities rather than a singular homogenised vision, but also for many because of its universalist terms that can allow people to forget the cultural specificities of masculinities. As Connell frames the relationship between 'hegemonic' and 'subordinate' masculinities exclusively in terms of power, so he allows for an abstraction from cultural and historical specificities as well as from the complexities of emotional lives and intimate relations. Rather, we tacitly work with a definition of masculinity defined exclusively as a relationship of power. This makes it easy to assume that masculinity needs to be deconstructed as the problem rather than revisioned as part of the solution. It also tempts us into thinking of heterosexuality as simply a relationship of power.

Part of a criticism of Marx's work has to be his acceptance of a universalism that is set in radical opposition to forms of particularism. The assumption that the universal is somehow ethically superior is part of a devaluation of culture and difference as forms of particularity that need to be 'transcended' in the move towards universality. This vision was already around in the 1970s when activists argued that an awareness of gender oppression was a necessary step to the realisation that capitalism needed to be overthrown. Gender was taken as a particularity when contrasted with the universal discourse of class. This analysis sought to reduce gender to class, so failing to appreciate that women's liberation was indispensable for a social revolution. It was not an oppression that an orthodox Marxism could leave waiting until later to be dealt with.

Bob Connell, in *Gender and Power* and in his more recent *Masculinities*, offers a more sophisticated structural analysis which gives due weight to different forms of oppression. But tensions remain between the more theoretical writing and the concrete studies of masculinities that follow. A rationalist universalism is still very much in play and gets worked out in his positioning of the personal as 'therapeutic', which is set in contrast to the 'political' and in some senses to the theoretical. As with Lynne Segal, who follows Connell's framework in *Slow Motion*, this produces its own temporal narrative which has the sexual politics of the 1970s being framed as a moment of consciousness-raising and personal exploration of emotional life that sought to reduce the political to the personal and so is deemed to be 'pre-political'. But this is a historical misreading that exposes weaknesses in the structural Marxism that informs this work. Somehow it refused to acknowledge the significance for men's lives of the feminist insight that 'the personal is political'. This works to devalue the pioneering work in relation to men and masculinities of *Achilles Heel* in Britain and movements in other countries concerned with explorations of men's politics. This movement contrasted with a concern with 'real' politics that supposedly emerges in the 1980s, marking a move from the 'therapeutic' to the 'political'.

This marks a failure in Connell's work to engage with the emergence of men's movements in different cultural and historical settings and their diverse relationships with both the women's movements and gay liberation. Despite his intentions, there is a reinscription of the very masculine universal assumptions that feminist theories had helped to challenge within a rationalist modernity very much constructed within the terms of a dominant, white, heterosexual masculinity. As there is a tacit advance from the 'therapeutic' to the 'political', so there is also a move from the 'personal' to the 'theoretical'. We are presented with a global theory of masculinities that can supposedly be 'adapted' to take in regional variations.

Emotional life

While it is important to both learn from and critique the sexual politics that emerged in the 1970s, we have to be careful not to accept neat temporal distinctions as if they do not obscure theoretical differences. Connell's work represented a particular reading of Marx, which through a reading of Gramsci could make available notions of 'hegemonic masculinities', establishing relationships of power separating different masculinities. This involved reading 'difference' in terms of power and so foreclosed the space in which different histories and cultures of masculinity could be theorised. In its own way it tended to sustain a particular radical feminist reading of masculinity which had been helpful in opening concerns with male violence towards women, but that tended to think of masculinity as exclusively a relationship of power.

Even if it is not Connell's intention to undermine the insight that 'the personal is political', his theoretical work produces dualities in which the 'personal', which he labels as 'therapeutic', is represented as a 'stage' on the move to the political and theoretical. Thus, rather than encouraging men from diverse backgrounds to learn to theorise on the basis of their diverse gender and sexual experiences, having learnt to distrust the rhetorical and often empty relationship to language they had grown up to take for granted, there is a refiguring of the traditional distinction between 'emotion' and 'reason' as a distinction between the 'therapeutic' and the 'political'. This is important because it can allow men to adopt a theoretical and rationalist conception of masculinity before taking the time to name their own experience as masculine. There is a flight into the theoretical and away from the emotional and personal that comes to be legitimated by the very discourse of hegemonic masculinities.

This not only makes it difficult to learn from past movements, rather than devaluing them from the point of view of the present, but illuminates dangers in the ways that critical work in relation to men and masculinities can develop. A split can open up between men who have become aware of gender politics through having worked on themselves emotionally as men, and men who have turned towards an analysis of masculinities as a new object of their research. Men who have had to engage with their own inherited masculinities have had to rethink the individualist assumptions that inform psychoanalytic and humanistic therapeutic practices as men learn to appreciate the significance of taken-for-granted masculinities in their emotional histories. But some men may also remain trapped within the psychological, unable to make connections with the structural relations that sustain particular gender relations of power. Sexual politics have been significant partly because they have helped sustain connections between the structural and the personal.

Sometimes it is through exploring tensions between their lived experience as men and the structured masculinities they have internalised that men engage in movements of social change. This helps to shape a psychosocial politics of masculinity that differs from the structural accounts of hegemonic masculinities with which Connell leaves us. Even if it is not his intention, his work can reinforce a distinction between the personal explorations of men and their grasp of structural relations of male dominance. It can produce its own forms of disavowal as men discover yet new ways to legislate what is good for others – even if this time it is framed in terms of a discourse of hegemonic and subordinate masculinities – before they learn to explore the contradictions of their own lived experience.

A tension can be found between those men who have done the emotional work to ground their own thinking about men and masculinities and those, possibly more theoretically inclined, who have adopted a language of hegemonic masculinities because they assume the theoretical task has to take precedence. They may be concerned to evaluate different theoretical positions in relation to men and masculinities with the idea that a new 'model' of masculinity can be shaped to replace an earlier model of patriarchal masculinity. Sometimes this can be a form of escape, especially if people feel uneasy with more personal explorations. Too often in very different cultural settings we can find men taking refuge in these abstract formulations that make it more difficult to explore discrete cultural masculinities. Of course there can be traps on both sides. You can be as locked into a discourse of personal suffering as you can into abstract theories.

Men who have learnt to work emotionally with other men may stop working on themselves. They can be trapped into images of themselves as 'new men', as if this is confirmed by their soft voices and refusal to express anger, which they take as a negative emotion. These traits were often produced by an unhealthy relationship to feminism, as Robert Bly also recognised in *Iron John*. There was too much of an uncritical relationship with feminism and often a culture of guilt whereby men had come to feel bad about themselves as men. Rather than engage in revisioning masculinities, there was often a tendency to deny their male identities.[14]

Theorising masculinities

When we are tempted to think about masculinities in abstract and universal terms, it is easy to lose touch with the diverse lives of men and their relationships. But as middle-class heterosexual men, we can feel easier with universal theories because they allow us to escape from the unfamiliar terrain of the personal and the emotional. We do not want to go there because for so long we have learnt to control and silence inner emotional feelings and desires. Within academic rationalist cultures we have learnt to identify with a notion of reason radically separated from nature. It is through objectivity and impartiality that male superiority is affirmed. Whether we think in Connell's terms of hegemonic masculinities or in the post-structuralist terms of discourses that constitute masculine and feminine as gender categories, there are dangers of evacuating the realm of the personal and the emotional or assuming that psychoanalytic theories can be mobilised to provide analysis of subjectivities that would otherwise be lacking.

Even when we frame the 'personal' in terms of an exploration of male subjectivities, we can discover that we have left our own emotional histories behind. It is the very universalism of theoretical approaches caught within the terms of a rationalist modernity while at the same time unsettling fixed notions of identity that allows us to forget cultures, histories and context, even if we pay them lip-service. Somehow it is a politics of gender and sexual difference that gets lost as men learn to move from the exploration of their diverse personal experiences to abstract notions of hegemonic masculinities. The exploration of particular cultural masculinities that can help think difference/s somehow gets forgotten in the exploration of diverse straight and gay masculinities.

We can find ourselves failing to learn from feminist critiques of modernity that recognise how expectations of 'theory' and 'methodology' are themselves shaped in masculinist terms that systematically devalue the 'personal' and the 'emotional' as subjective and anecdotal. Alternatively we can learn to talk in post-structuralist terms about the uncertainties and instabilities of masculine subjectivities as if these can be thought to be the effects of particular discourses. We learn to treat identities as provisional positions that people assume in relation to prevailing discourses. But if these visions of identification present themselves as fluid and fragmented in opposition to identities as fixed, they too can easily lock us into unhelpful dichotomies. The oppositions are themselves provisional and so easily become rhetorical.

We can learn from feminisms as well as from postmodern theories to be explicit about the positions from which we are speaking. This is a crucial challenge to the universalism of social theories that present themselves as speaking from neutral positions of scientific objectivity. Social theories set within the terms of a rationalist modernity often learn to speak from nowhere. As men, we find it easier to speak with the abstract voice of reason than out of the particular male positions we inhabit. There seems to be a significant contemporary resonance between universalism and the power of the United States within the globalised economy. Possibly this is echoed in the tendency in the United States for men to identify themselves as feminists before they settled for the designation pro-feminist. This was a weakness in the anti-sexist men's politics that developed in the United States and marked it out from movements in Europe. Often there was a clearer sense of what men were struggling against – the patriarchal domination of women and men's violence against women – than what they were struggling for. Sometimes men talked more easily about the sufferings and pain of women than they could talk from their own position and experience as individual men.

This is a significant weakness in the anti-sexist politics that developed in the 1970s. It was as if men could be clear in their discussions of male power and patriarchy that they were anti-sexist, anti-racist and gay affirmative so that they were defining themselves through a set of crucial abstract principles. Men had to learn to take responsibility for the terrible violence that is so often perpetrated by their gender, even if not by them individually. They wanted men to become aware of how male violence was so normalised that its legitimacy in diverse cultures was not questioned. As other men would adopt similar principles of action so they would identify themselves with the ending of patriarchy, homophobia and racism. But these positions tended to remain moralistic and they could leave men feeling guilty in relation to their own masculinities, as if masculinities understood exclusively as a relationship of power could be no part of the solution.

If masculinity is identified exclusively as a relationship of power, then the task is to deconstruct it. This can make it difficult for heterosexual men to speak out of their particular experiences as men, and so can tempt them to identify themselves paradoxically with feminism as 'male feminists'. The positions are more complex than I am presenting here, but I want to draw out the implications of universalist ways of thinking about masculinities. Whether the stress is placed on gender equality or upon the deconstruction of dominant masculinities, we think of masculinity in terms of privileges men can take for granted in their relationships with women. This is to theorise out of a generational experience shaped by the early relations between men and the women's movement in the 1970s. But it was a weakness of the universal terms in which it was framed that it tended to abstract from the historical and cultural specificities of gender and sexual relations. Within this framework it remains an issue of men being made aware of the sufferings of women and the privileges they take for granted as men. It becomes a matter of heterosexual men learning politically to identify with the struggles of women against patriarchy and so committing themselves to deconstructing male privileges.

But if this discourse speaks to the experience of the first generation of heterosexual men engaging with the challenges of feminism, it does not resonate with the experience of a younger generation who have grown up to take gender equality for granted in their schooling. There will often be contradictions between the verbal support men give to notions of gender equality in different generations and their willingness to actively participate in childcare and domestic work. But a younger generation will want to question an anti-sexist politics that focuses explicitly upon the sufferings of women while remaining strangely silent about the lived experience of diverse masculinities. As I explored in *Recreating Sexual Politics*, there was often a moralism in the appeals made to men which reflected a weakness in the sexual politics that prevailed in the 1970s. The positions seemed principled but somewhat rhetorical in their ability to speak about the sufferings of women while remaining silent about their own experiences.[15]

In some cultures young men in the new millennium seem to reject the guilt they feel they are being asked to take on for being men. They do not mind taking responsibility for their own actions, but they feel they cannot be made responsible for the actions of other men. They reject the notion that masculinities can be conceived of exclusively as relationships of power, and so they question whether the relationships between different masculinities can be imagined in such terms. They question whether, from their own experience of greater gender equality, masculinities cannot be revisioned. For a younger generation mostly more tolerant of gender and sexual differences, the issue becomes rather how they can be deconstructed in the name of a gender equality they are more likely to take for granted. If this is a commitment that cannot be reached through younger men learning to care for themselves individually by doing their own washing and cleaning, this does not necessitate an appeal to guilt which so often fails to motivate people to action. We require a different ethical vision which resonates with a commitment to gender justice while being able to engage with the ways in which new generations imagine gender and sexual differences.

3 Masculinities, power and social movements

Generations

How do different generations of men positioned differently within newly globalised relations and networks of mass communication learn to speak for themselves as part of their commitment to greater gender equality? The moralism that underpinned the sexual politics of the 1970s is strangely perpetuated in the ways people still speak about men and masculinities. In a sense it continues to inform the ways in which we think critically about men and masculinities. It can still feel easier for pro-feminist men to talk about the sufferings of women and the need for men to commit themselves to struggling for the end of patriarchy and for greater gender equality than to talk more directly out of their own experience. This is a position I have grown to distrust, for it reflects the ease with which they learn within a rationalist modernity to legislate what is good for others before learning to speak more personally about themselves. I think we need to question prevailing rationalisms and explore different theoretical positions in the ways we theorise men and masculinities.

This is not simply a generational argument, although it feels important to seek clarification because these issues around men and masculinities are now being taken up as global concerns. We need to be critical about the abstract and universalist terms into which we often slip when talking about masculinities within a refigured globalised world. These theoretical issues are far from settled and we have to be wary of assuming that these new theoretical models of masculinity, largely developed in the West, can be translated into diverse cultural and political settings. We find people talking about 'dominant' or 'hegemonic' masculinities as if the theoretical issues have been settled and we need simply to apply these formulations to different cultural and material settings. But if we are to appreciate how, since the attacks of 9/11 in the United States, Bush's 'war against terror' has been framed within the terms of a moralism that has insisted that this is a struggle between the forces of 'good' and 'evil,' we need to recognise how this reflects a global struggle between diverse masculinities.[1]

For some men it is a relief to read in Bob Connell's *Gender and Power* and again in *Masculinities* that we can move from the 'therapeutic', which supposedly characterised the consciousness-raising concerns of men's early engagements with feminism, to the 'theoretical' and 'political'. Even if this is not Connell's intention, his work can be used to legitimate both the devaluation of personal and emotional explorations for men and also a flight into abstract and universal theories that assume masculinities can be understood exclusively as relationships of power. Although theoretically Connell is much more closely identified with socialist feminism, he keeps faith with what very loosely – and it is hoped not too misleadingly – can be framed as a 'radical feminist' vision of men and masculinities. Again, put very crudely, the idea is that masculinities are the problem and need to be deconstructed so they can be no part of the solution.

This means that it makes no sense to talk about 'revisioning' or 'rediscovering' masculinities. Indeed, there would be no need to talk about masculinities at all once they had been deconstructed as relationships of power. For Connell there is no sense in which men can be 'emotionally damaged', let alone 'oppressed,' by their masculinities because it is through these masculinities that they supposedly enjoy all the benefits and privileges that have been denied to women. Since men have power within patriarchal societies, they cannot also suffer. They might suffer psychologically for all kinds of individual reasons, but this can never be structural and so cannot be 'political'. This might go some way to explaining the relative absence of a critical engagement with men and masculinities within anti-globalisation movements that echo traditional left analyses.[2]

In the different settings of Mexico and Spain, where men have been active around issues of men and masculinities, there has been a need to rethink the distinction between the 'personal' and the 'political'. It seems as if the early responses to feminism in the 1970s and 1980s died away but the new generation of men has recognised the importance of engaging with their own emotional histories. Often there is a tension between activists who are working with men around issues of male violence, for example Coriac, a project in Mexico City, and Cantera in Nicaragua, who want to value the emotional experiences of men in their theorisations of local masculinities, and more theoretically inclined academics who assume they have to reach agreement on a new theorisation of masculinities, often by engaging with theoretical positions developed in the West before they can engage with local NGOs and political activists.[3]

Sometimes this tension is productive, but at other times it can be difficult to resolve, especially if theorists assume that the new model of masculinity has to be established before it can be applied in concrete situations. This can express a traditional masculinist vision that assumes life can be controlled through reason alone. However, this rationalism that has characterised modernity in its relationship with a dominant Eurocentric masculinity needs to be questioned because it has tacitly reinforced the notion that men are the source of authority and knowledge. This legitimates a refusal of men to talk more directly from their own personal experience since the 'personal' and the 'emotional' are disdained within a rationalist tradition that sees reason alone as a source of knowledge.[4] This is a dominant rationalist vision which is sustained rather than challenged in Bob Connell's *Masculinities*. Although there is an attempt to theorise male subjectivities, there is a limited recognition of emotions and feelings as sources of knowledge. Rather, there is a tendency to integrate masculinities into a more universal theory, partly set in terms of a Marxist theory with little sense of how Marxisms are also often bound within a rationalist modernity.

Anti-sexism/pro-feminism

Somewhat paradoxically, a dominant rationalism has also sustained different kinds of anti-sexist politics that inherited its own forms of moralism. A rationalist analysis provides a critique of patriarchy and wants to insist that the struggle is against the oppression and subordination of women. Although they also value the emotional work men do, their focus is upon the sufferings of women. This partly explains the early hostility shown to Robert Bly's *Iron John*, which, despite its essentialist vision of masculinity, is too easily dismissed as mysogynistic. Both Bob Connell and Michael Kimmel were quick to dismiss Bly's concerns, though Kimmel later changed his view. Possibly they did not want to recognise the value of what he said about some men too readily identifying with feminism, taking on the suffering of women as their own and the difficulties this could produce.

Although Bly generalises about men's complex and diverse relationships with feminisms, as I argue in *Man Enough*, he also puts his finger on some crucial issues. He has helped to name the unresolved feelings that men in contemporary societies often carry for their absent fathers. He also names the anger they can feel for their absent fathers when they needed them as they were growing up. But if Bly goes on to focus too exclusively on men's relationships with their sons and fails to appreciate both what men can learn from their partners in heterosexual relationships and what they can offer to their daughters, he does give space for men to explore their own inherited myths and the complexity of their emotional lives. If he places the focus directly on the experience of men, this does not mean that he can thereby be dismissed as anti-feminist.[5]

Michael Kimmel revised his early opinions and did work with Bly in different venues in the United States. He learnt that it was mistaken to identify Bly and the movements he helped inspire with the strong anti-feminist men's rights movements that had developed and which were often centred around issues of divorce and fathering. He recognised the need for a more complex political reading that can understand the anxieties and frustrations also driving men towards an anti-feminist politics. Rather than rush into making moralistic judgements, we have to contest these positions and expose the reassertion of patriarchal power they represent as we challenge men to think again. This means we also have to learn to engage with the pluralisation of feminisms and the different positions taken up in relation to men and masculinities. We also have to question theoretical and activist movements of men that have left little space for them to revision their masculinities.[6]

In *Man Enough*, I argued for a new framework that learnt from both the strengths of an anti-sexist/pro-feminist men's politics as well as from a critical engagement with the mythopoetic men's movement, acknowledging that Bly could not always be held responsible for the directions these movements had taken. But it remained important for men to explore their own emotional histories and the diverse masculinities they had grown up to identify with, and so to learn how to speak out of their own experience and be able to relate to the wider structural relations of power. This would involve questioning a rationalism they had grown up to take for granted within modernity as well as the privatisation of experience that has been a feature of postmodern cultures.

We also need to engage with different global, regional and cultural histories so that we can appreciate the weaknesses of universal theories, which can present homogenised visions of masculinity as if they transcend cultural and historical specificities. This can be a weakness in Connell's conception of hegemonic masculinities which can easily be abstracted and presented in terms of universalist discourses of power. It is also a question of whether there is an unfortunate resonance between Anglo-American masculinities that have become 'hegemonic' within a globalised economy and the universalist forms of theorising masculinities that have felt so appealing. They can make it easier for men to feel that they are not speaking from particular cultural and historical positions but rather within modernist discourses from a universalist point of reason. As men invested with the tasks of theory, it is easy to speak with the authority that comes from reason at the very moment when we are supposed to be deconstructing male power and dominance.

We also have to appreciate that a discourse of gender equality carries its own universal assumptions. It is too easy to assume that we know what we are talking about when we speak about 'gender equality'. This is presented as a modernist aspiration for the future that allows us to forget the painful histories and traditions that people carry silently from the past. This is clear, for instance, in Spain and also in the Basque countries, where there is an anxiety to leave the traditional and authoritarian past so closely identified with Franco so that these nations can be part of a new Europe of nations. In itself this raises difficult questions about the project of state-building and how historically the Reconquista that sought to unite Spain under a single ruler was the project of a particular dominant Catholic heroic masculinity.[7]

Power/ethics

Spain was unified through an exercise of military power and subordination in which different regions were forced to submit to Castilian authority. The Spanish State was consolidated through expulsion of its 'others', namely Jews and Muslims. As New Christians – conversos – people forced to convert to Christianity could not be trusted and there was fear about an 'inner' enemy who could not be seen. This produced its own intense fear of difference, where the 'goodness' of Catholicism was contrasted with the 'evil' of the Jew, who was cast as doing the devil's work. There was a fear of ambivalence in a cultural tradition that was very clearly divided between the forces of good and the forces of evil. The purity of the Catholic State had to be defended and the Inquisition had to seek out hidden enemies who had to be destroyed so that the health of the body politic could be preserved. This helped shape a totalitarian culture that invested in heroic masculinities that were set against the threat of the female. But these dualities were hidden through the glorification of the mother, through the figure of the Virgin Mary. This helped sustain the sharp dichotomy between 'good women' and 'bad women', between virgin and whore that still echoes in contemporary Spain.

Traces of this moral dualism live on, hidden in the aspirations towards a secular modernity. This can make it difficult to discern how Catholicism can still shape women's and men's relationships to their bodies, sexualities and emotional lives. Thus 'gender equality' may be seen as an unqualified and universal 'good' that cannot be questioned and given context through its complex relationship with Hispanic, Catalan and Basque traditions. At the same time traditional patriarchal masculinities within the New Spain can be defined as 'bad', as what needs to be overcome and left behind. But within a rationalist ethics we can be tempted into making too sharp a distinction between 'tradition' and 'modernity', as if new 'models of masculinity' can somehow be discerned through reason alone. But this tends to ignore the need to remember traumatic histories from the past as well as the more recent Civil War in Spain if we are to appreciate the ordering of gender and sexual relations. Within modernity we think that these histories can be put aside as people learn to focus upon opportunities opened up in the present, but this can make it harder to discern forces silently at work within intimate and social relationships.

Within Northern Europe, where Protestant ethical traditions have largely defined the terms of modernity, there is a stronger sense that men need to be 'independent' and 'self-sufficient'. There is less space for the figure of the Virgin within Protestantism and therefore less attention given to the feminine. Rather, the feminine can be more easily identified with sexuality and so as a threat to male reason. This works to shape a different, more impersonal form of rationalism and so a different ethics of knowledge and power. There is a clearer sense that emotions can be suppressed as signs of the 'feminine' as a dominant masculinity learns to identify with an independent and autonomous faculty of reason. Ethical theory is largely shaped within Kantian terms that assume a categorical distinction between reason and nature, where nature has to be shaped to accord with the dictates and demands of reason.[8]

In the Scandinavian countries there is a much more widespread commitment to gender equality and it is largely taken for granted that women have an equal right to compete in the labour market. Feminisms have also had a much greater impact upon the state and upon welfare programmes. The commitment to gender equality was supported by widespread provision of childcare facilities. The state took responsibility for childcare so that both men and women could participate more equally in the labour market. But this vision of gender equality could also make it difficult for partners in heterosexual relationships to learn to negotiate dependencies created through pregnancy and birth. With the widespread expectation within post-feminist cultures that not only men but also women will exert control over emotions and feelings as 'irrational', it can be difficult to deal with the complex emotions which can emerge for women and also for men with a new birth. People sometimes have limited experience with negotiating anger, so that they tend to suppress it.

Alcohol may help people to feel more emotionally expressive, and alcohol abuse is widespread not only in some Scandinavian countries but also in the former Soviet Union and in Eastern Europe. The particular form of individualism that characterises a Protestant modernity can leave men feeling isolated and lonely, unable to reach out for support to others. Often they are trapped by the images they have created as rational selves in control of their emotional lives. They can be haunted by a sense of failure as they cannot live up to the ideals they have set for themselves. They can feel that they have failed to live up to ideals of gender equality that can be legislated for in Scandinavian countries. Sometimes there is an ideology of equality as sameness that can make it difficult to negotiate gender difference/s and activities individuals might engage in more easily. With the high divorce rates and the difficulties of exploring inner emotional conflicts that remain hidden because people do not want to betray their ideals of gender equality, people can find themselves drifting apart as they are encouraged to discover individualised solutions for themselves.[9]

Partly because of the institutionalisation of feminist claims in state welfare systems, there has been an increasing tendency in the men's movements in Scandinavia to reconsider issues of sexual difference/s. Men have been prepared to explore the difficulties they can face in participating in the domestic sphere, which has traditionally been one of the few sources of women's power. Men have also been prepared to question whether childcare and domestic work can be conceived in completely neutral terms as activities that can be equally divided, wanting to reflect upon whether fathering, for instance, brings particular challenges and gifts to parenting. This is not necessarily to question assumptions of gender equality, but to redefine its terms through the experience of changing gender relations. This can help question the idealisation of experience that can be a feature of a rationalist modernity.[10]

European masculinities

Being aware of the complex and traumatic histories in Europe can be part of a process of opening up a dialogue between diverse European masculinities. This involves appreciating the different cultures of masculinity rather than thinking in rationalist terms that differences can be superseded through a universal discourse of power. Men can learn from the diversity of experiences gathered in different movements concerned, for example, with practices men have developed to work with perpetrators of male violence or from their experiences as new fathers. This will involve a readiness to revision relations between work and intimate life, rather than assume that gender relations can be reorganised within the private realm alone. Instead, we can think across boundaries as we learn from the different ways in which public and private spheres have been imagined and shaped within different European traditions. A sensitivity to cultural differences has become even more necessary within an expanded European Union. It also helps us to establish more complex comparisons across global masculinities.

As men we have been too ready to accept a universal analysis of masculinities in terms of relationships of power. This has been partly fostered by men adopting as their own a traditional feminist analysis of patriarchy as power, so avoiding the need to engage critically with different ways in which feminisms have theorised men and masculinities. It has also allowed for a misleading parallelism with the women's movement, especially as a move has been made internationally towards gender analysis. The women's movement has developed theoretically and politically since the early 1970s, so we have to be careful to acknowledge the relatively small numbers of men in different countries who have been engaged critically with men and masculinities. We also need to be wary of imitating a postmodern analysis that would echo the critique of 'woman' as a category, before it has learnt how to name its own experience as masculine or explored the diverse inheritances of its own masculinities.

This tendency to rush into a postmodern analysis of unstable masculinities can itself emerge from a longstanding fear of the personal and emotional, which have quite different meanings within the constructions of masculine subjectivities than they do for women.

At the same time we have to acknowledge the hold of a revisioned rationalism for both women and men within a postmodern culture. Appreciating that they live in a world of far greater gender equality, they can be reluctant to name experience as masculine when it seems to accompany a fear of vulnerability. It is as if young men feel that they ought to be able to cope with more equal gender relations and that what matters is how they present themselves as capable and 'in control', at least in public.

In different parts of Europe men's movements have thrived for a few years and then died away to be reborn. Sometimes it can seem as if the difficulties men face within postmodern cultures of validating their own emotional histories as men is tied to a new emphasis upon being 'in control,' with men learning to negotiate a wide range of identities as they move between different spheres. Often men resist processes of self-exploration that potentially threaten images they want to sustain of themselves. This can make it difficult to discover *how* 'the personal is political'. This is an insight that different generations of women seem able to integrate without the same felt need for consciousness-raising groups. But then there has been a disavowal of the personal as younger generations of women have felt a need to regulate the boundaries between the private and the public if they are to be able to compete on equal terms. This has also shown itself in the difficulties of dialogue between different generations of feminist scholars/activists that hold different senses of the relationship between 'theory' and 'politics'.

Frequently the references we make to cultural and historical differences and to diverse cultures of masculinity turn out to be gestural; we find ourselves trapped in universal and abstract conceptions of masculinity as power or else in idealised visions of 'gender equality' as a transcultural and transnational aspiration. We assume that once we have analysed masculinities in the universal terms of male privilege and power, we can 'modify' the analysis for different cultures. Cultural differences are set as forms of 'particularity' that are transcended within the 'universalist' analysis of masculinity as power. This makes it easier to move too quickly from the 'psychological' as the 'emotional' to the universal analysis of masculinity as dominant or hegemonic power.

We need to insist upon spaces of reflection and to suspend the more universal and abstract analyses. We need to be much clearer about the cultural settings in which these diverse theorisations of men and masculinities have emerged. Rather than giving voice to our experience as men and so exploring our own voices so that we can be clear about the positions we are speaking from, we find an anti-sexist politics speaking more easily in general and impersonal terms. At the same time it has been crucial for men to learn to take seriously how violence against women has been normalised in diverse cultures. Sometimes it is a duty to men to discipline their wives through physical violence, for women supposedly cannot be expected to control themselves. As women are deemed 'closer to nature', so they are often figured as 'irrational' and so unable to control their own experience without the external intervention of men. In this way male violence towards women is legitimated as it is often hidden behind closed doors. As men critically engage with their own cultural masculinities, so they can begin to grasp the different moralities and institutions through which power is exercised.

Difference/s

Western conceptions of modernity are deeply implicated with rationalism as power of a dominant white, heterosexual masculinity. In this way knowledge cannot be separated from power, even if we need to think their relation in different terms than those favoured by the early Foucault. But this means we have to question a European modernity that frames a rationalist tradition in which discourses of masculinity as power can so easily be taken for granted. We need to explore how the categorical Kantian distinction between reason and nature has shaped the West's colonial relationships of superiority to its 'others'. This was a racialised process through which colonised others were identified with nature and separated from culture, which was identified with European reason, science and progress. It was only by accepting their subordination to European power that the uncivilised could hope to make a transition from nature to culture and so enter the modern world. This was also a gendered process through which European middle-class women were also traditionally silenced, expected to leave the dinner tables of the powerful so that men could be free to discuss important questions on their own. Women were to be seen and admired as objects of sexual desire, but they were not to be heard. Not only were women to be identified with children, but the weakness of their inner connection with reason marked them as also needing the protection of a dominant masculinity. As Kant makes clear, women could also not be expected to think for themselves and so they were destined to remain within a condition of 'immaturity' unable to benefit from the gifts of the Enlightenment.[11]

Sometimes men aware of the challenges of feminism find it difficult to discover their own voice. They feel that anti-sexist men's politics belongs to an earlier generation and that it has become too rhetorical to be believed. A younger generation of men often questions the moralism figured as pro-feminist men's politics. Sometimes it just does not ring true and they can identify with the suspicion women feel, as if these men are somehow presenting themselves as different from other men, when clearly they are not. They learn from their experience that they are living in a very different world, especially in their relations with young women and gay men with whom they were at school. They are suspicious of the easy universalism into which men seem so easily to escape. They might feel a need to honour the experiences of the past while also learning to voice the very different lives they live as young men in the present.

Reflecting on diverse cultures within Europe and the United States, we need to appreciate that patriarchal masculinities take on very different forms; for instance, they are shaped differently within Protestant and Catholic traditions. The history of the Reconquista in Spain, for example, shows the struggle to marginalise and exclude Jewish and Islamic masculinities that had existed in some kind of dialogue with Christianity in the Convivencia. But this was to change with the unification of Spain. The motherland had to be 'purified' of all alien elements and foreign bodies that threatened its centralised and homogeneous vision as 'Catholic Spain'. Those who were not Catholics were deemed to be a threat that needed to be eradicated through expulsion. This worked to silence other national traditions, for instance in Catalonia and the Basque country, which were demeaned in the eyes of the dominant cultural patriarchal masculinity. The expulsion of the Jews coincided with the externalised project of conquest that was also to serve as a point of unification. Masculinities were set within the heroic discourse of conquest, which served to unify the country in opposition to colonised 'others' in New Spain that had to be defeated for the glory of the mother country.

We need to engage with these different national, regional, cultural and religious histories if we are to explore the diversity of European and global masculinities. This means resisting the universal terms of a patriarchal analysis as a transnational theory in terms of which diverse gender and sexual differences can be analysed. We also need to explore how these traumatic histories of conquest, colonialisation and resistance have been disavowed and actively forgotten so that people within late modernities can identify themselves with the future as they turn their backs on the past. Often there are breaks in historical memory as grandparents and parents have refused to speak about their traumatic histories so that new generations can somehow be protected from painful pasts.

For instance, in Franco's Spain people in the Basque lands were forced to change the spellings of their names and give up using Basque names as part of an attempt to destroy their culture and traditions. An older generation often lost connection with their own language, which was only reclaimed when Franco died and a new democratic Spain was created. But tensions have remained, as the terms of national and regional identities have to be renegotiated. Perhaps it is easier to forget these painful histories, so that a new generation can make its own life in a globalised present, even when it insists on reclaiming local languages and traditions. But these histories have a tendency to return and can be crucial in maintaining a balance between past and present. As gender and sexual identities became refigured, so people reach for a new relationship with their pasts. As they learn to participate within global cultures through the Internet and other forms of mass communication, they can use virtual media in which to explore their own diverse identities. Feeling isolated in relation to gay identities within a homophobic culture, young men can take refuge within a virtual space that allows them to recognise aspects of identity that might otherwise remain hidden. They can explore virtual spaces of identity to discover relationships in which they feel affirmed, as well as to retrieve aspects of local histories that might have been silenced within other media.

As a dialogue opens up between diverse European masculinities, the past cannot be forgotten but needs to be acknowledged through the memory work people can do in the present. The twentieth century, which saw the devastations of Auschwitz and Hiroshima, produced death and destruction on a scale that has left deep scars in the relationships between peoples and nations. We cannot explore these diverse masculinities without seeing them through their relationship with imperial and colonial others. It is through these historical relations that masculinities have been defined. We cannot speak about 'new masculinities' until we have engaged with the complex histories which mark relations with our fathers and grandfathers. We have to be ready to think about displacements and migration so that we can understand the complex hybrid relations and identities that have emerged across the boundaries of nation-states. If we refuse the notion of 'Fortress Europe', we have to be ready to rethink its complex histories and relations with its others. Some of the fears and anxieties lived out in the present, particularly in relation to homophobic and mysogynistic discourses, have to do with complex histories of male supremacy and entitlement that need to be remembered through their specific historical and cultural settings.

In part this involves developing a critical relationship with the different ways we have learnt to think about men and masculinities. It forces us to question an easy universalism and the temptation to cast masculinity abstractly as some kind of homogeneous entity that transcends history and culture. However, while there are resonances between different traditions and across diverse colonialisms, masculinities are always framed within particular histories of class, nation, religion, 'race' and ethnicities. As we come to name our experience as men within newly globalised relations, so we can learn to question the prevailing individualisms of Western liberal postmodern cultures. As we learn to make connections that the larger culture renders invisible between the personal and subjective identities and the structural and historical conditions in which we live, so we can appreciate the need to think about the relations between the 'psyche' and the 'social' in new terms. But this will mean challenging views about the 'therapeutic' as the personal and emotional while the political remains identified with the structural and the impersonal. It will also mean rethinking the terms of male violence, as both structural and historical as well as personal and emotional. To this end we have to rethink the terms in which we have been tempted to understand male violence.

4   Rethinking male violence

Learning

How do we learn from our experience as men, in dealing with both our own violence and that of other men? When men witness violence normalised and legitimated in relationships, they can feel responsible for this terrible suffering. Men who have been engaged in working with perpetrators of violence tend to be most insistent that an anti-sexist politics needs to treat masculinity as the problem that can be no part of the solution. They may feel that their masculinity has been shamed and that it is only through an identification with the sufferings of women that they can be redeemed. They insist that men have to be made aware of this suffering and learn to critique a patriarchal culture that has legitimated it.[1]

But when women argue that they cannot trust men because of what they have experienced and learnt about men's violence, we need to critique an analysis that defines all men as 'potentially' violent in a way that resonates with the idea that all men are 'potentially' rapists. While we might understand the distrust women feel, we have to question the universalism of this analysis and the judgements it fosters. And while we recognise that heterosexual men can take their power for granted within a patriarchal society, we need to differentiate if we want to allow for a reflective space in which men can change.

In rethinking male violence, I want to draw upon two contrasting experiences, one from Europe and the other from Central America, that we can learn from. The first is a talk given by Michael Kaufman to the conference entitled 'Men in the Face of the New Social Order', which took place in San Sebastian in the Basque country in June 2001. Michael is a Canadian activist and writer who has done important work in the men's movement and has been centrally involved with the White Ribbon Campaign that started after a terrible incident in which women students were killed. This campaign has now spread to many countries. Even though Michael's presentation was clear, I felt uneasy about his analysis and about his relationship with the audience. What came over was a sense that Michael could speak authoritatively, but had little to learn. This sounds unfair even as I write it, but it had to do with the fact that he was speaking as a North American, as a Canadian who is otherwise very sensitive to the power of the United States. It affirmed that a man can still assume authority, even when he is talking about violence towards women. Of course he also remembered to say, invoking an analogy I have always felt uneasy about, that when you want to learn about racism in South Africa you speak to a person of colour, so when you want to learn about men's violence towards women you have to speak to women.[2]

For some reason the analogy does not help, although it has for a long time been part of a radical feminist analysis and has shaped assumptions about men and masculinities. I don't know whether my unease has to do with the distance it creates and the way it positions men who work against male violence in relation to other men. I also feel uncomfortable with an anti-sexist, pro-feminist analysis which seems more attuned to speaking about the sufferings and oppressions of women than speaking out of its own, male, experience. Michael Kaufman gave an example – one I felt he had given too many times before – of walking in a park with a woman friend who was verbally attacked. He felt terrible about the incident and felt he should apologise for the abusive language used by the man. It seems as if he felt shamed by his own sex in general and needed to apologise on their behalf.

But his friend turned round and said that he should not feel shame, nor should he apologise; rather he should feel angry at the man for having behaved in such ways. Michael took the point, or at least seemed to. But he did not seem able to think through the full implications of her challenge. He went on to say that it was an assault on her human rights and that men and women should be able to walk freely through public spaces without fear of abuse or assault. But there was something too quick in this shift towards a discourse of human rights, as if this does not carry its own gendered assumptions, and can be presented in gender-neutral and universal terms. The universalism did not ring true. It seemed to serve as a distraction from the point of her challenge.

Anger

Suppose a woman tells me that I should be angry that a man has spoken to her in a sexist way, and I realise that I do not feel angry, even if part of me might want to. What do I do then? It might be partly a matter of recognising that not only was the woman demeaned, but that in not being able to connect to my own anger, I was also being undermined in respect of my own humanity. Women have learnt to work on the difficulties they can have in expressing anger, if they have grown up to feel that it was inappropriate and a threat to their femininity. Thankfully, things have changed and many young women have learnt to express their anger directly. But men can also feel that anger is a 'negative' emotion that they should not express because it is read as an assertion of male authority.

If the focus is uniquely upon the sufferings of women, then paradoxically Michael Kaufman is excused from expressing his anger as a man. Rather, he can maintain a position of male authority by coming to the rescue of a woman in distress. This is a position that many women suspect – as, perhaps, did the woman walking in the park. But if men are to learn to speak more directly out of their own experience, we will need to ground men's politics in different terms. We have to be wary of shaming men because of their violence towards women and question those programmes working with perpetrators that focus too exclusively on shame and responsibility.

Rather than assume that masculinities can be theorised exclusively as relationships of power, as Connell tends to do in *Masculinities*, we have to engage with the lived experience of the men themselves. Of course men must take responsibility for their violent behaviours and accept the punishments that have been established through law. But at the same time we need to create spaces in which men can reflect upon their own traumatic histories as men, rather than assume that because they are the bearers of war this overrides whatever they have suffered. We too easily assume that if men are powerful, then they cannot suffer: it encourages us to take the view that whenever women are violent, it is their male partners who should be held responsible.

Within a patriarchy, men tend to take out their frustration and anxiety on the women they live with in heterosexual relationships. This was clearly shown in the BBC film recently made about the experience of a men's group, Cantera, in Nicaragua.[3] The film opens with a voiceover saying that because men are superior they have to be obeyed, and can rightfully tell their partners what to do. As men, they have a right to be obeyed. This expresses a dualism that is familiar within Hispanic Catholic cultures, where men are seen as superior, or as inferior if they allow themselves to be ordered around in a 'feminine' way. Since men are born to give orders and it is their duty to exercise their authority over women, they never have to listen to what their partners have to say. If you have masculine authority, there is nothing for you to learn.

The documentary showed the men's group giving out leaflets at a sporting event where one older man says 'Real men do not hit their women.' If the relationship is one of possession, there is another strand that can be drawn upon which acknowledges that men should not hit women, who are defined as weaker. Rather, as we say in England, 'They should pick on someone their own size.' But what it also emphasises is how violence hurts men too, and undermines their humanity. The men's own experience fighting as Sandanistas made them feel caught within violent patterns of behaviour. One man admits that he did not want to be violent towards his son as his father had been towards him, but he found himself acting precisely in this way. In the men's group he learnt to talk about his feelings and actions, rather than conceal them as he lived out traditional masculine ideals.

Sometimes, through role-play, men might discover that they were carrying anger towards their own fathers that they had never been able to express. Having been taught to respect their parents, they felt their anger was inappropriate and reflected badly upon them. But as they learnt to talk more openly and honestly with each other, they felt less guilt than they might have done within the Protestant North. Because of the Catholic tradition of confession, it was possibly easier for the Men to acknowledge their emotions and feel they could begin again. While perhaps also questioning Catholic notions of sin, especially in relation to women as bringing evil into the world and therefore as temptations needing to be avoided, they began to reframe their experience.

Shame/guilt

When thinking about working with male violence in different national and cultural settings, it might be helpful to contrast Catholic cultures in the South, more focused upon questions of shame, and Protestant cultures in the North that are traditionally more concerned with guilt. Even if you have grown up in the West within the different traditions of Islam and Judaism, it can be difficult to escape the influence of the dominant religious traditions, even if these remain largely hidden and unacknowledged within secular modernities. But when we explore how men and women feel about their bodies, sexualities and emotional lives, it often helps to remember these buried cultural traditions that can shape subjectivities even if religious belief has been disavowed intellectually.

Within the framework that Michael Kaufman presents for understanding male violence is male power within patriarchal societies. There is a sense that men themselves have created these structures of patriarchal power, so they should be able to undo them. But there is a tension between Michael's own readiness to share his personal experience, say of the wonder he felt at the birth of his son, and his theoretical analysis of male violence. He draws on this experience to mark the difference between his son, who was welcomed by the nurse with the words 'What a strong boy!', while a girl is often welcomed with 'What a beautiful baby!' He felt that his baby could be both strong and beautiful, and that it did not help to separate out genders with such powerful expectations at birth. He also draws on his experience to question why theft from a shop might be regarded as a public concern, but violence against a partner is often regarded as 'private' and thus beyond the reach of law. Men may express individual remorse, saying to their partners 'It will never happen again', but it does, and sometimes gets worse.

When it comes to the theoretical analysis, we are given a straightforward presentation, unchanged since the 1970s, of men's social power within a patriarchal society. Thus men have to recognise the power they have over women and the different ways in which this is normalised so that, for instance, it is a man's duty to discipline his wife because supposedly 'she is emotional and cannot know her own mind'. But somehow this patriarchal analysis is presented in universal terms, even if Kaufman willingly acknowledges that it has to be reworked in particular cultures.

However, Kaufman goes on to say that it is not his intention to shame men or make them feel guilty, although this is just what his analysis has served to do. In part this is tantamount to a realisation of its inadequacy. After the talk I questioned how he could continue to say things that he did not seem to believe wholeheartedly. This is a form of self-betrayal, and goes against the spirit of the men's movement, which must speak from personal truth and integrity. Later he acknowledged that these were the things he was expected to say to maintain his movement's political profile. Unless he started with what is taken as an 'unproblematic feminist analysis' of patriarchy, even if its universalism has long since been questioned by feminist theorists and activists, he would be opening himself to attack. No doubt there was some truth in this, but it was not a satisfactory situation to get into. The White Ribbon movement would still flourish even if he had focused on the present, rather than reiterate past positions that have become almost rhetorical.

In the second part of Kaufman's analysis he talks about the individual experience of men in terms of their powerlessness, not their power. But it is only when the traditional patriarchal analysis is in place that he goes on to mention the lived experience of men who have either suffered violence at the hands of their parents or been witnesses to domestic violence which they felt powerless to prevent. In this part of his analysis violence is understood as a 'compensation' for male powerlessness and impotence. But this unhelpfully separates the analysis into two discrete parts. As a theory of 'compensation' he draws upon such patriarchal expectations as that 'real men do not allow themselves to be bossed about by women' and that 'real men are supposed to be in control'. The idea seems to be that because men cannot realise these traditional patriarchal aspirations, they resort to violence to affirm their male identities.

Implicitly working within the terms of a secularised Protestant tradition that typically informs modernity, Kaufman appeals in somewhat moralistic terms for action to end male violence towards women. I felt uneasy as the tone of this appeal towards the close of Kaufman's speech to the conference at San Sebastian. I did not expect it, and it encouraged me to reflect upon its sources. The impression was given that men were positioned within a patriarchal analysis as guilty because of the power they inherited, and so could draw upon it in their relationships with women and gay men.

Difference/s

Within an anti-sexist men's politics there remains an echo of the Protestant assumption I sought to explore in *Recreating Sexual Politics* that men are born with evil natures and that they cannot trust their own emotions, feelings and desires. This Protestant tradition was given a secular form within modernity through Kant's ethical writings. This feeling of guilt emerges from the exclusive identification of masculinity and power, so that it becomes difficult to acknowledge that men should accept their condition as a group, but should take responsibility for their actions as individuals. This helps to question the guilt that men are made to feel within anti-sexist men's politics, as if their masculinities have to be rejected for them to experience freedom as men. This produces an impossible situation, which works to demonise masculinities and does not resonate with younger generations of men who have grown up to experience more equal relationships with women. They are less concerned with relationships between men and feminism, which was such a formative theme in the sexual politics of the 1970s and 1980s. In the West, as a younger generation of women resist identifying with feminism and assume that gender equality has been realised, so men can also feel estranged from men's sexual politics, isolated in their emotional concerns.

Kaufman's analysis starts with a commitment to gender equality while at the same time holding that men's work to end violence against women is accountable to women and women's groups. He is clear that violence is never legitimate, is always unacceptable and must be stopped. There can be no justification for individual acts of violence. Women's safety and dignity must come first. Men have to learn to take responsibility for their violence towards women and they have to be held accountable. At the same time Kaufman goes on to argue that we have to recognise a diversity of men and masculinities, and acknowledge that different men have different beliefs and behaviours and cannot be treated as part of a homogeneous group. This is already in tension with a radical feminist analysis of men and masculinities that tends to explain women's violence, say towards their sons or daughters, as a consequence of their subordination to male power. It is also in tension with the insight that violence towards women cuts across boundaries of class, 'race' and ethnicities.

Younger men are often keen to involve themselves in the campaign against violence against women but they question the moralistic analysis. They sense that it can be patronising at the very moment that it presents itself as supportive of women. Its focus on the terrible sufferings of women works to silence its own reflections on the contradictions of male experience within a patriarchal culture. If you refuse to position yourself as superior, you are showing yourself to be not 'man enough'. In this sense violence does not work as compensation, but as a straightforward assertion of male dominance.

Kaufman draws upon the notion of a 'psychic armour' of masculinity which is partly explained by a father's absence in the early years of his son's life. Such an armour protects them from the pain of absence, and they learn a narrative which says that as boys they can be independent and self-sufficient, and do not need love and recognition from their fathers. Kaufman asks his audience to imagine what it is like to relate to others wearing armour, taking this metaphor literally to make his point. It helps to produce emotional distance and is shaped within a fear of intimacy that is experienced as a threat to male identities. Armour also makes it difficult for men to experience empathy with the sufferings of others, so that they may not feel the consequence of the suffering they produce through their violence. Since he cannot feel her pain, it is easier for him to insist that 'I did not hurt her'.

Sometimes when men have witnessed violence when they were young, say exercised against their mothers, they can either identify with their fathers or feel horror at their own powerlessness to intervene. Some might resolve never to be violent themselves, but this may fail: a Nicaraguan man in the documentary *Macho* revealed that his father was never around for him since he had children with different women, but he found his resolve never to be violent was at odds with his own behaviour towards his own son. This tension between ideals and behaviours encouraged him to join the men's group. He recognised that he had to work on himself and that he needed the support of other men. But what is striking in this Central American Catholic culture was the insistence that shaming men was not the aim, because it would not produce change. Rather it was stressed that violence also worked to dehumanise them. This undermines the moralism found in Anglo-American writings. The Nicaraguan man says that although he is poor, he is rich in the love that he expresses towards his son and towards others.

In this catholic culture, rather than an implicit moralistic appeal to curb the 'evil' natures of men, there is more a sense of what men can gain for themselves by expressing more of their potentially loving natures. This is an interesting reversal since traditionally it was women who were regarded as the source of evil and who therefore had to be disciplined by men because they could never be trusted not to lead men astray. It was through a dominant Christian tradition that Genesis was read as a text that affirmed, through Eve, women's distrustful and evil natures.[4] In a reversal within a moralistic sexual politics we can find the idea of women's innocence and men's guilt through their identification with patriarchal power.

Within the Nicaraguan men's movement there was a crisis when Solamerica, the daughter of the Sandanista revolutionary leader Daniel Ortega, accused him of rape and sexual violence over many years. He had come to power as Daniel, 'the fighting cock', and he had used his power against his daughter. It was difficult for men who had identified with Daniel to recognise the truth of the accusations made against him. At first they did not want to believe them, but then they recognised these strategies of denial. For it was crucial to the work they were doing against violence that they acknowledged their own violence and how it had dehumanised them. The only difference between them and other men was that they acknowledged their violence and wanted to change it. They felt ashamed to recognise that they had been violent; growing up within a macho culture meant that violence was expected of them, as a legitimation of their male identities.[5]

The men's group came out in public support for Solamerica and they demonstrated alongside her. She appreciated their support and the work they were doing with young men in the shanty towns, and in helping to change attitudes in the police and the army. They were concerned to question inherited masculinities and the superiority they had learnt to assume over women and gay men. They recognised the need for young men to get together in gangs, but this should not mean the abuse and humiliation of others. Operating within a Catholic culture, they could appeal to notions of forgiveness, recognising that it was also important for men to learn to forgive themselves for the violence they had perpetrated. They could question the dualistic conception of women as virgins or whores, as well as the suspicion they were brought up to feel towards women. It was because women could not be trusted that they did not have to be listened to. Rather, if a man refused to demand obedience, he was not a 'real man'. Masculinity was tied to a specific vision of activity, so that even if men have sex with other men they are not deemed to be homosexual.

We need to question the universal terms of a patriarchal analysis that can make it difficult to appreciate cultural patterns of violence and humiliation. We need to grasp the material, social and cultural formation of male violence and how this emerges out of particular conceptions of male superiority in relation to women and gay men. This means exploring diverse ways in which heterosexual masculinities are set within a fear of the 'feminine' and homosexual desires. It also means appreciating the different stages that boys go through in their transition to manhood and the anxieties they live with in relation to their sexual and gender identities. Often it can be difficult to work with boys between the ages of 10 and 14 because their fears have been so internalised that they will not easily share them with others. It feels too risky, though in later years they might reflect on what they have lived through.[6]

We need to acknowledge not only the violence that men perpetrate against others, but also the violence that they do to themselves when they block the expression of their vulnerability, fear and intimacy. Within specific cultural and historical settings we need to find a balance between these different concerns so that men do not 'close down' emotionally but feel safe to explore some of the complexities of their own emotional lives. If they have witnessed violence and humiliation at an early age, they may have unconsciously resolved never to place themselves in a similar position. Sometimes they may perpetrate violence before allowing themselves to be victims of violence.[7]

In different cultural settings men can grow up feeling that they are not lovable. Sometimes they exercise power as a means of gaining sex, which they have learnt to identify with love. Within the Protestant North there is often a refusal to engage with issues of feminism because men feel uneasy about the guilt they know they carry and feel they should have 'solved' these questions of emotion and desire for themselves. There can be an uneasy tension between their inner feelings and the ways they behave towards others. In Scandinavia, where there is a widespread acceptance of gender equality as an ideal, men feel they should be able to regulate their behaviours accordingly. They do not want to acknowledge their violent desires towards women because this would threaten the modern image they want of themselves. Thus they live in denial, knowing that they cannot easily be forgiven their desires and behaviours, which merely confirm their 'evil' natures. This can partly explain the interest there was for a time in Bly's mythopoetic work in countries like Denmark: it seems to provide a space in which men can explore issues of gender difference which are often closed within neutral visions of gender equality.

But while we acknowledge diverse cultures of violence, we must also be aware of the material conditions that sustain unequal relations, as Catherine Reilly wrote in a piece entitled 'Girl power is Africa's own vaccine for HIV' (*The Guardian*, Tuesday 26 June 2001) in relation to a United Nations meeting in New York on HIV/AIDS. As Reilly has it, 'Africa's unequal gender relations are now deadly. HIV/AIDS has advanced human rights violations, such as rape and discrimination, from merely brutal to fatal. Threatened by physical violence and a life of hunger and poverty, young girls in Africa cannot say no to risky, unwanted sex' (p. 12). She gives examples, saying that 'Child brides cannot say no to sex without a condom to their older, sexually experienced husbands, who could respond with violence or desertion. Orphaned teenage girls who are heading households of as many as six younger siblings find it hard to say no to sex with a "sugar daddy" in exchange for a good meal or payout of a month's school fees' (p. 21).

Reilly warns, 'Condoms and AIDS education are of little use to girls who lack the economic bargaining power to negotiate safe sex' (p. 21). But she helpfully draws attention to Uganda and Senegal, which have had most success in stemming the spread of HIV/AIDS through the political and economic empowerment of women and girls that has been instrumental in changing risky sexual practices. These countries have opened up access to productive resources, starting with universal girls' education. Through income generation and micro-credit they have pursued the empowerment of women and girls. In Uganda women have been appointed to key political positions to reinforce gender equity policies and efforts have been made to change attitudes towards sexual violence and increase boys' respect for girls' rights. In Senegal's AIDS risk-reducing strategy there have also been incentives for alternative employment for commercial sex workers.[8]

Teenage African girls are up to six times more likely to contract HIV than boys, and the UN secretary-general, Kofi Annan, has called for a 'deep social revolution that transforms relations between women and men, so that women will be able to take greater control of their lives – financially, as well as physically'. Catherine Reilly also reports the president of the World Bank, Jim Wolfensohn, expressing outrage at the sexual violence that infects younger and younger African girls: 'In too many communities men believe that having sex with a virgin will cure them. The human tragedy surrounding that belief is staggering – in South Africa today, 95,000 children under the age of 15 are HIV positive, most of them girls' (p. 21).

While we can welcome these words from such global figures of power, they have been a long time coming. It has taken enormous efforts to move these concerns up global agendas. They can sustain their own moralisms as 'good' men recognise these concerns to do with male violence while 'bad' men still live in denial. There is little sense of humility or self-critique which would help explain long years of silence. At the conference in San Sebastian a UN representative talked about the different projects they were working with in Central and South America with men and masculinities. It was the first time I had heard of some of this work, but it was only because of the critiques made by students in the audience that he specified the particular conditions in Nicaragua that allowed them to work with the police and the army. Even then there was no mention of Cantera and the men's groups which had made the initial contact with the army to question their work for peace while upholding male violence. For some reason they were not acknowledged, although their work was acclaimed by others. This is part of a top–down vision that can also be perpetrated through universalising Anglo-American theorisations of men and masculinities so as to sustain refigured post-colonial relations of knowledge as power.

There is a danger that we have identified within the very well-intentioned pro-feminist work of developing rhetorics that do not speak accurately out of the contradictory lived experiences of men. This means that even Michael Kaufman is bereft of adequate criteria by which to evaluate projects he deems 'good' because they do not seem to rely upon shaming men about their behaviours. His patriarchal framework that is set within universal terms threatens to become part of the problem because it produces its own forms of cultural insensitivities at the very moment that it talks in abstract and homogenised terms of masculinities as power.

At the same time as we empower women and girls, we also have to explore ways of working with men and boys, so that they learn to recognise themselves as colluding in this tragedy. But if we want men to change, we cannot simply import models of work with male violence as if they can be applied in different cultural and historical settings. This makes it important to question the universalism of a patriarchal analysis that paradoxically seems to resonate with the universal reach of global power. As women and girls are empowered economically, so they can negotiate sexual relations on more equal terms, but these negotiations are not a matter of economic power alone. Nor is it always helpful to identify masculinity as exclusively a relationship of power because it too easily blinds us to the diverse cultures of masculinity and ways they are framed in mysogynist and homophobic terms.

In different cultures, because of the global anxieties around HIV/AIDS and an increased awareness of issues to do with male violence towards women that have for so long been marginalised as 'personal matters', there is a readiness to think critically about men and masculinities. But often this means an uncritical translation of Western theories, which are presented as 'scientific' and thereby 'universal', as if they can be 'applied' in local cultures, even if they have to be reworked to take account of cultural differences. Even if these concerns are worked through in regional conferences, they can reproduce the universalist theories imported from the West since sometimes the local intellectual elites are more connected with universities in the West than with local activists who are working with men in diverse settings. If they are too concerned with working out a correct theoretical position, they will often not be working with the specific historical and cultural masculinities in which they are seeking to intervene.

This somewhat generalised approach to men and masculinities resonates with a current discourse within many international organisations that seek to balance universal human rights with a respect for cultural differences. But this can be a simplistic formula that conceals complex ethical and political concerns. For too long the discourse of universal rights has been framed in masculinist terms of the public political realm as the space of reason and power set apart from the personal realm, rendering less visible the sufferings of women and gay men. Paradoxically it can also work to silence the contradictory relationships that men often have within inherited masculinities, identifying men with the masculinities they would otherwise question.

5   Authority, hegemony and emotional life

Power and control

Men sometimes grow up in different cultural settings feeling that they have to control others if they are not to be controlled themselves. But they learn to exercise control in different ways and can learn from reflecting upon the experiences within different cultures. Within the kind of macho culture we can find in Central America, as explored by the men's group Cantera in Nicaragua, there is an intense fear of the 'feminine'. Men learn to fear their own emotions and feelings because they might betray their identity as heterosexual men. They feel that they have to control 'their' women, even if they cannot control other areas of their lives and labour. They can expect to give orders and be obeyed by their partners. Sometimes they will use violence to make sure of the obedience they believe they are entitled to. Often the structures of male power are clearly visible even if they are so taken for granted that they are hardly seen by the men themselves.

Since the 1970s the structures of patriarchal power in the west have been questioned and in various countries there is a new idea of gender equality. But this can make it harder to discern the play of power and control that is at work within relationships. The fact that young women have entered the labour market and often have incomes of their own has radically shifted the terms of their relationships. Women now have very different expectations of relationships, and if they do not work out, they are more ready to move on. There may still be a feeling of regret when relationships fail, but as long as women and men can feel they have worked on their relationships, there is a wider acceptance that people can fall out of love. People within contemporary urban cultures are less likely to keep relationships going when love has died.[1]

Though crucial class, 'race' and ethnic differences remain, there is a feeling that has moved across the boundaries of class that relationships must work for both parties. Women are less likely to stay in relationships for the sake of the children if they feel that their own emotional needs are not being met. Marriage is no longer so much conceived as an end in itself but as a framework within which individuals can expect to seek their own fulfilment. If a woman feels that she is being taken for granted within a relationship or that her partner is emotionally closed off, she will insist on change. There is a different vision of entitlement – a radical shift – where it is no longer considered enough that a man is good provider and breadwinner. Women have come to expect more emotionally for themselves within relationships.[2]

A different economy of time now prevails, in which women expect their partners to be more present in relationships. They might have put up with long hours of overtime when it was a question of economic survival for the family, but when these patterns continue in a different present, women feel dissatisfied with their partner's absence. They expect their partners to be there for them as well as for the children. But men can still feel uneasy in the domestic space, as if they do not really belong there. They can feel more at ease with their male friends at work, and so are ready to take on whatever overtime is offered, but find this difficult within the space of the family. It is as if the family has organised itself without him and he cannot find his way in. But there have been transformations in gender relations for both women and men, so that women can feel more identified with work as a space of order, where they can equally feel is their escape from the uncertainties and demands of children and home.[3]

When fathers could expect to be respected as traditional figures of authority within the family, they had a position that was reserved for them. Mothers would appeal to fathers as a source of discipline and authority – 'Just wait till your father gets home!' Talking to some young women who had grown up in migrant Bangladeshi families in East London, it was clear that different patterns were emerging. Where grandparents were not around it was often easier for new patterns to be established, especially if women were working outside the home. Some young women talked about how their mothers were relatively silent and would not speak up for their daughters. Others remarked that more equal relationships had been established. Some shared the view that it was the mother who was responsible for bringing up the children and she would provide discipline if they misbehaved. It was made clear that boys enjoyed freedom to go out and come back late that was denied to young women, who were made to feel that they carried the honour of the family.[4]

When we think about the diversity of cultural masculinities, we can be struck by both similarities and differences. We might note the different ways in which men maintain their power and control and the different sensitivities they carry. Often it is only when we are aware of how patriarchies have been sustained in diverse religious and spiritual traditions that we can begin to grasp the nature of gender relations. We can unwittingly reproduce dominant Christian assumptions about a singular source of power and authority. In this tradition the chain of authority starts with the father as representative of God's authority within the family. His word has to be obeyed as law.[5] This tradition still echoes within liberal democratic states where there is a singular source of authority and legislative power – for example in England the idea of the Queen in Parliament as the exclusive source of authority. For years this remained the ultimate source of authority and final court of appeal for former colonies of the British Empire.

While this hierarchical vision of authority resonated with the different legitimations found in the Indian caste system, it was easy to misread diverse religious traditions. It could be difficult to appreciate the power of female deities within Hindu traditions. Women were not submissive to male authorities in the way they were in the West, but these gender hierarchies had their own unresolved tensions. Women's power was to be feared and women's sexuality could be deemed as a threat to male potency. Women had their own identifications and could exercise their own forms of control over their sons and daughters in the religious sphere.

We could characterise different forms of patriarchy in which men learn to exercise their power in different ways, but this suggests a universalism that too easily becomes reductive. It is a weakness in critical work in relation to men and masculinities to define masculinities exclusively as relationships of power. It can suggest that cultural traditions are presented in orthodox Marxist terms as ideological legitimations which have to be uncovered to reveal the gendered relations of power. This was the very kind of orthodox Marxism that Gramsci was seeking to question in his examination of the workings of hegemony. But there is a danger that in Bob Connell's discussions of hegemonic masculinities we are framing them exclusively as relationships of power, both between men and women and also between diverse masculinities. Even if it is no part of Connell's intention, his work fosters a universalism that too easily sustains Western conceptions and solutions and makes it difficult to theorise diverse cultures. We are left thinking that power somehow represents the 'truth' of masculinity that has to be exposed, rather than exploring the complex relations between power and emotional life.

Power of emotional life

Bob Connell's formulations in *Masculinities* tend to echo the distinction he draws between power and emotional life which itself reflects the misleading distinction between politics and therapy. Rather than engage critically with the individualism that can inform therapeutic practices or explore why men felt the need to break with the intellectualism which limited experiments in consciousness-raising in relation to emotions, Connell tends to identify consciousness-raising as a therapeutic practice. This is unfortunate since men adopted this practice to explore for themselves the feminist insight that 'the personal is political' and how a liberal moral culture had encouraged them to construe as 'personal' and 'subjective' experience what was in fact shaped by larger relations of power and subordination.

We need to explore why men in particular class and cultural settings felt trapped in their own rationalism, unable to break away from the intellectualisms they had taken for granted. This was a difficulty Freud had identified in his realisation that men can escape from emotions and feelings they have learnt to interpret as threatening to their male identities into a rationalism that maintains emotional distance. This could be a difficulty that consciousness-raising sustained and which traditional psychoanalysis also reproduced. It explains why in diverse cultural settings men sought more expressive forms of psychotherapy, less engaged with regressions to early childhood experience and more concerned with exploring directly unresolved emotions and behaviours in the present. They looked for therapies that could support a different future in which men could feel more at ease with the complexities of their emotional lives.[6]

If we are to explore diverse cultures of masculinity, then we have to open up complex relationships between power and emotional life. We have to question Connell's willingness to distinguish between what he takes to be the therapeutic politics of the 1970s with the 'real' politics that supposedly comes afterwards. This is an unhelpful historical distinction that does not really serve to mark out different historical moments in the critical exploration of men and masculinities. Rather than engage critically with the experiences of the past, it closes them off and presents a radical break from emotions to power, from therapy to politics. This emerges out of a particular reading of Gramsci that needs to be contested.

Rereading Gramsci

In *Recovering the Self*, I suggested a different reading of Gramsci and set him in terms of Marx's complex relationship with an enlightenment rationalism, showing how Marx was both inside and outside of modernity.[7] In the 1970s Gramsci was understood through an Althusserian reading which insisted on reproducing a misleading distinction between an earlier 'humanist' vision which supposedly rested upon a given conception of human nature that needed to be 'realised' and a later scientific conception of Marxism as a 'science' of history and politics. This Althusserian reading of Gramsci had a particular resonance in the early writings of Stuart Hall and Chantal Mouffe.[8] Connell does not emerge from this tradition of structuralist Marxism but there is a moral rationalism he tends to share from his structural reading of Marx. Even though he makes some space for emotional life, it is positioned within a larger structure so that a fear of the personal and the emotional seems to persist.

Sometimes it is helpful to be reminded of these traditions of intellectual work for, even if they are disavowed in the present, they continue to resonate and even shape the ways people think about bodies, sexualities and emotional lives. In the shift social theorists made in the 1980s from Althusser to Foucault there was relatively little self-criticism that could help explain the shift and so account for the silences in people's work. Rather, certain continuities were largely policed through a notion of 'anti-essentialism' and a framework that assumed that experience was discursive, which helped maintain suspicions about the 'personal' and the 'emotional'. Gradually some of the confidence in post-structuralist traditions also began to weaken as people became concerned to think about histories, bodies and emotions. Gramsci himself was working with a relational conception of subjects, in which individuals were to understand themselves not in terms of an inner nature that had to be expressed, but in terms of their relationships with others. He wanted to think of individuals through their fragmented identities and social relationships as they came to appreciate the different histories that shaped a 'common sense' they often took for granted. In the *Prison Notebooks* he explores conditions for developing a critical self-awareness and what it means to 'know thyself', not simply as an inner psychological exploration but in terms of a network of social relationships. If people are to develop a critical consciousness, they must understand themselves not in the individualist terms of an inner psychology but in relation to a complex of historical relationships.[9]

As you read some of the crucial footnotes, you can feel Gramsci struggling with issues of how to think differently about the relationship between the 'personal' and the 'political'. It is only in the later *Prison Letters* that you see his dissatisfaction with the kind of structural account that characterised prevailing Marxisms, which treat experience as an effect of prevailing discourses.[10] He was seeking new ways of thinking about emotions in relation to the 'psyche' and the 'social'. Gramsci was already questioning a rationalist tradition that would dismiss Catholic religious tradition as 'irrational', recognising that in Italy at least, you had to engage critically with the power of Catholic traditions to shape particular identities. He appreciated how the very meaning of time was structured within the Catholic calendar and how this shaped identities and a sense of the present and future. Rather than dismiss religious traditions as forms of superstition, we had to explore the truths they also carried and the ways they could sustain people in oppressive and humiliating conditions. This would also mean exploring how the feminine was both idealised in the figure of the Virgin and experienced as a fearful contamination for men. In the Catholic reading of Genesis, Eve was experienced as a temptation to be identified with the serpent that needed to be resisted. As men could not trust women, so they also learnt that they could not trust the 'feminine' within themselves.

If we are to learn from Gramsci's later writings, then we must realise that masculinity cannot be exclusively defined as a relationship of power. Gramsci introduces the notion of hegemony in order to escape this idea, wanting to focus upon questions of legitimacy in relation to diverse sources of power. This means that, for example, we have to engage with Catholic traditions and the ways they sustain particular visions of male power. This has to do with notions of purity as well as with notions of the 'masculine' that are somehow untainted with the 'feminine'. We need to explore how particular heterosexual and homosexual masculinities are set against each other. Unless we engage in detail, we will not appreciate how male subjectivities are organised in relation to themselves and others, and in particular the homophobia that can emerge when men are close to each other.

Unless we engage with particular fears and anxieties, we cannot appreciate how male subjectivities are sustained. Rather than assume a vision of individual freedom and autonomy that is already set within the terms of a Protestant moral culture, we have to explore different visions of modernity. In *Rediscovering Masculinity* I focused on the relationship of a dominant white masculinity within a Protestant modernity, which legislated a particular relationship between reason and emotional life. This vision of masculinity cannot be translated into different cultural settings, but rather has to be revisioned within Catholic traditions. Within postmodern cultures people sometimes insist that these histories no longer resonate within more secular cultures. But we have to be careful before making this assumption; otherwise we might encourage universalism in the ways we speak about 'hegemonic masculinities' that Gramsci came to question in his thinking about Italy.

Hegemony and emotional life

If we persist in thinking about 'hegemonic' rather than culturally dominant masculinities, we may fall into a universal discourse that treats masculinity exclusively as a relationship of power. In different class, 'race' and ethnic settings there are visions of masculinity that need to be carefully explored. The way men, for instance, identify themselves with physical strength can at the same moment be discounted through a contrast between intellectual and manual labour. We might feel uneasy if we are not strong enough, but at the same time middle-class men can be brought up to disdain physical strength alone. There are complex histories that need to be explored. When Gramsci talks about the hegemony of capitalist institutions and moral cultures, he mentions different spaces in which to create alternative relationships and ways of living that together represent a counter-hegemony. In part this can be seen in the anti-capitalist movements that have emerged to contest globalisation. People want a different vision of the relationship between culture and nature, mind and body, matter and spirit as well as between work and intimate life.

Gramsci is concerned to stress that it is not a matter of alternative values and beliefs alone, but of creating alternative relationships and lifestyles that can sustain these visions. He presents this as part of a complex historical process in which people would gradually come to appreciate the connections between different spheres of life they had learnt to see as separate. When people talk about 'hegemonic' masculinities they tend to forget the cultural and political settings in which Gramsci's theorisations developed. He was concerned to challenge the spread of fascism within the working-class community as support for Mussolini developed. He was aware that you could not focus upon the mechanisms of capitalist exploitation alone. It was crucial to explore connections between power and culture, so that we have to question an analysis of hegemonic masculinities that focuses exclusively upon relationships of power and works to sever connections with culture and emotional life.

In this way Connell's work remains within the terms of a structural analysis. When he talks about masculinity as power he does not engage with the contradictory experiences of men themselves. Although we can learn from Connell's more empirical studies, he does not tell us how these masculinities have emerged and the abuse, violence and humiliations some of these men had to endure as boys. Nor does he make a link with the more theoretical discussions of masculinities, so that the different sections do not really hang together: there are not enough terms to help in the analysis of what is going on in the more empirical studies.

Postmodern social theory has taught us to question the universalism that for so long informed previous theories. We have learnt to question the position from which subjects are speaking and where they are in relation to prevailing discourses.[11] In part this has involved using the insight of sexual politics that people should speak from their own experience, rather than in rationalist terms about what is best for others. Rather than assume that 'experience' is somehow given, there was a realisation that it is already fragmented and that identities are complex. This was in tension with the universalism that could encourage women to speak for others, whom they assumed shared a situation of subordination and oppression. As women from diverse class, 'race' and ethnic backgrounds learnt to speak from their very different experiences of otherness, so an implicit universalism was brought into question.

At the same time we now have to be careful not to present homogenised and unified visions of masculinity. We have to question universalist discourses of power and the terms of male dominance. If we insist on articulating Gramsci's insights in whatever structural terms as relationships of power, we fail to connect with the contradictory experiences of diverse masculinities. What is more, we tend to identify men with the masculinities that they are often struggling with or attempting to distance themselves from. We must be careful not to lock men into relationships of power both with women and with each other, without creating spaces in which they can explore their contradictory relations with dominant masculinities.

In the *Prison Letters* Gramsci began to question the universalism that was often implicit in Marx's writings, and particularly the authority that Lenin assumed in relation to working-class experience and consciousness. Gramsci was seeking to explore his own individual voice in these letters to his family, and he was reflecting critically upon his own political experience on the left. He was rejecting a contrast often at work in earlier writings between 'knowing yourself' personally and knowing yourself politically through your relations with others. This had become a false opposition for him as a man attempting to share his prison experience with his family.

When we think about hegemonic masculinities, we are already disavowing the personal and the emotional. Men's personal struggles with their own inherited masculinities can be disavowed as 'therapeutic' and so deemed to be not political within a reductive analysis that speaks only in the language of power. This makes it easy for 'masculinities' to become a new object of scientific research, without the need to question the masculinist assumptions that treat the personal and emotional as sources of 'bias' threatening the 'objectivity' of scientific research methodologies. Rather, the temptation in social research is to follow the direction of hegemonic masculinities because it serves to silence and disavow the personal and the emotional. It allows men to reproduce a theoretical realm disconnected from the exploration of their own lived experience as men.

This echoes Marx's own difficulties with his personal experience of Jewishness, which he had to disavow in order to speak in the universalist terms of humanity. Without really appreciating it, Marx assumes that his Jewish difference cannot provide a position from which he can speak. Rather, it is a particularity that in secularised dominant Christian terms needs to be transcended so that he can speak in the universal terms of reason. Instead of appreciating that a universal discourse of reason, established in radical opposition to nature and emotional life, legitimates and speaks from the experience of a dominant white, heterosexual, Christian masculinity, Marx takes this to be a sign of unquestionable progress. Marx's Jewishness is something that has to be transcended in the move towards a universalised 'being human'. To assert a particularity of 'race', gender or sexuality is already to threaten and compromise the universalism of a humanism identified with reason and rationality alone. This explains why Marx assumes that he has to somehow be liberated from his Jewishness to exist as a human being in his own right.[12]

Unless we can critique the universalism implicit within diverse Marxist traditions, we will find ourselves reproducing these assumptions within the sexual politics, which is figured in its terms. An abiding strength of Marx's writings is his concern with justice and his struggles against exploitation and oppression. But at the same time Marx saw injustice and oppression as only 'real' when taking place within the public realm of work and politics. This was a critical assumption which feminism helped to challenge as part of its critique of modernity.[13] Not only did it question abiding distinctions between culture and nature, reason and emotion, but also between public and private spheres in its critical insight that the 'personal is political'. This was not to reduce the political to the personal, which was the false critique that both Connell and Lynne Segal were to make against the Achilles Heel project in the early 1980s. But it betrayed a refusal to acknowledge that when it comes to men, an exploration of emotional and personal lives can be part of developing a men's politics, which can question the rationalism that has shaped thinking on the left.

This means that in thinking about masculinities, questions of difference in relation to culture, religion, 'race' and ethnicities tend to fall away as forms of particularity that need to be transcended as we move towards the more universalist discourse of power. But this too often weakens our thinking about men's complex relationships with inherited masculinities and silences the lived experience of men as we find ourselves trapped in the abstract terms of hegemonic and subordinate masculinities. If Connell's work helpfully shifted towards a more pluralist discussion of masculinities and away from singular visions of the masculine, which often embodied particular class, 'race' and sexual assumptions, it also served to limit the exploration of diverse cultures of masculinities as people fell back into the universal and homogeneous discourse of power. Recognising the play of power within gender and sexed relationships is a vital beginning rather than an end in itself. It is by grasping how power works to undermine self-worth and reduces people to mere matter, as Simone Weil appreciated, that we show how power also works through emotions, bodies and institutions.[14]

This paradoxically resonates with a discourse analysis that has moved away from thinking about the power that men have in relation to women and gay men to thinking about how these different 'subject positions' are articulated within prevailing discourses. This has helped to bring masculinity back into the frame of a post-structuralist feminist analysis at the same time as it questioned notions of given gender and sexual identities waiting to be expressed. It is the personal and the emotional that are disavowed as we think in terms of subject positions and reject identities as anything more than provisional assemblages of traits and qualities. In their different ways such positions paradoxically make it difficult to explore how heterosexual men can also change, for they seem to be uniquely fixed in relation to relationships of power.

Rather than encouraging men to speak from their own experience and explore the complexities of male subjectivities, we find ourselves with an abstract and universal discourse of hegemonic masculinities. This has presented theories that global organisations have invoked because it seems to provide an analysis that does not necessitate listening to men themselves. We do not have to listen to what men might want for themselves, say in relation to reproductive health, or engage in the difficult process of negotiation across differences. Rather, we assume that because men have power they cannot have virtue on their side.

Paradoxically, a hegemonic analysis of masculinity has often silenced the men to whom we need to listen and made them feel guilty and ashamed of their masculinities. We should make them aware that, while inherited patriarchal masculinities may be part of the problem, revisioning masculinities can be part of the solution. There is no space for such a realisation in prevailing discourses of hegemonic masculinities. Rather, their universalism and global reach has become part of the problem.

6 Honour, shame, nature and peace

Self-esteem

An activist in the men's movement in Nicaragua said that the only difference between himself and Daniel Ortega, the Sandanista leader who has been accused of raping his daughter Solamerica, was that he wanted to change his violent behaviours while Daniel was still living in denial. He talked in the film *Macho* about the difficulties he faced in recognising the truth of her claims, for Daniel had been his hero and he had modelled his life on him. There was a connection between the image of the revolutionary he represented and a macho masculinity that remained unquestioned. He felt that it was important for men to realise that they can change, and that shaming them about their masculinities rather than their violent behaviours does not help the process. He also shared his feelings about how his violence had served to brutalise him, as he never felt good after hitting his partner, even when he had learnt to think that she had somehow deserved it, or that he owed it to her to discipline her and force her to respect his male authority.

He had come to question the male supremacy that he had grown up to take for granted in Nicaragua. He knew how it worked to undermine the possibilities of a loving relationship with his partner. Rather, violence created distance and left him feeling bad about himself. He felt similarly about his violent behaviours towards his son. Even though he had sworn never to repeat the violent beatings that his father had given him, he felt violent towards his own son. He knew that it was not a matter of will and intention alone. He also knew that to force obedience did not create harmony and peace, but served to produce its own resentments.

In Nicaragua, when fighters returned to their homes after the civil war they realised that they had learnt habits in the war that meant they had little patience and expected to be obeyed. They felt bad about the conflict and disharmony that they created, even though they had not wanted to. They appreciated that they took out their anxieties and frustrations on the partners and children. They had learnt a discourse about women's rights and said that they wanted peace, but they recognized that they persisted in this behaviour.

If masculinity is defined exclusively as a relationship of power, this does not help men's self-esteem. They feel that they are oppressive to women and that they cannot change. They know that they do not want to be violent towards their partners, but they have learnt to expect respect and obedience as men. Even if they have questioned some of these notions intellectually, they may still feel gripped by them emotionally. They find it difficult when their children answer back. They assume that this denotes a lack of respect which, as fathers, they feel is their due.[1]

Within a largely Catholic tradition respect is largely positional: it is the status as husband or father that deserves respect. It is not to do with thoughts and behaviours, as it might be within a Protestant culture which is organised more around notions of guilt and responsibility. Within a Protestant culture it is sometimes a matter of shifting blame between partners so that someone is made the guilty party. When a relationship breaks down, the 'responsible person' can be blamed and the other person feel blameless. This Protestant vision is questioned in the notion that 'It takes two to tango', as my Brazilian mother-in-law used to say.

Within patriarchal cultures a man can feel shamed if he thinks he is not being respected. Often there is a sharp distinction between public and private spheres, so that within a Catholic moral culture there is greater emphasis on how people are supposed to behave in public. There are codes of behaviour that people are expected to conform to, whatever their feelings. Men expect to be treated with respect by their partners and children within the public sphere and they do not expect to be questioned or their authority challenged. Men may behave quite differently in public than they do in private with their families.[2]

Honour

Within cultures that emphasise codes of honour, individual behaviours can reflect on family names. Since women often carry the honour of their family, their behaviours are often regulated and policed. Their virginity can be crucial to the honour of the family within the community, so that their fathers and brothers feel responsible for their protection. Often they are not allowed to go out in public alone and their freedom to meet other people, especially from the opposite sex, is severely restricted. Again we have to be specfic about the cultural settings we are referring to. We have to think in different terms about a Hispanic culture in Central America, where Catholic traditions still inform and give shape to more secularised cultures, than we do about South Asian cultures in Britain. We might detect certain resonances, say in the ways young women are treated, but then we have to explore the influence of being brought up and schooled in the West and the kind of conflict this often produces with traditional values.

Young Asian women in Britain talk about the difficulties of communicating their experience to their parents. They can feel isolated, especially if they are not schooled with other young Asian women. They can feel that they are being made to carry not only a responsibility for themselves, but also for the honour of their whole family. They see it as unfair that their brothers can go out and stay out, when their own freedom is so restricted. They might also be expected to help with domestic work and childcare. Sometimes they learn to accept these differences as given, but at other times they might resent their brothers, especially if their brothers identify with the father's authority and tell their sisters what to do. Young women may turn their unexpressed anger in against themselves, leading to a high suicide rate among young Asian women.[3]

Within different traditions the 'feminine' can be regarded as a threat or as a contamination that is to be feared. Thus men are encouraged to disavow their own 'feminine' qualities, learning to fear their emotions of tenderness and vulnerability. In the West this has been expressed within modernity in Rousseau's terms, where women's sexuality is deemed to be a threat to male reason.[4] This vision of a dominant male reason has been given a particular form within a Protestant modernity where men have assumed the authority to legislate for others. This is the result of Kant's identification of morality with reason. Morality is conceived of in terms of impersonal and universal principles that can be discerned through an autonomous faculty of reason that in Kant's terms is radically separated from nature.[5]

Within the Kantian tradition there is an emphasis on guilt, in which individuals learn to internalise their moral experience. They might feel guilty about the ways they behave towards others, which does not mean they will change their behaviours. Catholic cultures emphasise honour and shame, and the importance of outward behaviour: there is less anxiety about consistency between inner thoughts and feelings and external behaviours.[6]

Sometimes this means that men behave well towards their partners and children in public while being abusive and violent in private. If they feel dishonoured because their partner might reject their abusive language, they may feel not only entitled but also obliged to use violence to restore their authority. The demands of children can provoke violence if fathers feel that their authority is being challenged, or they may take it out violently on their wives, blaming them for the children's behaviour. If women are held responsible for bringing up the children, fathers can blame their partners if they feel dishonoured and shamed by their own children.

Within a Catholic moral culture men often feel closely identified with their mothers, and the culture draws a sharp duality between 'virgin', identified with the 'mother', and 'whore', who is both desired and feared. This duality creates conflicts for men who need to protect the honour of their sisters but are driven to pursue sexual relationships themselves. Even if the cult of virginity has been widely questioned in urban settings, it can still be strong in rural areas. These images can still operate unconsciously for men, especially when their partners become mothers and are thus removed symbolically from identification with the Virgin Mary.[7]

When we think about the symbolic order of male dominance we need to question the universalism of a discourse of patriarchal or hegemonic masculinities and think more about 'contextualising' masculinities. Where there is a sharp duality between the 'masculine' and the 'feminine', there is a greater anxiety about 'contamination'. Masculinity also comes to be defined in contrast with homosexuality, as if to be gay is not be 'man enough' but to be defined 'as a woman'. So homophobia is often invoked to police dissident masculinities and force men to regulate their own experience. Men thus come to fear their own impulses as signs of an animal nature that needs to be controlled. Although masculinities are often identified with self-control, the form that control takes is figured quite differently. There is less of the overt repression of emotions that we discover in Protestant cultures where emotions are thought of as 'feminine'.

Within Catholic cultures men are often tied into networks of familial relationships and assume responsibilities for family members. Here masculinities are defined in more relational terms, as men feel duties and obligations towards others. Gay men live one sort of life in their families and their gay lives with their friends. They are used to crossing boundaries and assuming expected identities, so there is less guilt and anxiety about consistency between inner experience and outer relations. If young men have come out to their friends, they might feel less urgency to come out to their parents, who might well know but remain silent so that they do not have to confront the issues.

But where there is space for more emotional expression, partly because of Catholic confession, there can also be a greater fear of gayness as 'contamination'. Closeness can be threatening where young people believe that gayness can be 'caught', so they deal with their anxieties by homophobic joking. Within Spain, for example, there is a tradition of heroic masculinities that has to do with the Reconquista and the expulsion of Jews and Muslims who had been there for generations. As part of the project of nation-building, as we have already indicated, there was a centralising Castilian vision in which mother Spain was identified with the purity of Catholic blood. The Inquisition was used against 'others' who were deemed to be threatening because of their difference. Others were to be expelled in order to maintain the 'purity' of Catholic Spain.[8]

As violence was deemed to be an acceptable way of resolving conflict for the state, so a dominant masculinity learnt to exercise violence within the domestic sphere. There was a sharp boundary that had to be continually policed where the 'feminine' was deemed to be a contamination that had to be controlled. The 'feminine' came to be projected as the abject other that needed to be expelled, so that Jews and Muslims were 'feminised' as they were racialised. Since the nation was to be defined in religious terms, they could not belong, but if they refused to convert they were to be expelled. Traditionally this also meant that women were confined to the private sphere within a hierarchy in which men were seen as the sources of authority, power and knowledge. Where there are notions of personal honour that attach to prevailing masculinities there is a different shaping of gender relations. Men and women will be concerned in different ways with how they present themselves in public and how they behave towards others.

Having grown up in post-war Britain, I have learnt to read a very different cultural situation and very different gender expectations. This helped to make me wary of abstract and universalised discourses about masculinities and gender equality that transcend social and cultural contexts. Often we cannot recognise the issues we face in both personal and political relationships because we are talking across cultural differences that have yet to be recognised. We escape into yet another abstract language.

Nature/s

An interesting paper was given at the conference on 'Masculinities in the Face of the New Order' at San Sebastian by D. Vincent Martinez Guzman, Director Catedra UNESCO Filosofia Paz, Universitat Jaume 1. Castello 'Roles Masculines y construccion da una cultura da paz'. It discussed finding our way towards a peaceful coexistence, not only that between states, but also that between genders, 'races', ethnicities and sexualities. Martinez Guzman questioned Max Weber's definition of states, which talks of their legitimate use of violence. He recognised how using violence can rob us of a sense of our own humanity as it brutalises our relationships and makes us less sensitive than we could be. He also acknowledged that when we talk about knowledge as universal, we are often speaking in the exclusive terms of a dominant, white, Eurocentric masculinity. Within modernity, as I have argued in *Unreasonable Men*, as reason is set against nature, so knowledge is often set against 'experience', which is defined as 'subjective', personal and anecdotal.

Martinez Guzman reminds us that 'culture' derives from 'cultivate', which means to grow and to harvest. This enables him to speak about 'culturing' our relationship with ourselves, with others and with the planet. It also helps him to pluralise a vision of cultures that embody their own knowledges, grown and cultivated over time, which cannot be measured or reduced to a singular scale, as a Western rationalist culture would want to assume.

Rather than setting culture against nature, this reminder of derivations helps us restore the lost connections between the two. It also helps us to question a post-structuralist tradition that not only sets culture against nature within the terms of an Enlightenment rationalism, but denies nature its independent existence by insisting, through discourse, that nature itself is a cultural construction. In his talk Martinez Guzman drew on the example of the orange trees of Valencia that have been dying over the last few years, partly because of intensive productive methods used in a competitive, globalised economy.[9]

Intensive forms of agriculture have meant that trees have been planted too close to each other. We have not understood their needs; rather we have exploited nature as a resource. We have failed to reflect upon our relationship with nature and have treated it as mere matter, thus as dead. The fertilisers we have used have drained the earth of its own nutrients. We have sought to dominate nature and defined the 'humanist' project by its control of both inner and outer nature, of human nature and the natural world.

Martinez Guzman also helps us to see the linguistic relationship between masculinity and violence. Exploring the connections in Spanish, he shows the link between violence and the Latin 'vis', meaning strength. There is also a philological link between virtue and strength related to 'vir', which links to virile qualities and so to man. Thus we inherit a tradition in which both virtue and violence are related to a dominant masculinity. Such a link is also present within the Greek tradition where these qualities exclude women and the 'uncivilised' from citizenship and so from the dialogue of ethics and philosophy.[10]

If this helps us understand how women have been silenced, and their exclusion from knowledge production, it helps us recognise a singular tradition that has been resistant to the voices of others. The Christian Roman Empire had a hierarchical vision of knowledge, in which a singular divine authority was taken to the source of all authority. As Elaine Pagels explored in *The Gnostic Gospels*, this came to be constructed through a male line where the voices of women were deemed to be subversive and were silenced. Women were to learn the values of silence and obedience, discounting their own needs and desires as selfish, and putting the needs of others before their own.[11]

The Latin language has connections between *vis* and *vita*, between violence and life. It was supposedly men alone who could give life as active subjects, while women were deemed to be the passive carriers who had little to contribute themselves. Although Thomas Lacquer has traced this tradition, from a view of the body in which women's sexual organs were deemed to be internalised male organs towards a view of sexual complementarity, there was still a sense that women's sexuality was somehow lacking. On this view, in Kantian terms, women lacked an inner connection with reason that only men possessed. This has also been figured within a Freudian tradition and in Lacan.[12]

If male violence towards women has been rendered invisible by being normalized, we have to be careful not to explain women's own violence as always a direct response to the violence they have endured at the hands of men. This is to make women passive, and to fail to appreciate their own emotional histories. At the same time we can appreciate that when a man beats up his wife, he is re-establishing patriarchy, which is not simply an external structure that bears down upon men, but is implicated in the ways men grow up to think and feel about themselves and in how they relate to women, gay men and lesbians. Masculinity can become a way heterosexually identified men learn to affirm themselves at the expense of others who are deemed not 'man enough'.[13]

Peace

In our efforts to create peace cultures we are not aiming to end conflict, since this is often structured materially over long historical periods and cannot be wished away by good intentions alone. Rather, we have to learn to live with conflict, allowing men and women within the realm of gendered relationships to express their own anger, need and loss. People may need to learn new skills of emotional communication in which they learn to relate across differences of power. Often these skills are also needed within the public realm as people learn to live with differences they might earlier have experienced as threatening. This is the challenge of a multicultural politics which refuses to categorise people into pre-existing cultural groups but which acknowledges the flows that take place as people from different generations learn from each other.

Rather than treat peace cultures as fixed in time and space, we have to engage with both the opportunities and challenges of a globalised culture in which new media and new technologies are circulating images and ideas across national boundaries. The nation-state can no longer hold to territorial visions of homogenised cultures but must look to new definitions of cultural pluralism. This means that nations must come to terms with their own complex histories and the dominance they have taken for granted in relation to colonised others. As movements of population take place across borders, so peoples will have to learn to live together in new ways.[14]

This is not a matter of merely tolerating differences, but also of learning to listen and to celebrate. We have to be wary of making judgements before we have listened carefully to the voices of women, gay men and lesbians. As people learn to make peace with each other and intimate relations become more open, fluid and democratic, so a new respect for cultural differences can emerge.

7 Negotiating gender and sexed identities

Fear

We need to explore in different cultures how masculinities are defined in heterosexual terms. How do boys grow into manhood and in what ways is this still governed by a fear of homosexuality? In what cultures are men predominantly defined negatively in terms of 'not being soft', 'not being weak', 'not being a woman'? If we think of masculinities exclusively in terms of relationships of power, then we can be left with limited visions of how men can change. We might assume that men can only change if masculinities are deconstructed and men give up their powers and privileges. At least this gives us a framework for understanding the difficulties that men have had in changing their attitudes and behaviours towards women, gay men and lesbians.

Young men often disdain their own vulnerability and emotions, fearing that these can threaten their male identities. Sometimes the fears they carry about the revelations of their own inner natures are projected as contempt for gay men. In the early years of secondary schools, when young men feel particularly vulnerable in relation to their sexual identities which are still taking shape, there is widespread reference to 'softies', 'sissies', 'poofters', 'queers', when boys talk about others. While they feel unsure about their own sexualities, they may need to establish clearer boundaries and may fear that they could be 'contaminated' by gay behaviours. They tend to keep such fears to themselves, as too threatening to share with others. If they suspect their own emotional attractions they will often internalise them. They may fear rejection by their friends, and feel impelled to defend themselves by engaging in activities that traditionally affirm a heterosexual identity. If they do not feel attracted to girls, they may seek the protection of a close friendship with a girl that they have perhaps known since early childhood. But they may still carry a fear that other boys will suspect their difference and reject them. It is as if they can develop a double skin in which they develop a sensitivity towards others that they conceal from them.[1]

Boys often watch each other's behaviours, especially between the ages of eight and fourteen. There seems to be a crucial time towards the end of primary school when the genders separate, and young boys who have grown up feeling easier playing and relating with girls find themselves stranded. At this time boys can feel that they have to find their way back to relating to other boys, even though they feel little attraction for traditional male activities, such as football. They may feel they have to pretend or show an interest because they want to be accepted, and at the same time can feel shut out by the girls' awakened gender-exclusiveness. This is a point of vulnerability for young men who can feel rejected in their efforts to belong. It is a time when bullying intensifies.[2]

At this time it is crucial for parents to give time and space to listen to these fears and anxieties. It might also be valuable for fathers to admit their own early fears, so that their sons do not feel so isolated, believing that nobody else has ever felt this way. But sometimes boys will refuse to open up or it might be too hard for them to do so, even if part of them wants to share the pain of their school lives. By this stage they may already have locked away their inner emotional lives, so they will have little access to them themselves. They will have learnt to repress their own emotions and possibly to take out their insecurities on other boys, weaker than themselves. A bullying culture emerges.[3]

Diversity

Sometimes a singular masculinity dominant in a particular school gives way to alternative masculinities. This process develops in same inner-city schools, for example in North London, where alternative models of masculinity arise. Boys have always fallen into different groups and selected their friendships accordingly. But this is different from a wider tolerance that can sometimes emerge. Where alternative ways of being masculine emerge there may be intense resistance to what is perceived as threatening and so in need of attack by those representing the dominant masculinity. Traditionally school culture has reinforced and policed the distinction between male and female, masculine and feminine, at least publicly, where signs of homosexual identities are suppressed.

Since the 1980s a plurality of youth styles has developed, and new technologies have enabled young men to seek support in different spaces. Sometimes there have been sharp antagonisms between different groups of boys, as in recent shootings in the United States, such as in Colombine High in Colorado. A group of trenchcoat-wearing boys identified with gothic styles and felt antagonism towards the sporting jocks who were given public recognition in the school. The availability of guns was a factor, but, more important, boys were ready to use them. Some of the boys spent hours every day in front of the computer and lived in a virtual space of their own, drawing on images and identifications new technologies made available to them.[4]

There were conflicts between these diverse masculinities in Colombine High that could not easily be settled. Within the official space of the school it seems as if it was masculinist-sporting culture that was publicly respected and acknowledged. In cultural shifts that developed in the wake of the 1960s, many of the other students did not identify with this culture or aspire towards it. They pursued different values and they resented the recognition given to those engaged in sports. But what was dangerous, and difficult to explain, was the resorting to arms as a way of resolving conflicts. The shootings took place not in the context of inner-city poverty but within the relatively affluent suburban middle class. The shootings were not about class hatred but about different resentments to do with lifestyle that had developed over time.

Similar shootings have taken place in other high schools in the United States and Canada, and we must be careful not to generalise. But a documentary shown on the BBC that interviewed some of the pupils from Colombine had a revealing image of a young man doing rifle practice by shooting a television set. He was talking about being part of a generation that had been brought up by television, with both parents anxiously working to provide a good standard of living for the family. He expressed resentment at being left with the television, and was made to feel that he had no grounds for complaint because his family had provided so well materially. Thus his demands to spend more time with his parents were somehow 'irrational' and selfish, because it seemed as if he only cared about himself. He withdrew into the world of new technologies and the Internet.

This young man had given up making emotional demands because he knew he would not be responded to and that he would be left feeling worse about himself, as if it was wrong for him to have emotional needs for contact. On this view emotional needs are a sign of weakness and a threat to male identities. So young men learn to attack their own emotional needs, silencing them so that they cannot betray their masculinities.

There is more space within postmodern culture for young men to explore their needs and desires. But this can still be a dangerous process because men might discover emotional needs or their love for other men. Within a dominant culture that defines masculinities in heterosexual terms it can still be difficult to discover spaces in which young men can safely explore their emotions.

Weakness

Why is it felt as threatening for young men to acknowledge their weakness or vulnerability? Many young men grow up to affirm their experience through constantly evaluating themselves according to prevailing masculinities. Gay men, for example, acknowledge at an early age that they cannot live up to prevailing masculinities, even if they wanted to. This makes it easier to recognise that masculinities are masks that men are forced to adopt.

With the emergence of feminism many young men have had to deal with more equal relationships with young women. Even if young women often do not think of themselves in terms of feminism, they are now less prepared to be put down or remain silent. Early on they can have a clear sense of what they want for themselves. But at the same time straight boys can exert considerable power through the judgements they make about girls' attractiveness, where this remains defined in terms of being attractive to men. In a recent article entitled 'Give us back our bodies', Susie Orbach, a feminist psychotherapist and author, writes: 'Every 12-year old girl I know can regale me with a tally of the crash dieters and the anorectic wannabes in her secondary school. Every one of the girls is gorgeous. Most of them are skinny. Certainly none is fat. But every one of them thinks herself gross.' (*The Observer*, 24 July 2001, p. 27).

After discovering that eating problems and body image were the major preoccupation of adolescent girls, sapping their self-esteem, the Cabinet Office and the Minister for Women in the first New Labour Government held a body image summit. They were recognising how these issues were affecting young women, and increasingly young men, 'skewing their ways of eating, away from hunger and appetite and towards watchfulness and wariness.' (p. 27). The government brought together 'those in a position to transform the situation from one of obsession and self-hatred into one of acceptance and pleasure.'

(ibid.). As Orbach recalls, 'what made the summit exciting was that arguments explicitly linking personal experience and private life with the political and economic structure were entering the mainstream of political power. Politics was moving from something out there being done to us to something that might take on those industries which breed body insecurity in girls and women for profit, by first selling it to them and then purporting to solve it' (ibid.).

Of course the corporate pushers of this aesthetic ducked responsibility, saying that fashion and design are harmless fun and do not create insecurities. They could only be influencing the few who would be screwed up anyway. In any case they are successful export industry and British design sells. As Orbach recalls, 'Leave off. Girls, we were told, just want to be beautiful.' And indeed they do.

> The tragedy is that they are. But the overwhelming number of daily images foisted on girls means that they can't register their own beauty unless they see a facsimile of it represented around them. If beauty comes in only one size and shape, then they will try and reconstruct themselves to measure up. They will reject who they are and cast about for ways to restructure themselves, by whatever means. This is not a sign of female passivity or weakness per se, but a woman's attempt to have a body that is acceptable when the one she has has been deemed not to be so. (Ibid.)[5]

As Orbach explains, 'The magazines, TV, billboard and print advertisements, the constructed girl pop groups featuring femininity as ever more skinny and sexy, were the legal routes by which the purveyors of an ideal more legal than heroin, which kills fewer people than anorexia, entered the consciousness of our female population' (ibid.). As she readily acknowledges, these images are increasingly shaping the experience of young men, who are also in a struggle against 'fat', even when they are thin. They often watch their food and feel anxious about what they take into their bodies. This is linked to a new body consciousness that is shaping men's lives too.[6]

According to Orbach, we now have damning evidence from Fiji of 'the impact of Western ideals of beauty where, in a three-year period after the introduction of TV (mainly US programmes), 15 per cent of the teenage girls developed bulimia. The penetration of Western images, coupled with an economic onslaught, has destabilised Fijian girls' sense of beauty, infecting them with a virus far more lethal than the measles Britain exported to the colonies 100 years ago' (ibid.).

We need a diversity of images that will help to reshape the currently limited aesthetic which reproduces dominant Western white, heterosexual, images. According to Orbach, we also need to intervene in 'the process by which mothers unwittingly pass on to their daughters their own fears about their bodies and the female appetite' (ibid.). She had done important work to introduce emotional literacy programmes in schools that, as she has it, 'provide girls with the means to deal with the problems of growing up directly rather than translating them into food and body-image problems' (ibid.).[7]

We also need to work with young men and the ways they translate the anxieties they carry. Boys may find it even more difficult to use an emotional language to explore what is happening for them. There is a tendency to silence their emotions and turn them in on themselves, or else to project them as anger and violence they can take out on others. But increasingly boys are also translating emotional issues they have into food and body-image problems. They are also withdrawing into new media and the Internet in the hope that they can express themselves in more impersonal and so less threatening ways. There has been an increase in the sites where young men can explore their issues of sexuality, depression, self-harm, drug abuse and suicide. These are issues about which they do not feel easy talking to their parents. They are scared of what they might discover about themselves, especially as they are growing up in a culture that often works to individualise experience and make people feel that theirs is unique. On this view there is little point in reaching out to others, because it is assumed that others have never suffered in these ways.[8]

At the same time young men are also exploring sites and chat rooms on the Internet relating to their emotional lives and issues. They can assume identities that allow them to check out their inner emotions and feelings without risking personal rejection. They can make connections with others who are living with similar fears. If they have taken the risk to reach out to others, they can sometimes question an individualisation that isolates them and learn to draw valuable support from others.[9]

Beyond gender

The changes in gender relations within a postmodern culture resist neat classification. There has been a shift away from the sexual politics of the 1970s when people were more concerned with affirming different genders and sexualities to a greater recognition of the fluidity of these identities. People are concerned with exploring their desires in the present, rather than committing themselves to an identity that they will live with in the future. Rather, there is a sense of complex identities where people are constantly negotiating their emotional needs and desires. People often feel unsure of what they want for themselves and wary of notions of identity that might fix and constrain possibilities, but they also recognise that they need time and space for exploration.

This has meant questioning implications of fixed identities, say between 'butch' and 'fem' as lesbian identities, or active and passive sexual identities. A young man might feel unsure about his sexual identity, whether he is straight, gay or bisexual. He needs the space for exploration and wants to feel validated and affirmed for whatever choices he makes for himself without feeling that he is foreclosing possible futures. But at the same time these are not fixed categories, but unstable identities that can shift with time. We must also question overly rational notions of choice that can be implicit, as if it is a question of exercising an independent faculty of reason. Rationalism that can still inform ideas that gender is 'socially constructed' leads to a detached view that can trap people as observers of their own experience.

People are often exploring embodied forms of knowledge and thus choices that connect to emotions, feelings and desires. It is commonly through reflection upon the lived experience of relationships that people discern what they want and need for themselves at particular moments in their lives. If they have recently come out of a relationship, they may need more time and space for themselves. This does not mean that they will reject a relationship if it comes their way, but that for the moment at least they need something different in their lives. This helps us to appreciate that desires are not fixed and given, somehow waiting to be discovered. At the same time people can sometimes realise that they have lost their way or sense of themselves.[10]

As young people explore their genders and sexualities, they will question the dualities they have inherited in relation to 'masculine' and 'feminine', though they might feel some freedom in the Jungian notion that people have both 'masculine' and 'feminine' qualities, even though they might reject the hierarchies in Jung's work that implicitly value the masculine. But at least this provides a more fluid framework in which they can explore a range of qualities they may have little contact with. In this exploration they move beyond the realm of the ego and the personality, possibly touching a Jungian conception of their higher selves.[11]

As we create spaces to explore the complex relationship between men, male identities and inherited masculinities, so we acknowledge the time that young men need for this exploration. This works against the prevailing culture that expects men in particular to know what they want and so make choices for themselves. Men from different class and ethnic backgrounds can thus feel a pressure to make decisions before they are ready, or make choices to satisfy the expectations of others. They find it difficult to live with ambivalence and uncertainty.

A young man might feel unsure of his sexual identity and feel the need to hide his sexual desires from his family. He might have known from an early age that he wanted to have sex with men, and could not believe that this meant he was 'failing' as a man. But it unsettles prevailing heterosexist notions of masculinity to recognise that men are no less men if they have sex with other men. As they come to terms with their homosexual desires, they may appreciate masculinity as a performance that they could refuse for themselves.[12] As they see heterosexual men trapped within the expectations of a dominant masculinity, they might recognise their lack of freedom and spontaneity: they have not had the freedom to create a masculinity for themselves. Rather they are living out the expectations of the dominant culture, unable to reflect upon what they want for themselves.

Social construction

If gender roles are not given in nature, but are features of particular cultures, then they are socially constructed, so surely they can be deconstructed. Within a structuralist tradition we read a categorical distinction between nature and culture as the founding myth of modernity. This means that we are tempted to accept a duality between gender identities being 'given' in nature and being 'constructed' within the terms of culture. If gender identities are given in nature, then supposedly they are fixed and cannot be changed. Since the idea that gender distinctions are inscribed within nature was historically used to legitimate women's subordination, we may feel that a duality is inescapable. We recall how it was argued that it was written in to women's nature to have children since they have the 'maternal instinct' to care and look after them. Traditionally this was connected to a gendered instinct for doing housework and looking after the domestic space.

It was because women's subordination was legitimated through an appeal to nature that it became important for second-wave feminism to argue that there was nothing 'natural' in the ways traditional gender roles were organized, with men identified as breadwinners and providers within the public sphere while women were to be confined within the private and domestic sphere. But we can be too quick to argue that if gender distinctions are established within the realm of culture alone, then we should accept a duality between the categories of 'nature' and 'nurture' and state that biology has no place in the structuring of gender relations. So it was that a vision of gender as 'social construction' was established in radical opposition to biology. This seemed the only way to allow people to establish their own gendered identities. It also allowed for a radical critique that wanted to move beyond gender and argue that gender roles had to be negotiated within relationships with no prior assumptions.

At the same time we might want to argue that if people are born into particular genders, this implies that they should not feel any guilt on this account, but they should feel responsible for actions they take as individuals. As men we are then responsible for the arrangements we set up with our partners in gay and straight relationships. We might have agreed a certain division of labour which had to take into consideration the power that individuals had in the labour market, but did not assume that it would therefore be 'rational' for the person with more earning power to be working because the family could be said to benefit most materially. There are other considerations that need to be brought into the equation that have to do with opportunities to develop careers as well as the need for people to work less so that they can be more involved in the everyday life of the family. Since these are negotiations which do not take place abstractly but within particular material situations over which people will have limited control, people must be prepared to renegotiate whatever agreements they make. At different times women and men will have different needs and may want to envisage different futures for themselves and their relationships.

This is not to wish away gendered relationships of power and subordination, but to recognise the material contexts in which more equal relationships are being negotiated. Some people may feel easy with strict egalitarianism while others may want to take more account of what individuals enjoy doing. Of course this can serve to consolidate traditional hierarchies, but it can also open up a space to negotiate individual wants, needs and desires within relationships in which people can learn new skills and abilities. It is easy for men in particular to say that it will take time for them to change, to get used to looking after children. This may be merely a rationalisation, and we must recognise that within traditional gender relationships men have continually devalued the labour that has gone into looking after children. Men will still come home and feel angry if their dinner is not on the table, accusing their partners of 'doing nothing all day'. It is only when men are left with sole responsibility for the care of the children that they recognise the labour involved.

This is why it has been crucial and often transformative for men to be involved in preparations for pregnancy and birth. As this becomes routine and expected it can lose its significance, especially if men are not also expected to learn how to look after babies from the moment of birth. Rather than assume that men's partners will 'teach them later', when they will be too busy, it is preferable for both partners to be learning and exchanging skills at the same time. In the early months of a baby's life we can also see the limits of a social constructionism which in the 1970s was ready to dissuade women from breastfeeding because this could create an inequality in the relationship. Some partners insisted on bottle feeding so that a more equal relationship with the new baby can be sustained. This grew out of the notion of equality as sameness.

Difference/s

It can be difficult for new fathers to accept that their role might be in supporting the primary relationship between mother and baby in the first few weeks. This does not mean that the relationship with the father is not crucial from the outset, especially if he has learnt to care for the baby from the first. But it does mean that the relationship is different because of the importance of breastfeeding. Again, this does not mean that two gay men cannot share a loving relationship with their child through bottle-feeding. We should be able to recognise differences without thereby making comparative evaluations. I know from my own experience that there were distinct moments when my own relationship with my son and daughter came into focus after the first few months. As parental figures my partner and I seemed to move in and out of significance.

The sexual politics of the 1970s resisted thinking about difference, and tended to think of childcare and domestic work as neutral activities that could be equally shared between the partners involved. There are often preferences that cross boundaries of gender, where women do not like cooking but their male partners enjoy it and so readily take it on. An Oxford University researcher, Man-yee Kan, presenting a survey of 2,000 couples which did not look at childcare but at the division of labour in unpaid household work such as cooking, cleaning and grocery shopping, found that men pay lip-service to gender equality while letting women do the bulk of the housework. On average women do more than 18 hours per week, compared with about 6 hours for the average men. But men were more inclined to pitch in if their partners worked long hours. Women's earning power made a difference, as did how educated she was and how young. A higher income gave women more bargaining power in the family. The study showed that educated women tended to do less housework than women who left school at 16, and expected their partners to do more.

In a report by Jeevan Vasagar in *The Guardian* commenting on research, Fay Weldon is reported as saying that what such studies omitted is that housework could be fun. 'The idea is that housework is a terrible burden, but it is just something you do to make your house look nice.' She is more ready to think difference when she says 'More women like doing housework than men. It's a nesting instinct. Some women don't and don't do any, but more men don't care what the house looks like ... Women who are better off just employ other women to do the housework – the rich have to find more energy to earn more money.' (*The Guardian*, Friday 6 July 2001, p. 5). Apparently in Fay Weldon's household the division of labour includes her husband taking out the rubbish while she cleans up the cat sick.

Within same-sex relationships similar negotiations take place, individual desires and preferences are allowed for, and it is also recognised that everyday life can become routinised so that some-times tasks need to be reallocated. At the same time some good intentions are never realised. At least in traditional relationships the division of labour was supposedly clearly defined. In a piece for *The Observer*, Lauren Booth, in 'That fish still doesn't need a bicycle', reports:

> Friends in the City talk sadly of the trade-off between men and women, a contract that was poorly renegotiated in the Sixties. It was never a fair deal, in the first place, but once upon a time women had doors opened for them, meals paid for and perhaps

jewellery bought in return for a life of servitude to their husbands. Your sense of worth, so goes the legend, came from keeping a clean stoop and cooking a fine flan. Now we work longer hours, buy our own jewellery and are forced to stand on the Underground even when pregnant. (*The Observer*, 1 July 2001, p. 25)

But far from living in a world dominated by ice queens and businesswomen who are ball-breaking careerists, according to Booth, 'Among my peers, there is an alarming return to the 'But I love him' anxiety and desperation of our teenage years' (ibid.). She reports bright successful women who are emotionally immature and battling with 'Does he fancy me? Why doesn't he fancy me?' insecurities. She tells a tale, supposedly common among her friends.

Julie is a 30 year-old TV executive whose partner of five years disappeared two weeks ago. She got home from work late one night to find everything he owned gone; their joint life-savings have vanished too. In the Nineties, such scandalous cowardice and abuse would have led to screams of 'get outta there, girl friend' and 'anything he's left, you burn'.

But Julia is keeping her life, their room and everything just as it is because: 'I don't want to make it difficult for him to come back.' Her identity as so-and-so's girlfriend is far more important to her than her career and her 'freedom'.

Then there's Amanda, a stunningly gorgeous PA who goes to bed and cries every night while her boyfriend runs up a huge bill having phone sex with women in Thailand and the West Indies. He even boasts about it to her friends: 'I just have to do it and Mandy understands, don't you babe?' Back turned to him and doing the washing up she silently nods.

As Lauren Booth has it,

Trust me, she doesn't, but the confidence and happiness that can come from being intelligent and sexy is being undermined by her need to have a man around, any man.

With sex on the menu at every bar and club in every city, the pressure to be 'cool' about sexuality, porn, phone sex, whatever, is immense and immensely diminishing... A few years ago, the ladette was considered to be the low point in the life of the emancipated sisterhood, but at least she was having a good time. (Ibid.)

8 Fatherhood, class, 'race', power and sex

Masculinity and power

In the early responses of men to feminism there was often an internalisation of responsibility for the pain and suffering that women had endured over time. Men came to feel ashamed of their own masculinities, thinking that they owed it to women to forsake their own male identities. There was little space for men to reflect upon how they might change and a sense that if they could change at all, it was by giving up their power as men and so surrendering their masculinities, defined in much early feminist theory exclusively as relationships of power. This allowed men to feel that if they were to deconstruct their inherited power, then there would be little sense of talking in terms of masculinities at all.[1]

Helping men to name their experience as men – itself a complex task that they often resist – becomes a matter of teaching them to recognise the power they take for granted in relation to women. But we have to appreciate that male power takes quite different forms and that it can be misleading to assume in a dualistic way that men always have power and that women are always subordinate and thereby powerless. Within the West the way we conceive patriarchal power grows out of particular cultural histories and settlements through which an Enlightenment vision of modernity has been shaped by a distinction between public and private spheres. Traditionally within modernity the public sphere was defined as a masculine space of reason and power. This was the sphere of politics and work which men learnt to call their own.[2]

As we have seen, women were to be restricted to the private sphere, that of domesticity, childcare and emotional labour. The change came with Mary Wollstonecraft, who claimed that reason was not to be assumed to be masculine faculty.[3] She who insisted, against Rousseau and Kant, that 'Public education, of every denomination, should be directed to form citizens; but if you wish to make good citizens, you must first exercise the affections of a son and a brother. This is the only way to expand the heart; for public affections, as well as private virtues, must ever grow out of private character.'[4] If she argued for more presence of women in the public world, she also made the crucially significant demand that men should be judged in private as well as in public terms. She was concerned that men would learn to identify themselves with their achievements within the public realm of work, and thus learn to devalue other realms of experience.

The power which men wielded through their assumed relationship to reason and rationality became invisible because it was assumed to work in the interests of all. So within the West men learnt to identify themselves as 'individuals' or as 'persons' whose reason transcended gender and allowed them to speak within the universal voice of reason. When fathers spoke in traditional families, they were not expressing their personal opinions as men, but speaking with this authority. They were deemed to be God's authority on earth, and their position at the head of the table symbolised their authority within the family. As the head was to govern the body, which was identified with an 'animal nature', so fathers were expected to govern their families 'for their own good'.[5]

Power and love

Fathers had a right to be obeyed, and women and children had to learn the discipline of obedience. For a wife or child to question the head of the family was already an act of disobedience. It was only because men had authority that they had power within families; their word was treated as law. But at the same time they were not expected to relate closely to their children: this might threaten their impartial authority. The upbringing of children was to be the responsibility of mothers, apart from decisions in relation to education, especially within the middle class. Fathers expected to be obeyed and loved, following directly from their position: 'Of course you love me. I'm your father.'[6]

However, in middle-class families there is often considerable emotional distance between fathers and children, especially where children in England were brought from the nursery in order to say goodnight to their parents. They lived in a separate space of their own and were made to feel that their fathers were 'too important' to relate emotionally to them. Fathers in their turn believed in 'independence' and 'self-sufficiency', where emotions and feelings were deemed signs of weakness. They would never cry in front of their children: it was their duty to discipline and set an example, for their sons in particular, that 'boys do not cry'. This disciplining of the emotional lives of men was not always so, but we are still living with echoes of Victorian imperial manhood.

So when a man reflects upon his upbringing within a middle-class English family, he might be aware of the emotional distance still separating him from his father. As a young boy, for example, he might have been taught that love was something that had to be earned through effort. He might feel terribly isolated and alone when he was sent off to boarding school when he was eight. He might have known that his mother did not want him to go, but she remained silent and did not question her husband's wishes. The father might assure him they were making sacrifices so that he could have 'a good education' which would 'make a man of him'. He was not sure that he wanted to be man when it was expressed like this, but there seemed little alternative. It was a testing time and he had to prove himself.

At school he might be given gifts if he did well. These came to represent the love that was not easily expressed in the family. Often there was coldness between his parents and rows were bitter. He did not want to listen to them. It was the one thing that made him glad to be away at school. He felt that his mother had not wanted him to leave for school, but that it was too late to do anything about it. He could not really talk to her about it. And his father had always been a more distant figure. He respected his father, but had never been able to love him. He had wanted his parents to love him as a child, but felt their difficulties in expressing direct physical affection, and could hardly recall being hugged and kissed by his parents. He knew that they wanted the best for him, but could not express the love that he needed.

If his parents separated, he could not but feel in some way responsible. He did not want them to separate but also felt that it might be better, at least for his mother. The rows that he had witnessed had left their mark and even though his parents kept saying that they 'had nothing to do with him', he wished that he had not had to witness them. When suppressed anger broke through it was so terrifying, since it seemed so much at odds with the usual restraint they showed. If he was an only child there was no one in whom he could confide. He just wanted the anger to stop. This background made it difficult for him to feel intimate and trusting in his own relationships. In his heterosexual relationships, it was hard for him to feel that his partner was really there for him, whatever she said. He still felt that he had to work out his emotional life on his own, which could leave her feeling excluded.

Because showing love was associated in his life with giving gifts, he felt unsure about his own capacities to love. He did not feel particularly lovable himself. When he was ill he did not allow his partner to look after him or touch him. He felt that he needed to be on his own. He was too vulnerable to accept the love and care she had to offer. This could make her feel resentful, as if she was useless to help him because he seemed to reject the love and care she had to offer. This was also reflected in their sexual relationship; he went for penetrative sex when he did not seem to know what he wanted. Sometimes he just wanted to be touched, but felt fearful that he might be rejected. He had learnt unconsciously to identify love with sex. It was only after sex that he realised that just being held was sometimes enough.

Men sometimes fear intimacy, finding a sexualised relationship easier than expressing physical needs to a partner. Intimacy can be threatening to male identities, partly because emotions have already been defined as 'feminine'. Since men can grow up to experience their emotional needs as signs of weakness and thus a threat to their male identities, they can find it difficult to recognise their own needs and desires.[7] This can create confusion between love, sex and care, and tempt men into thinking that if they are having sex, this means they are loved. Sometimes they show their love by buying gifts or giving money. They may not think about whether this is pleasing to their partner, assuming that such gifts are a sign of their love. This can echo how, as children they were given toys as a demonstration of love.

In some working-class cultures men grow up to assume that being a 'good' husband involves being a good provider for your wife and children. It is through work that they can affirm their male identities. This is why unemployment can prove so difficult for men to accept: they can no longer show their love by giving their partners money.

Women's power

Fatima Adimo, in a paper entitled 'My wife's tongue delivers more punishing blows than Muhammed Ali's fist: bargaining power in African Muslim society', given to a conference on 'Gender Flux' at

Chester College, 19–21 November 2001, questions assumptions in the West about the powerlessness of women who are forced into exclusion.[8] Although she might want to adopt a generalised framework which argues in terms of men's power and women's subordination, as if the theoretical terms of analysis can be presented before the concrete analysis is given, she forces us to think anew about relationships between power and gender. Although women in her setting can rarely leave the compound, they have their own sources of income, even though they expect their husbands to provide for them. Should a husband fail in this respect, a wife can complain to her own family and divorce proceedings can be initiated.

Fatima's parents paid for her education, which gave her a special position, even though her husband had other wives. It was partly because there were other wives that she could leave northern Nigeria to teach and research in Bradford. In her research she reported that some of the men she interviewed said that she should not talk to a particular person because 'he was not a man'. When she explored what this meant, she found that, as he was no longer able to provide for his family, he ceased to be considered a man. He was excluded from the company of men and was shamed.

Adimo stresses the power that women have in Hausa society, which is different from other Muslim societies. She shows that there is a more fluid distinction between the public and the private sphere, and even though women are rarely allowed to leave the compound they do not hesitate to leave their houses if they are involved in a row with their husbands. Other people will come into the compound if they hear the argument, and women can shame their husbands in public if they have been violent to them or if they have failed to satisfy them sexually. This means that there is relatively little male-to-female violence, although there is violence between women, as different wives can compete with each other. Women will immediately leave their houses if violence is threatening and make a public issue of it. Thus they can use masculinities against men, for example if they have failed to satisfy them sexually. There is a recognition of women's own sexual desires, and no shame if women seek divorce in a society in which it is accepted that women will separate and divorce a number of times.

Adimo insists that women are not simply victims of male power, but that they can use their own sources of power, even within a society that teaches the absolute obedience of women to men. The women are living in a patriarchal society, but they retain their own power, which also has a basis in their own material power. Women might lend their husbands money, but Adimo followed through a case where a women sought a divorce because her husband had made use of money that was intended for her brother's operation. She was angry to discover that he had used the money for himself, and complained to her extended family about what had happened. In the end she decided to divorce her husband.

A man from Somaliland who was living in exile in Britain talked in a workshop on masculinities and drug abuse at the same conference about his experience of living in a Muslim society where women's sexuality was not respected in similar ways and men saw themselves as protectors of their sisters' honour. He said that a sister he was close to was being physically abused by her husband. He intervened on her behalf, but was told that it was not his concern. But when the husband, who was also his cousin was visiting his father, he dishonoured him by pouring some water on him seemingly by mistake. He took his revenge on the man and the elders did not intervene but felt that the man was receiving what he deserved. This was a traditional Somali setting in which there was a warrior image of masculinity, where a family's honour had to be defended.

Gender difference/s

In a workshop run at Orexis, a programme against drug abuse in Deptford, South East London, November 2001, a woman from an Afro-Caribbean background talked about the power that women often exerted within the family.[9] She said that her mother insisted that her word be obeyed when she gave instructions to her husband. He was expected to provide for the family but this did not entitle him to rule within the sphere of the family. Rather, women maintained considerable power and would not trust their husbands to decide for them. They were the centres around which family life was organised. Often different generations lived together in the same house, but the mother remained the centre of love and power.

Another woman said that her father left home and she and her brothers were brought up by her mother alone. This confirmed in her a sense that men could be irresponsible, although she paid tribute to her mother for having brought up her brothers to be so. They have families of their own where they have proved themselves in this respect. She knows that many young Afro-Caribbean women choose to bring up their children on their own, often living with their mothers in the same house. Sometimes fathers will make great efforts to maintain a regular relationship with their children, even if relationships with their partners have broken down. And although they are not living together as a family, the children are often brought up within the love of the extended family. She is also aware of the racism and exclusions that many Afro-Caribbean young men face. They can have a harder time in school because teachers so often misinterpret their behaviours and expect the worst from them. Sometimes boys who have performed well within primary schools can feel estranged from secondary-school cultures, when they feel more of a need to confront potentially difficult issues of racial identity.

In the workshop a woman explained that slavery had taught Afro-Caribbean families that love is the most precious gift and that, if everything else can be taken away from you, love cannot. So love acted as a point of resistance within the spiritual movements of the church.[10] A particular interpretation was given to Christianity in black churches that emphasised the gift of love, even if in Protestant traditions love went together with a fear of sin that was identified with the body and sexuality. This could be a reaction to the sexualisation of Black women in slavery and how they were abused by their white slave-owners. The black church became a space of resistance in which people of colour could reclaim their own power and dignity.

The unconditional love preached by black churches was given to both girls and boys, who could be held and kissed. But within the first generation that came over with the Windrush, there were also strong moral codes that children were expected to obey. Sometimes this could produce conflict between the generations, especially as young men felt that their families did not understand the racism they had to deal with at school. They were not prepared to 'turn the other cheek' or defer to whites as their parents did. Rather, they wanted to explore what it would mean for them to grow up as 'black British', not having the same allegiance to 'back home' that their parents felt. They felt forced to make their homes in Britain and they wanted the respect that was due to them as citizens.[11]

Affirming racialised male identities

A time comes in young white men's lives when they can no longer expect to be held or hugged by their parents. For example, a father may no longer be prepared to hold his son's hand in public: he may, with no explanation, refuse to take the hand that is offered. This can be experienced as rejection that the boy does not understand, even though he has to accept it. He might think that he has done something wrong or has angered his father in some way. Young black men experience a similar break in their growing up, which can be more intense the more accustomed they have been to loving contact when children. Young women do not experience a similar break with their mothers, and this might be a source of strength for them.

If you do not have to deal with the everyday realities of racism, it is difficult to appreciate what this involves. Young black men can feel that they have to defend themselves, and so are continually on guard. Sometimes it can be easier not to try to work hard at school than to work and to fail, since they have to deal with enough rejection in their lives. Often it is through their bodies that they learn to affirm their male identities, since there can be so few employment opportunities. But this can make it harder for them to acknowledge their own vulnerability, which is seen as threatening to male identities.[12]

Afro-Caribbean women can feel betrayed if black men are more interested in relationships with white women. Or they might feel in contemporary Britain that they have moved ahead as women and that it is difficult to meet men with similar work aspirations. Perhaps black men still carry the traumatic histories of slavery that so often involved their emasculation and the denigration of their bodily integrity. It would be significant to explore how these histories have been gendered and sexualised. Maybe it can be tied to a particular fear of homosexuality within the Afro-Caribbean community – a fear shared with many other cultures. It seems as if where male identities have to be affirmed and cannot be taken for granted because the traditional supports of being a breadwinner and provider are not available, there is more centring of male identities on bodily experience. This seems to connect with a particular fear of homosexuality.

Also relevant here is the experience of Jewish masculinities, where Jewish men were feminised and identified in various ways with African experience. It might be that this fear of being feminised serves to produce a tougher masculinity, since you can be continually engaged in an inner rejection of feminised stereotypes. These identifications were affirmed in Otto Weininger's *Sex and Character*, where Jewish men were deemed, like women, to be 'closer to nature' and so unable to reason dispassionately and objectively for themselves. They fell short of being able to live out the moral ideals Kant had established for the West.[13]

Some of these connections were re-imagined within the Nazi unconscious that tended to identify Jews and blacks, say in their production of 'degenerate' art forms such as jazz. But this meant that Jewish men, like black men, could never take their masculinity for granted but constantly had to prove themselves. This might go some way to explaining the number of Jewish men who have been involved internationally in the men's movement since they have been positioned, somewhat paradoxically, both inside and outside traditional Western masculinities. As they could never take their 'whiteness' for granted, so they also had to affirm their masculinities.

Without reinstating homogeneous conceptions of culture, we can trace how these connections cross cultural boundaries. Living within a multicultural society in Britain, there are complex influences that cross generations. Often there are radical breaks between different generations of migration, where the older generation holds to loyalties that no longer have the same meaning for young men and women educated in British schools. They feel they are living a different reality and that the traditions that their parents might be keen to hand down to them no longer speak to the conditions of their everyday lives.

Young men may feel isolated, unable to speak to their fathers or mothers about the realities they face. They might not dare to speak about their experiences of drugs or sex, which they can share with their friends. They can feel torn between different worlds, as if they have to behave in particular ways at home that make little sense when they are in public. They might feel, as a younger generation, that they have more in common with the experience of other young migrant groups than with their own community. They may also identify with images from the mass media and the Internet, feeling more connected with distant spaces where other young migrants are shaping their identities through contemporary music and dance styles. Again, these are often experiences they cannot share with their parent's generation. But at the same time they remain vital if we are to grasp the shaping of new masculinities within diverse contemporary cultures.

9   Diasporas, histories, drugs and love

Diasporic masculinities

How do young boys grow up to be men? How do they learn to affirm their masculinities? We have seen that in a dominant white culture masculinities are affirmed by men proving themselves to be independent and self-sufficient. In white working-class culture it is often through physical strength that male identities are affirmed; middle-class men who do not seem strong can be deemed to be not 'man enough'. When I went to grammar school in the 1950s in north London I felt some sense of security through the friendships I established with working-class boys who were more willing and able to defend themselves.

At Orange Hill County Boys' School, which was originally built for a large working-class estate in Burnt Oak, there was an ongoing tension between boys from the local estate and a largely Jewish community that used to come to the school from Hendon and Edgware. In part this tension had to do with class, but it also had to do with different versions of masculinity. To be interested in your studies was already a threat to your male identity. You learnt to pretend to others that you were not trying very hard. Sometimes there were open clashes between different groups of boys, but there was limited anti-Semitism, as I recall. There were some strong friendships that crossed class and ethnic lines and there were enough pupils from different groups for people not to feel isolated.

If we were aware of ourselves as Jewish, this was largely as a religious identification. We used to have separate Jewish assemblies while the rest of the school gathered in the hall. Sometimes we would join them for announcements and end-of-term assemblies. But if some of the Jewish boys were third generation, their grandparents having migrated from Poland and Russia at the beginning of the century, and others were more recent migrants, their parents having fled from Nazi-occupied Europe, such distinctions were hardly registered. In our different ways we wanted to be 'English' and assumed we were entitled to think of ourselves as such if we were born in the country. We did not think of ourselves as 'British Jews', although some might have thought of themselves as Jews living in England. In general there was an aspiration towards assimilation. We wanted to belong and were prepared to make the effort that this required.[1]

This meant watching other boys, first at primary school and then later at secondary school, to see what was expected of us. We could not trust our own spontaneous behaviours since these might betray a difference we very much wanted to conceal. We learnt to be 'Jewish' at home and 'English' at school. This was why we could be so easily embarrassed if our parents came to school with their foreign accents. We preferred to keep these different worlds apart. There were very few Afro-Caribbean or Asian children in the school, as I remember. We were concerned with working out our relationships with the English boys and proving that we could 'get on' with them. We watched their behaviours and imitated their ways of being. We did not want to be different, because difference was deemed a threat.

If we experienced ourselves as 'outsiders', this probably connected to the traumatic histories that our parents carried silently. They did not want to tell us about what they had lived through because they wanted us to be 'normal' – to be 'like everyone else'. If we could be accepted, then possibly we could be safe. As second-generation children, we realised that it could be dangerous to be Jewish. We carried dangerous identities, so we had to be careful about how we handled ourselves with others. Some of these lessons were passed on silently, rather than verbalised. We learnt not to draw too much attention to ourselves and to conceal our Jewishness, which came to be shamed within the public sphere, even if we could feel some pride in the private sphere of family and community. We looked away from ourselves to learn from other boys how we were supposed to be as young men.

Shamed histories

I wonder how these hidden and traumatic histories affected the kind of masculinities we could sustain for ourselves. Some Jewish families who had originally settled in the East End of London were aware that their grandparents and parents had fought in the two world wars. They had died for their country and their families could be proud of the sacrifices they had made. This was important when masculinities were largely affirmed through war. They might have felt that terrible things had happened to the Jews of Europe during the Second World War, but they knew that they had a different history. They might also carry anger at the prevailing myth that was circulating in the 1950s and 1960s that the Jews had somehow gone 'like sheep to the slaughter'. It was partly to erase these disquieting myths young people learnt to identify with the heroic masculinities that were part of Zionist tradition and history.[2]

But as children of refugees we often carried traumatic histories. We knew that our parents had come from continental Europe to find a safe haven in Britain. They remained grateful throughout their lives and would rarely tolerate a critical word about the country. Often they did not want their children to know what they had lived through; rather they needed their broken lives to be redeemed through the efforts of their children. Sometimes they were very ambitious for their children, hoping they would fulfil the dreams they couldn't live out for themselves. They did not want to pass their pain on to their children; they insisted on carrying it themselves. They wanted to protect us as children from the past, which supposedly did not exist for us. As children we had a present and a future, but we did not have a past.[3]

In some of the Jewish refugee families I knew when I was a child, many of the eldest sons do not seem to have survived. I am not sure whether they carried too many expectations or whether the pressures were just too great. Sometimes the families were haunted by terrible fears and over-protected their first-born, who may have carried the unresolved memories. Sometimes fathers who had lived through painful experiences would take out their rage on their children.

Growing up in the shadows of the Shoah, it was difficult to know where you belonged. My father was the only person to survive from his large family in Warsaw, and only my mother, her brother and their own mother survived in her family. She did her best to invent a family for us, with close friends being called aunts. But we were to live as if nothing out of the ordinary had happened: the past was to be sealed off from the present. We felt little connection with where our parents had come from; they had an unspoken sense of rejection for having been forced to leave cities that they loved. In Vienna my mother had been made to feel unwanted and rejected by the city she had grown up to identify with.[4]

I wonder whether these unspoken legacies affected us deeply because we knew that our relations were humiliated in their own countries. Even if we never got to know what happened to them individually, we had learnt about what happened to Jewish men and women at the hands of the Nazis. We could not help wondering what our own families had been forced to live through. This knowledge was denied to us as children: we were left to imagine the worst. We knew about conditions in concentration camps and how people were murdered. Only years later, as an adult, did I learn more of the truth about what had happened to uncles, aunts and cousins in Warsaw and what my uncle and aunt had lived through in Vienna. I learnt to relate to them as individuals rather than as part of the 'six million' – a figure that continued to haunt us. The number was overwhelming and impossible to come to terms with. It could so easily become a means of not having to reflect on individual lives and the sufferings they endured.

It is through this experience in my own family that I can understand what Afro-Caribbean women and men say about the legacies of slavery and how they continue to echo in the present. This is a history that affects men and women differently. I listened to a woman saying that her grandmother could recall that her own mother had known slavery. She talked about how families were broken up and how people were forced to take the names of slave-owners. Often you did not know who you were related to. Women had a particular responsibility to keep the family together through difficult times and people learnt different ways of sustaining their lives, often through recognising that love was the one thing that could not be taken away from them. Christianity came to be reframed so that it could sustain a faith in a different order of human relations. People could feel that whatever the humiliations endured by the body, the soul could somehow remain pure.

Since slavery worked to emasculate men (slave-owners insisted on treating their male slaves as children), there was a rage that could not easily be expressed. Men were forced into deferring to whites and it could be difficult not to feel that whiteness was identified with 'goodness' and that people of colour could measure themselves on a scale of whiteness. The whiter your skin, the more status you could claim in the community.[5] A white skin was something you learnt to feel proud of, as you learnt to disdain those with darker skins. As men were forced into dependence they found it more difficult to affirm their masculinity, and a legacy was left for future generations who were never to allow their masculinities to be compromised. This created a particular fear of homosexuals, who were treated as 'not real men'.

It might be thought easier to regard slavery as locked away in the past, but many Afro-American and Afro-Caribbean men have had to revisit it to appreciate the particular fears that can emerge in the present. They can find it difficult to affirm their masculinities when they have failed at school and do not have a job, or cannot fulfil their role as breadwinners or providers – the roles their fathers had assumed when they came over from the Caribbean. Sons have refused to defer to whiteness as their fathers did, and cannot share with their fathers their different experiences of being 'black British'. With mothers taking central authority within the family, fathers can exist on the margins of family life, taking refuge with their male friends in playing dominoes or cards.

Discipline

Afro-Caribbean fathers who enforced discipline on their sons have distanced them emotionally. They wanted their sons to behave properly and conform to a strict ethical code that was sustained through church, but their sons often felt estranged. They were not prepared to put up with the everyday racism they endured on the streets. Sometimes they learnt more from their fathers than they readily acknowledged about how to handle themselves emotionally. They felt that they needed to be strong in order to affirm their male identities because this was the only way to maintain a sense of self-worth.

Sometimes it was through affirming their male identities that they took responsibility for a shamed past. They were determined that their masculinities would never again be shamed, and they would not tolerate disrespect. They would hold their heads high and never allow others to see their weakness or vulnerability. They would withdraw, rather than allow themselves to be humiliated.

As Dee Riley-Buckley, an Afro-Caribbean drugs worker with Orexis in southeast London, expresses it, 'No matter how empowered, strong and in control men may appear to be, one of the contributing factors which goes against the grain of masculinity is often when women in general express emotion with tears the male species of our race feel inhibited to cry as this may be a flaw of their masculinity and a sign of weakness.' They may believe that it is their duty to remain strong so that they can support others who are dependent on them. This is an intense form of self-discipline.

Black men who have inherited the traumatic histories of slavery have to find their own ways of coming to terms with these pasts. They might also feel a particular responsibility to redress the balance, determined that others will not get the better of them. They may therefore withdraw into themselves while presenting a particular 'front' to the world. Sometimes they can be taken in by their own fronts, unable to let go but trapped into feeling they have to constantly fight back. This can make it hard for them to trust others, knowing that they live in a hostile world. They are constantly testing people to see whether they can trust them, and often expect the worst.[6]

Drugs

It is in this situation that men can turn to drugs as a way of controlling emotions that are beginning to surface – as a form of self-medication. Drugs take their place within technologies of self-discipline, through which male identities can be affirmed. Since it is crucial for men to sustain their self-image in front of others, they have to exercise discipline over their inner emotional lives. Masculinities thus come to be identified with particular regimes of self-discipline in which substance abuse has a particular part to play.

As an earlier generation of working-class white men used alcohol as a way of both releasing inhibitions and controlling unwelcome emotions which were beginning to emerge, so their children in Deptford turned to heroin and amphetamines in the 1980s and 1990s. They perhaps rejected alcohol because they experienced for themselves the violence this could provoke in family life, and still carry the scars. But they know that heroin and methodone can help them control their own violent behaviours, which they have identified with their fathers whom they no longer see. Often these white working-class men have idealised images of their mothers.

It is striking that the Afro-Caribbean community in southeast London is identified with smack rather than heroin, possibly because of the stigma that attaches to needles and injecting practices. Of course people use substances for particular reasons, but there is often an emotional history that needs to be explored. An Afro-Caribbean man accompanied his partner to a clinic because she wanted to give up using drugs, but all the time continued his own use. He found it difficult to talk about his own emotional history, especially since it involved having been raped by a close friend of the family. This was a shaming experience that carried a particular meaning because of slavery. It was an experience that he could not face, but used heroin to calm himself. It took him years to be able to talk about the childhood violence and abuse he had endured and to make connections with how he had learnt to use heroin.

Another, more educated middle-class Afro-Caribbean man had been sexually abused by a family. He desperately wanted to win the love of his father and went into the army as a way of proving himself. But in the army he was humiliated and forced to go on his hands and feet as an animal in front of other soldiers. Eventually he left the army and tried to prove himself by buying expensive cars and a house. All the time he hoped to impress his father, but these possessions did not mean much to him or bring him joy. Gradually his heroin use took over, he lost his job and the means of supporting himself. He was separated from his child who lived abroad and was unable to sustain a relationship with her.

Another young Afro-Caribbean man had grown up to hate himself. He was shy and often felt uneasy and awkward with others. But when he was on crack he felt as if he was six feet tall. He felt that people noticed him. He got involved with a gang, knowing that this would be another way in which he would be noticed. But he got involved in a robbery and had to serve his time in prison. It took time for him to trust his counsellor enough to be able to share his feelings with her. He found it difficult to give up using crack because he had to deal with his feelings of inadequacy. If he needed to feel 'six feet tall' he could always return to using crack.

Even where people were sharing the discipline they experienced as children, they found it hard to cry and thus feel release. If they allowed themselves to cry, it could leave them feeling further humiliated and threatened in their male identities. As Dee Riley-Buckley sees it, 'If only most men knew that to cry and to express such an emotion takes courage and inner strength to give tears the respect they deserve which can then provide an opening of release of freedom to begin that journey of self-healing and new perceptions of thoughts' (Orexis, December 2001).

In her own experience she recalled a miscarriage and all the tears that provoked. She remembers her partner visiting her in hospital and the tears gathering in her eyes. She recalls that at this moment her father, who had always loved her dearly, put his arm around him as a way of helping him to control his tears, saying 'You can be strong'. Her father felt that it was the duty of her partner to 'be strong' so that he could support her in this time of need. It was through strength that he could affirm his male identity and prove his love for her. But she knew something different and knew that it would probably take years for them to return to this moment when they could heal together. She knew that she wanted her sons to learn that there was nothing to be ashamed about in crying and that it was good to learn to honour your tears.

People use drugs for a variety of reasons. Many young people use them recreationally as a way to relax and lose inhibitions. In club culture many people take ecstasy and ketermine so that those who are not taking anything can feel isolated. Ketermine can help people intensify their sexual feelings and give them a different experience of embodiment where they no longer discern where their bodies end and those of others begin. It gives them a different feeling to alcohol and can make it easier for them to have sex without love as they can allow themselves to 'let go' and play more easily.

Love and care

Some men say that lust and sexual attraction come before love in relationships. Both straight and gay men say that you have to get to know someone before you can begin to love them. In contrast, women have traditionally held that you need to feel loving towards someone before you can have sex with them. But attitudes have changed and young women now seem to share the attitudes we have traditionally associated with men. This has gone along with young women drinking and smoking much more than in previous generations. They feel that they can keep up with the lads, even if they sometimes drink spirits rather than pints. This marks a shift in gender relations, where women might equally go out with friends determined to get drunk and pick up men. A similar separation between sex and love seems to be taking place.

bell hooks admits that it took her time to distinguish between care and love. She realised in her experience with her mother that she was cared for, and had identified this care with love. But now she can more readily acknowledge that she was cared for but not loved.[7] Many people in various cultural settings think that we show our love for people by caring for them. But some people have grown up in families in which they have only known that their parents cared for them when they received negative attention. This can have damaging effects on future relationships, as some men can only feel sexually aroused if their partners are angry with them. If they are calm, then they feel indifferent themselves.

I could relate to what hooks was saying from my own diasporic experience. The traumatic history my mother had lived through meant that being vulnerable was a risk: she could not bear any further rejection. Thus she learnt to order her children around, as if we were somehow objects at her disposal. She found it hard to demonstrate love; rather she gave us things and ensured that we ate the food she prepared. As long as we ate, she could feel reassured that she was loved.

Possibly we should connect difficulties with loving to the traumatic histories that can be passed on from generation to generation, for example the legacies of Slavery and the Holocaust as they are played out in the lives of women and men.[8]

It was the transformations encouraged by the notion that 'black is beautiful' that allowed women of colour, in particular, to feel differently about themselves. Rather than accepting that the ways individuals feel about themselves are linked to individual psychologies, we need to make connections between emotional lives and the larger social and cultural settings in which they are lived. This is not simply a matter of individuals as a matter of will and determination changing the ways they think and feel about themselves. Rather, it can involve sustaining social movements that give support and recognition to challenging structures of racism and anti-Semitism as people learn to accept aspects of their histories and cultures they would otherwise want to disdain and forget.

As young Jews learn about the different forms of resistance that Jewish communities throughout Europe used against Nazi rule, so young Afro-Caribbean and Asian communities can also learn about the soldiers from the Caribbean and South Asia who fought alongside the British in the armies of the Second World War. Too often these histories have also been forgotten, and young people can be left bereft of histories by which to identify themselves. This allows people to recognise that there are different histories rather than a singular history of slavery, just as Jews learn to recognise the reality of histories and cultures that go back before the Shoah. For many Jewish men and women it is as if history did not exist before the darkness of the Holocaust. It takes time and emotional energy to prepare ourselves to recognise these connections so that we can feel, possibly for the first time, the reality of those in our families who were brutally murdered. This is part of a process of both historical and personal healing.

10   Memories, bodies and
         hidden injuries

Generations

Men returning from war may feel that they have to maintain a silence about what they have lived through. Many who returned from the Second World War felt that it was their duty not to speak about their experiences. Partners and children learnt not to ask too many questions because they feared the reactions. Even when men continued to wake with nightmares about what they had witnessed, they would often not speak too much. They would not show the hurt and the fear they carried, feeling that it served to threaten the male identities.[1]

The generation that returned from war also felt that they had to carry these memories on their own. Sometimes this could provoke a depression that was unconsciously passed on to the next generation, leaving men unsure about where their depressive feelings had come from. An individualistic culture that encourages people to frame these emotions as a mark of individual inadequacy fails to appreciate how unresolved emotional histories can be passed from generation to generation.[2]

Men may feel dissociated from the past, as if these pasts must have happened to someone else. Even when they recall their wartime experiences, they can feel as if they are talking about a past that no longer connects to the lives they live in the present. It might only be with old comrades that they can share what they have lived through.

When the composer Handel lived in London, he accompanied a woman friend to the docks at Dartford to say farewell to her 11-year-old son who was going on a dangerous sea voyage around Cape Horn. As the scene is described, the mother owes it to her son to show no emotion so that he is not left with any difficult memories. She has to be strong for her son, and he has to be strong for her. Handel refers to the control that the young boy has to exercise over his body and emotions. This is reflected in the awkwardness of the conversation between mother and son. It is only afterwards that she acknowledges how terrible she feels about not having reached out to her son. She could not allow herself to express her feelings because she wanted to spare him this burden. At the same time the boy had to exercise self-control: he had already learnt to carry himself in a particular way and knew, both mentally and bodily, that emotions were a sign of weakness that threatened his male identity.

These somatic traditions are passed from generation to generation, and mothers play a crucial part in sustaining them. They were bred into different levels of the class system through schooling as Britain assumed dominance over its empire. The 'stiff upper lip' was produced over generations as young men learnt to hold back their tears. It meant that they could not allow themselves to register somatically and emotionally the experiences that they were living through.[3] This produced its own forms of dissociation between an inner emotional life that had to be controlled and how men learnt to present themselves publicly. It was as if their inner emotional lives were 'buried alive' so that they could no longer be claimed. Men were left not knowing what they were feeling, having learnt to disdain emotions as 'feminine' and thereby as a threat to their male identities.

Disciplining bodies

Reich, a student and follower of Freud who developed somatic forms of psychoanalysis, argues that disciplining our thoughts and feelings is tied up with disciplining the body. We learn to hold our bodies in particular ways, so as to be able to block particular emotions more effectively. It is no accident that, at school, we were taught to stand up straight whenever a teacher came into the classroom. This was a sign of respect but it was also a bodily discipline that helped produce attitudes of respect towards authority. Tightening of the body was part of what Reich described as 'armouring'. It is a process that takes different forms and is especially relevant to the experience of men.[4]

Because boys are not supposed to acknowledge the hurts they feel, they learn from an early age strategies of denial. So if a young boy falls in the playground he will learn to minimise his experience, saying 'it was nothing'. Young boys learn to dissociate themselves from their experience from an early age. If I feel upset, this is something that I am so used to denying that I no longer know whether I am upset or not. This creates its own forms of confusion as boys discipline themselves in ways that make it harder to name their own experience.

As fathers who might have fought in the Second World War learn to 'hold on' to their own painful memories, not wanting to 'pass on' the pain they have lived through, so their sons also learn to prove their male identities by withholding the pain they feel. For example, a young man might have been sexually abused by a friend of the family, but feel unable to tell his family what happened to him. He is shamed by his experience but feels that it would be more shaming to talk about it. Rather he carries burden on his own, though years later he might be involved in a gang rape as a way of seeking revenge for his own humiliation as a child. He sought to pass on this hurt, hoping to free himself by passing on the pain to others.[5]

Sometimes a father has violently abused his son, hoping to assuage some of the memories of war he has felt forced to carry silently. He later regretted his action, knowing that he had gone beyond the boundaries of discipline. He caught himself enjoying inflicting pain and was shocked. But a pattern had been established, and he would act out his violence on his son while feeling bad about it later. He always picked on the older son, perhaps feeling that he was the one strong enough to take it. This created a distance from his son, who would do his best to absent himself whenever his father was around.

Sometimes children from different backgrounds witness violent behaviours at home that they feel they cannot tell anyone at school about. Again, fathers beating up on their mothers and felt bad about what they had witnessed. Children can feel shocked by the emotional intensity wishing that it was not happening and feeling powerless to do anything to stop it. Their parents might try to reassure them saying 'don't get upset' and 'this has nothing to do with you'. But the children can feel disturbed and feel terrible that they cannot do anything to stop their father. Sometimes children can withdraw into themselves as a form of self-defence, as if they have withdrawn from the skin surface and taken refuge in an inner place of safety or they may dissociate themselves from what is going on, bullying other children as a way of 'passing on' their own pain.

Children can feel very insecure when conflict breaks out in the family, especially if there is no one around they can talk to. Girls may be able to talk out their fears with other girls at school, drawing support from their friends, but boys can find it more difficult to reach out for support, fearing that it will give other boys grounds to reject them. So it can be easier for boys to act 'as if nothing has happened' at home, while taking out their hidden hurts on others through bullying.

If a boy is behaving badly at school, talking back to the teachers and not paying attention to what is going on in class, the authorities may well treat it as a school discipline issue. They will punish the boy to bring him into line, but this can make the boy feel more isolated and alone. The school might suspect what has been going on at home, but have no way of addressing it, and the boy might refuse to talk about what has been going on, not wanting to betray his parents.

Moreover, boys often do not have the trust to speak openly with their teachers. They do not expect to be understood and sometimes feel unable to speak about the hurt and pain they carry. A primary school in New Cross, South East London, found that when they placed someone next to a boy who had been particularly trouble-some, able to gain his trust so that he could share what had been going on for him, it made a significant difference to both his school work and his behaviour. He felt that someone cared enough to listen to him, which was a new experience for him. It made a difference to his self-esteem and how he felt about himself.

Drugs

Sometimes drug users, as Dean Whittington's research has shown, can talk about the community they feel part of. Not only is their time structured, but life seems to have a purpose, organised around getting sufficient funds to finance their habit. This takes the place of a job and so assuages the feelings of inadequacy that can accompany unemployment. In some areas of London young men have never had a full-time job and do not expect to get one. Working in a full-time job is something their fathers' generation might have taken for granted, but something they have never known. This means they have not been able to affirm their male identities through being providers and breadwinners. They have been forced to shape different lives for themselves. This can also explain why it can be so difficult for men to withdraw from their drug habit. Suddenly they can feel empty, as if their lives have no meaning. The moment when they are clean is not when the process is over, as government drug programmes assume, but often when they will need most support and help to work on the difficult emotions and memories which have suppressed for so long through their drug use.[6]

In working-class Deptford, southeast London, where Orexis does its counselling work with drug users, there are few opportunities for employment. Many young men are involved with petty crime to support their habit. Orexis also works with the Vietnamese and Somalian communities who have recently settled in the area. Both communities have had to deal with war and migration. In both, older men have had to deal with challenges to their traditional status, as their partners and children no longer rely upon them in the same way. In the Vietnamese community emotions are commonly internalised, with older men getting depressed. There are difficulties of isolation and language, and both older and younger men have turned towards heroin use. If there is domestic abuse, this is largely contained within the community because people do not want to bring further shame to their families. Sometimes young people are sent back to visit Vietnam so that they can begin to appreciate the benefits of living in Britain and also to learn to return to more traditional visions of discipline and authority.

In the Somali community, which has a strong honour code, there has been considerable tension in relation to fathers who are expected to provide even though their wives get support from social security. This is money that the women take as their own and they can feel resentful when their husbands withdraw to Khatt houses where a traditional drug is used. If there is tension in the family the men will withdraw for days, isolating themselves from their wives and children. They might threaten to take revenge as soon as they return to Muslim countries, where the police and social services will not intervene. Sometimes families are reluctant to call on social services, fearing that their children may be taken into care if there is domestic violence.

In different ethnic communities conflicts between the generations take different forms, though they can also learn from each other. A Vietnamese man who had been in England since he was sixteen talked about returning to see his family in Vietnam after many years and the pain he felt when nobody recognised him. They had expected him to smoke and drink in Western ways. He shared the pain he felt at the unease and awkwardness he felt with his father, as if they were strangers to each other. It was difficult for him to feel that he belonged in his own family. He had made a new life for himself in England, though he felt torn between different places and different communities.

A Somali man who had also lived in England for some time shared the difficulties that the older generation often have with their children. He talked about how children growing up in England often felt isolated and experienced difficulty in finding themselves in a different culture. Sometimes they tried to ground themselves by asserting their male identities. They could find it difficult to share their vulnerability and could feel estranged from their parents' generation. Sometimes, if they were 'going astray' and getting into trouble with the law, they would be sent back to Somaliland in the hope they would feel more connection with their own culture.

Parents frequently failed to appreciate the difficulties their children faced in coming to terms with the reality of British schools and local communities. Children would not respect their parents in traditional ways and would often see the children they met at school as role models. Sometimes they would be drawn into the drug cultures as a way of feeling a sense of belonging that would otherwise be denied them.

11   Narratives, fears, drugs and violence

Histories

In October 1981, *The Observer Magazine* published a feature called 'The Writing on the Wall', featuring children from the Ford Estate, a run-down housing estate on the outskirts of Birkenhead, on the Wirral across the River Mersey from Liverpool. As Lynne Clare, Parents against Drug Abuse, Liverpool, recalls, 'The Ford Estate was notorious in the Eighties. I wouldn't have wanted to live there. Always in the papers, always being vandalised, loads of drug use. One of the worst estates in Birkenhead. There was no purpose for those kids, no point, because there was no jobs. Norman Tebbit told us to get on our bikes, but it's quite hard to ride a bike on heroin. There was absolutely nothing for them... They're a lost generation.' (*Observer Magazine*, 30 May 2004, p. 26).

John MacDonald was 16 at the time and he remembers having his picture taken. He happened to be sitting on a grass verge with a few friends who had grown up together. Photographer Mike Abrahams snapped them as they sat, smoking cannabis and chatting. Twenty-three years later, MacDonald wrote to *The Observer* wondering if they would be interested in finding out what happened to him and his friends. He felt their stories needed telling. He had been looking at the picture, reminiscing. It was discovered that of the fifteen people in the picture, just two were not now using drugs. Four are dead and the rest are addicts of one sort or another. Possibly they didn't stand much of a chance as they were working class in an area of mass unemployment and low priority. Traditional local employers such as the car plants were under real pressure and the Cammell Laird shipyard was closing down. At the same time a new drug to relieve boredom was on the way in.

In 1985, Howard Parker, then a reader in social work studies at Liverpool University, wrote *Living with Heroin*, with many of the case studies coming from the Ford estate.[1] He sees Britain's heroin epidemic of the early 1980s as part of a cycle that began in the United States in the 1960s and 1970s. He describes a global flow of heroin use across national borders:

> 'The heroin epidemic in America had a natural life of 10 or 15 years. And then demand started to go down. As with any drug epidemic, the next generation won't go near it. They've seen the impact. So the market was finished there, and Afghanistan and all those places needed a new market. They hit Europe. After heroin it was crack in the States and with it the same kind of cycle.' (p. 27)

This is an insight that is reflected in Dean Whittington's work in southeast London, which shows that alcohol was often the drug that young people saw their parents abusing. Having grown up with domestic violence and forced to witness the abuse of their mothers, they turned to heroin as a drug that seemed to still their emotions, making the anger and violence they associated with alcohol less likely.[2]

John MacDonald's family moved to the Ford estate in the 1960s. 'It was new then,' he tells Ursula Kenny. 'We'd been living in downtown Birkenhead, in a place that was pretty bad. This was luxury by comparison. Three bedrooms and our own bathroom.' His dad worked for the gas board, his mum for Cadbury's and though things were insecure financially, they were much better off than some. He was 21 and had left home by the time his parents divorced. As he relates trouble started outside the house:

> 'There was a lot of violence on the estate. Regular violence. There was a pub opposite my school called the Buccaneer and we used to watch them spilling out of there. I've never forgotten one time seeing this really bad fight. It went on for ages and it affected me a lot. I know it affected other kids. I was in a gang, everyone was, we were always fighting and there was always a feeling that this was a hard place to live.' (Ibid.)

According to Parker, 'there was a lot of crime, vandalism. There were gangs, tough men. It wasn't a place to mess with. I think there was a lot of dumping of problem families on to Ford. Certainly it got into a mess for a while' (ibid., p. 28).

John knew the estate like the back of his hand. 'There were lots of alleyways that were used to get away from the police. I was never at home and my parents didn't have a clue what I was up to.' He started smoking dope at about eleven and was a regular user by 13.

> The older boys would always have weed to sell and a load of us would throw in 25p, and we'd get a £4 or £5 deal. And that would last a few days. We'd do it round the back of the school, or round someone's house, a single parent that we knew. Get stoned, put some records on and just laugh. It was all quite innocent.

As John remembers it, 'the change' happened more or less overnight. All of a sudden you couldn't buy dope.

Heroin

As John recalls it, 'You couldn't buy cannabis, couldn't buy weed. All you could buy was this cheap brown heroin. Within six months of that photograph the estate was flooded with heroin. Everyone started smoking it.' People on the estate thought it was a fad and that heroin would disappear as quickly as it had arrived. They thought the weed would come back. But what actually happened was that 'everyone got strung out, everyone got bad [drug] habits. You need more and more, so you resort to crime; dealing or begging, borrowing or stealing from your parents.' John was 16 or 17 when he started to steal. 'I had a habit. At first you're terrified, but after you've done it a couple of times the fear wears off.' Micky was 14 when the picture was taken. As he recalls, 'We were all pot heads then. We used to throw our dinner money in for a £5 deal. Then the heroin kicked off. I smoked gear every day for four years and I didn't really know what it was until I went to jail.' He has been taking methodone for 14 years.

Louis was 17 or 18 when he started taking heroin. 'I use methodone, hash and booze these days.' He lived in London for a while, working on building sites, but 'I got in too much trouble down there.' He recalls how he felt when he was young. 'I just thought there was nothing for us. I didn't think about how my life was going to turn out because there was no opportunities anyway.' Carl is 37 now and has been taking drugs since he was 14. 'Sometimes I got into jail for a break. Just to get meself off the gear, to get meself back up again, and I come out and I'm back to square one again. The temptation is just too much.' He still lives on the Ford Estate with his girlfriend. 'I don't like it, I'm trying to get away.' Julie, one of the few girls, now 40, has been taking drugs more or less continuously since the picture was taken. As she explains, 'I stopped for a while when I had my children, but always because someone else like my mum wanted me to.' These days she's working with a local drugs agency and says, 'I'm in a better place. I don't go out of my way to get crack. But if someone brings me round a smoke I'll do it' (ibid., p. 29). Her children, now in their twenties, don't take drugs. 'They've seen what I've been through and they wouldn't touch it' (ibid., p. 31). She thinks times are better for the kids on the estate nowadays. 'I don't think these kids are into what we were into,' she says. 'They can get jobs now, we were still all just dossing about. No one would touch us.'

John is the one who got away. He hasn't used drugs of any sort since he was 21 and moved away from Birkenhead. 'I got clean and to stay clean I knew I had to leave the area.' He has lived in London since he was 21, going to Narcotics Anonymous meetings and living his life the 12-step way. He originally came across Parents Against Drug Abuse (Pada), started in 1984 by Joan Keogh, who lived on the Ford estate when he was 19. She had found out that both her children had been taking heroine. He had been in borstal for eight months and had come out clean, off drugs for the moment. He had a job as a trainee scaffolder. But then he started sniffing speed, and eventually using heroin again. 'Still, my probation officer thought I was clean, he saw me as a role model, so he asked me to speak to this parents' group.'

John recalls his life back then: 'It was such a community, you can see from the photograph; despite all the madness, you know there's a real togetherness' (ibid., p. 32). As is the case with many ex-addicts, moving was crucial: 'The last time I used heroin was the day before I came down [to London]. The last time I smoked dope was on the way down.' He is married now and has a six-year-old son. He has worked as a resident social worker and has a private practice as a therapist.

Others in the picture were not so lucky. Joanne, Julie's best friend, died in a drink-driving crash, and one of the boys hanged himself in prison. Another died from an overdose, and another was murdered as a victim of a gay hate crime. The rest who survived are using either drugs or alcohol, all bar two. What can still strike a visitor to the estate, according to Ursula Kenny, 'is the isolation. Stuck in the middle of nowhere, with its own school, desolate pub and shopping precinct. "A prison with no walls," as MacDonald puts it. Crack cocaine is the drug of choice nowadays...' (ibid., p. 31).

When people tell their life stories they can often be concerned to offer a kind of coherent narrative to others, somehow moving over the breaks, disappointments and displacements. Young men can find it difficult to share the emotional pain they are carrying, not wanting to compromise their male identities. There is a tension between forms of narrative analysis that explore how people present their histories to others, bringing out, for instance, the different terms in which generations of men might present their stories. An older generation might share the feeling of loss that accompanied unemployment, possibly in relation to the community of mates at work or their politics shared through the trade union movement or Labour politics. They might look back with a sense of pride about what they had together and possibly feel anger about how so much could have been taken away from them with the closing of the shipyard or the car plant.[3] They might speak out of a collective sense of their struggle to sustain a sense of self-respect in the face of humiliation at work. But this kind of language is unavailable to a younger generation who never shared opportunities to work. Their language tends to relate more to individual choices and decisions and they may be more likely to blame themselves for what has happened to them. They may feel as if they have only themselves to blame, thus expressing a disconnection they feel with any sense of the social. Rather than being able to speak in relation to the larger community and class relations of power, they reflect in more individual terms about the friendships they used to have as children on the estate and what happened to others.[4]

Post-structuralist theories have often been impatient with notions of human needs and desires, taking refuge in an idea that identities are shaped within discourses of power and that it is through language that they are articulated. This tends to limit how people can express themselves, for there is suspicion about a sense of self imagined outside the realm of discourse. This often goes along with a rejection of any notion of depth, as if meanings can always be read from the surface of relationships, so that the text of what people have said is imagined as constructing 'reality' and there are no levels of experience that are hidden and waiting to be explored. There is no coherent self that is seeking expression through language so there is no space for tensions to arise between 'language' and 'experience'.[5]

But there is an inevitable tension between a post-structuralist framing and a recognition that it is not enough to trace languages in which people narrate their lives and so offer a coherent account that slips over breaks and dislocations. A man in his early fifties who had to accept that he would probably never find another job after the closing of the shipyard confronts a different reality from the young men on the estate who have never worked. A narrative account can be locked into an individualist framework that finds it hard to open to the difficulties in, say, relationships between fathers and sons. This is partly to do with difficulties of communication but also with the flow of love and recognition between the generations. As father's fall into silence, so sons might feel abandoned in their own time of need.

Relationships

In Dean Whittington's study into drug use in southeast London the young working-class men often speak with tenderness about their mothers, who have often stuck by them in difficult times. In contrast, they often feel distant from and angry at their fathers, especially if they recall the violence their mothers had to endure because of their father's drinking. One man put his hand through a window and cut himself to distract his father from hitting his mother. He felt powerless to intercede because he knew his father's rage would be turned against him, so he turned this anger against himself. He was prepared to cut himself to have a chance of protecting his mother from further violence. As he felt able to share this memory with Dean he was no longer defending himself with a mask, but had allowed it to slip. He was sharing experiences that he had never shared before and it took courage and trust. Of course this could have affected him and led to the emergence of different feelings and experiences. Although the 'truth' of what he was saying could be felt in the encounter, that does not mean that it is in any sense a 'final' or 'complete' truth. At the same time it can be revealing in helping to orientate more quantitative research because it makes visible levels of experience that might remain closed within interviews.

There might be hidden resonance between an orthodox Marxism that works with a notion of 'false consciousness', implying that working-class people can come to a 'true' understanding of their position within a capitalist society, and a Freudian psychoanalytic theory that holds that there is a 'true' interpretation that people will accept when they are ready to hear it. But neither view allows for an exploration that validates a process of understanding whereby people come to terms with aspects of their experience and so with the emotions and feelings that emerge. Men often grow up learning to fear their own emotions as a sign of weakness and so as a threat to male identities. Within working-class Deptford men know they have to put on a 'front' that is part of the local vernacular. They must not back down in face of other men but must be able to 'front them out'. This is not just discursive since they have to be prepared to 'back up' their words with actions. They have to stand their ground with what is locally called a Mexican stand-off. They have to maintain their hardness at whatever cost and keep their front. This 'front' was taken at face value by Bob Connell's study of bikers in *Masculinities*, where he could see nothing else.

Rather than recognise that there is a genealogy that has to be explored if we are to grasp how boys learn to adopt a front and so organise their bodies to defend themselves, Connell allows counter-transference to get in the way. He expresses a moral disapproval of their values and relationships. He misses the point and leaves us with a moralism that cannot illustrate the development path that these young men took towards their violence. We need to explore how the front is itself a defence against a vulnerability that is too threatening for young men to show to themselves, let alone to others. From an early age young men can learn that it is only through being 'hard' that you have a chance to survive. If you show vulnerability or any sign of weakness, you soon learn that others will ruthlessly exploit it to their own advantage. You will be made to suffer as you lose your position in the competitive orderings of masculinities.

Young men growing up in working-class Deptford often knew that their fathers were drowning their sorrows with alcohol. They might have sensed that there was a wartime experience that they could not share. A silence haunted the family and made the atmosphere brittle whenever their fathers were around. Young men learnt to be cautious around their fathers, anxious not to provoke them because they knew the violence that could erupt. As children they sometimes witnessed their mothers being physically abused and humiliated, knowing that if they intervened the violence would be turned towards them.[6] In some cases they learnt to behave as if 'nothing was happening', but this produced its own forms of disconnection. If they felt close to their mothers, they could feel guilty at not having been able to do more to defend her. This could produce an emotional distance from their fathers, whom they often feared and hated.

But at the same time they also knew that they had to become 'hard' like their fathers if they wanted to survive. They had to learn to stand up for themselves and be proud, knowing that the Millwall club they often identified with had a slogan 'Everyone hates us, but we don't care'. Some fathers had to live with wartime traumas they could not speak about in their families. They maintained a stoic silence that worked to create a tense atmosphere that could be difficult to relax in. The pub was a central space in men's lives in post-war Deptford where they would 'drown their sorrows' in alcohol, later coming home drunk and violent.

Violence

Having experienced the violence that was induced through alcohol, the next generation of men often wanted to have little to do with it. They knew they had to be on guard, always ready to show themselves as 'hard' men, but they also wanted to protect their mothers. They learnt a different form of stoic masculinity as they turned towards drugs. Often there was tension between fathers and sons, as fathers were no longer able to offer traditional work in the docks. An older generation in southeast London, traditionally heavily dependent upon work in the docks, were disappointed that they no longer had regular work when the docks moved downstream to Tilbury with the container revolution. Work had been a source of male identity and pride, and had guaranteed their position as providers and authorities within traditional families. But unless they could set themselves up in alternative work with their redundancy payments, they felt stranded and unable to draw upon traditional sources of support. They were angry at the loss of work and it was through violence that they sustained their position at home.

Unprepared for these radical dislocations in their lives and the loss of community that followed, men were left to deal with these traumatic events on their own. Families could feel the silent desperation, but were unable to intervene in a helpful way. Sometimes, inevitably, anger was taken out on wives and children.

Feeling bad that they could no longer secure work for their sons, they often blamed their sons for not securing work for themselves. There were arguments in the house when young men turned to drugs and to a lifestyle that seemed hedonistic and self-indulgent to an older generation that had shaped its identities through a strong Protestant work ethic.[7]

A traditional Marxist analysis takes it that masculinities were created and sustained through production, so it might find difficulty in understanding how male identities became significant in different ways, when work was no longer present. Masculine identities as sources of self-worth could become more significant, rather than less. Young men could feel a greater urgency to prove their male identities in contexts where it could no longer be taken for granted. Within the family young men could feel more anxious to affirm their male identities in the face of their father's challenges and attacks. How could you be 'man enough' without work? If you do not have regular work that allows you to feel a sense of independence, how is your male identity to be sustained? These issues haunted young men and violence seemed the only solution available.

Listening

In a working-class world sharply divided between 'us' and 'them', where doctors, social workers and probation officers are all professions that want 'to work on us', it can be difficult to trust anyone. Dean Whittington had to earn the trust of the men he was working with in Drugs in Deptford (which became Orexis) and they tested him continually. He was able to carve out a different space by asking them what the matter was and what their lives felt like. Often they were so unused to someone showing any kind of interest in their individual lives and experience that it could feel shocking and at the same time a challenge. If they had never been listened to in their families, it could be difficult to accept that someone *could be interested* in what they had to say. It could be daunting but also an enormous relief.

Within a space in which they could feel listened to they could allow their masks to slip as they shared their experiences of home and school. Talking about their mothers, their feelings seemed to emerge and they often expressed gratitude for everything their mothers had done for them. They were allowing themselves to explore their own histories, sharing what it felt like for them. As trust developed they could share more of themselves, knowing that they were speaking in confidence. In time they began to show their vulnerability, as they felt that in this space, at least, it would not threaten their male identities. Gradually they felt less isolated as they began to recognise that other young men felt similarly, even though they had never realised this before. You could argue that this was just revealing another kind of mask, as if they were just peeling off a layer of the onion, but a humanistic therapy sees this as a movement towards a core feeling of the self.

If they did not talk about drugs a great deal, it was probably because other things were emerging that it was more urgent to share. They had learnt to defend themselves against their own painful feelings through drugs, but now they felt more able to share what was troubling them, and this seemed to bring relief. It meant they were not carrying the same tensions inside their bodies but could let some of it go. It could also bring relief to talk about how they were treated at school and in young offender institutions, where people seemed concerned to discipline them constantly and so teach them proper ways of behaving. If they were angry or violent they would be punished 'to teach them a lesson'. But nobody seemed interested in understanding the everyday violence and abuse in the family. Often boys were so upset by this that they did not make it to school on Monday morning.

Boys learnt that it was through violence that they could prove themselves to others and so affirm their status in the community. They had to be capable both of giving violence and enduring it at the hands of others without complaint.[8] Within a strong homophobic culture there was a fear of 'softness' or 'vulnerability' that were identified with being 'queer' – a 'poofter'. Boys would discipline each other and pull each other 'into line' by accusing others of being 'poofters' if they did not behave appropriately. Often this meant that young men grew up with little contact with their inner lives and with a fear of discovering their emotions, feelings and desires.

Transformations

How can men change? Is it partly through the validation of their experience that they can begin to transform their thoughts, emotions and behaviours? If they have grown up in working-class communities where violence is a currency that works to win respect and esteem, it can be difficult to learn different ways of relating. If they have suffered in institutions that have sought to break their spirits as a means of disciplining them, they will have learnt to show their front to the world. They will have endured stings that might have meant it was difficult for them to 'open up' to others.[9] This means that trust has to be continually renegotiated and that counsellors and therapists who work with working-class men will have to have learnt to work on their own masculinities if they are to work effectively with their clients. They will need to be in touch with the sources of their own psychic pain if they are to help others.

Within more fragmented communities that are no longer organised around trade union and labour party politics, young men can feel more isolated in their experience. Hard on themselves emotionally, it can be difficult for them to feel any empathy or compassion for others. A difficulty with empathy has also characterised middle-class masculinities, where, for example, fathers might have little feeling for what their partners are going through in bringing up children. They might find themselves on the edge of family life with little contact with their children, never having taken time to look after them on their own. Rather than feel empathy for their partners, men can feel dismissive and patronising, underestimating what women have to deal with and the difficulties they face. Often it is only when men have exclusive responsibility that they can begin to understand but also transform as they appreciate the love they have been missing through the lack of relationship with their children.

Often there is little contact between men and women in heterosexual relationships, where they cannot understand each other. She thinks he is 'so moody' while he thinks she is 'so needy'. He might want to show his love by buying her expensive presents, unable to accept that this is not what she needs from him. She might want him to give up stealing and show that he is more committed to the relationship, but he might have little idea of what this involves.

The 'hardness' some men feel they need to survive in their communities can make it difficult to establish contact and love within intimate relationships. Young men can feel trapped into masculinities that they find difficult to make visible because they have been taken for granted. But as they watch the devastation that drugs have wrought on their friends and the trouble they have got into themselves, they might welcome the chance to change. They might also want to help others younger than themselves learn from their own painful experiences. Survival can be an emotionally driven force and it can close down other ways of being. They might want their children to have different opportunities and feel the loss of the contact they did not have with their own fathers. Some fathers might have been physically abusive while others were merely cold and distant, but the sons might explore connections between their family histories and their own experience with heroin and methodone. They might learn to look after their own health in a way they never did before, and learn how to identify what makes them happy. They might learn to say sorry to their partner or take the time to send a birthday card.

Through these small changes young men can feel more connected with themselves and so more aware of tensions between what they want and need and patriarchal structures of power. As they understand the violence they have suffered, they can also see how they continue to collude within relations of power that need to be transformed if young men are to explore more equal relationships in which they can both give and receive love.

12 Conclusions: Gender, power, ethics and love

Transforming male power

The women's movement emphasised the power that men had within a patriarchal society in relation to women. Often the workings of gender relations of power were rendered invisible within a liberal moral culture that thought in terms of the respect due to individuals. This meant that women were not used to thinking about how their identities were shaped by their experiences as women within a society of male dominance. Rather, they had to learn to name their experience as gendered as a way of refusing to internalise guilt and responsibility themselves. Rather than blame themselves for how they felt, they learnt to recognise how the ways they were treated helped to make them feel as they did. They recognised how their experience as women had been systematically devalued within a patriarchal culture formed in the image of a dominant, white, heterosexual masculinity.[1]

It was harder for men to recognise that their experience was gendered because they had often grown up to think of themselves in 'universal' terms. When men looked in the mirror they saw an image of themselves as a 'human being'. This also made it difficult for men to acknowledge the power they had in relation to women because they were reluctant to think in gendered terms.[2] Rather they saw power as a matter of individuals being more or less successful and making different individual choices for themselves within the terms of a liberal moral culture. But feminism challenged men to name the power they took for granted and to recognise the ways in which a capitalist patriarchy was organised in their interests. At that stage it was not easy for women to enter the labour market and professions were often still closed to them. There was little sense that they had a right to be more or less equally represented within the public sphere.

As feminism challenged the prevailing modernist distinction between public and private spheres, so it refused to accept the women were somehow 'naturally' suited to the private realm of domesticity and childcare. It questioned the notion that the public sphere was a sphere of reason and power while the private sphere was the space for emotion and love. Women insisted that the responsibility for children should not rest with them alone, just because they had given birth. They insisted that men should take a more or less equal responsibility for childcare, even if this might compromise their advances at work. They refused the logic that said that if men earn more money, then it was 'rational' that they should continue to be the providers and breadwinners, with women taking responsibilities for the home. Rather than accept a traditional gendered division of labour, feminists insisted that men had to rethink their phallic privileges and also recognise what they had lost in not having closer emotional relationships with their children. If feminism involved a challenge to male power, it also offered opportunities for men prepared to revision their masculinities.[3]

But a traditional patriarchal analysis, especially as it was framed within a radical feminist tradition, could position women as the victims of male power. It was a continuing strength of a radical feminist tradition that it refused to take attention away from the realities of male violence. Rather than treat questions of male violence as marginal, as traditional forms of social and political theory had done, reflecting a breakdown of social order, they insisted that it was a central issue in sustaining gendered relations of power and subordination.[4] They rightly insisted on showing the suffering that women were forced to endure at the hands of men and demonstrated how male violence had so often been normalised in notions such as 'she had it coming to her', 'if she hadn't nagged so much, I wouldn't have had to hit her', 'you cannot reason with women; only force brings them to their senses'.

In cultures where there are strict divisions between public and private spheres, much of this violence might be taking place behind closed doors. In public men might behave quite respectfully towards their partners, but they behave very differently in private. This makes it very difficult for women to speak out about their sufferings, especially if it is deemed to bring shame to the wider family. They might learn to endure, as the particular cross they have to carry, keeping their silence even when asked directly about it. It is a 'private matter' and so is not to be spoken about in public. But sometimes a patriarchal analysis fails to appreciate that women are not only victims of male power, but have their own sources of power they can sometimes draw upon. In the 1980s there was dissatisfaction with the theorisation of power as something that men always had and women always lacked.

But although Foucault's analysis of power was vital in questioning zero-sum conceptions, so that it was only when men were forced to give up their power that women could supposedly gain power over their lives, there was also a weakness in Foucault's difficulty in thinking about how power is so often used to trivialise, undermine and humiliate. His analysis seemed unable to come to terms with the emotional complexities, even if it allowed for a shift in the theoretical vision that brought masculinities into the figuring of gender relations. For many it was no longer adequate to think about gender relations of power in terms of a zero-sum conception. Rather, Foucault allowed people to theorise a shift towards gender through thinking that 'femininities' and 'masculinities' are articulated through discursive practices. But this inclusive vision can work to render invisible the power that men can exercise in heterosexual relationships as well as the different kinds of power that people can exercise in diverse relationships.

Gender and power

Foucault's *A History of Sexuality* helped to shift the emphasis away from power as something that men can take for granted in their relationships with women within a patriarchal culture and so as something which is concentrated in the hands of men, towards a more decentred vision of power, where power is deemed to be 'everywhere'. Rather than think of power as centred in men, with women positioned as victims of male power and violence, power is decentred and no longer conceived as gendered. With power existing 'everywhere; there was a challenge to traditional orthodox visions of power that conceived of it as centred in the state. To capture the state, in Leninist theory, was to appropriate the means of power.

But a decentred vision of power made it difficult to theorise men's power in relation to women and how this is constituted within diverse historical and cultural settings. However, it did enable us to recognise, as feminism and gay liberation had argued, that power was not confined to the public sphere and that it also operated within the private sphere of love and emotional life. This was part of the appeal of a Foucauldian analysis that seemed more able to discern the complex workings of power within different regimes of discipline and regulation. It also helped to move attention away from women as eternally victims of male power towards a recognition that both femininity and masculinity are constituted in relation to each other within prevailing discourses. This helped to bring a consideration of masculinities into the picture, but at the very moment that we could no longer theorise the workings of men's power in relation to women. Power thus came to be conceived in universal terms, rather than through the workings of class, gender, 'race' and ethnic relations of power and dominance.[5]

At the same time, in social and cultural theory in the 1990s uncertainties were developing about the implications of 'identity politics' as necessarily implying an undesirable fixity of identities and so foreclosing opportunities and desires people might wanted to explore. This also fostered a shift towards thinking 'beyond gender' that was partly encouraged by the influence of Judith Butler's important *Gender Trouble*.[6] Many students talk about the impact of this text not only on their thinking but also on the ways they were choosing to live their sexual lives. It allowed people to recognise the contingent and fluid nature of gender identities they had often grown up to take for granted. It shows the hetero-normative assumptions and allowed a generation of young women to feel that they could allow themselves to be shaped by their own desires. Butler helped people to question the notion of a self that made decisions and choices in accord with its own desires. Rather it could foster an idea that there were no subject positions, but people were chosen by free-floating desires that they could explore for themselves.

Some young women have shared how reading Butler had an enormous impact on their lives, but that it could also be unsettling, especially if you have a troubled family history and paradoxically a weaker sense of your own identity. The subversion of identity can work to produce its own forms of gender trouble as people explore their desires – or rather allow themselves to be explored through their desires. The deconstructive impulse can leave people stranded, with a sense that they can no longer trust the love they have had in relationships. They can be left uncertain about their own desires and feel troubled about what they might want for themselves.

On the other hand, women who had grown up in more secure family backgrounds where they had experienced love and recognition as small children seem more able to welcome the opportunities to explore diverse sexualities and desires that Butler seemed to be offering. But often they had a securer sense of personal identity. Of course it is difficult to generalise, but it can be helpful to explore the lived implications of gender theory and the implications of subverting notions of identity, although many people already feel haunted by a sense of uncertainty. This brings into focus the complex relationships between psychoanalysis, psychotherapies that in different ways imagine visions of an embodied self, and social theories that help to recognise how identities are shaped through social, cultural and political relations but can also serve at the same time to deconstruct identities.

Foucault has allowed us to recognise that women also have sources of power, both within the private and public realms, and got us away from thinking that, in every sphere of life, power is something that men have as a kind of possession which women lack. Rather than think of power in zero-sum terms or as a possession particular groups could take for granted, Foucault helped us think that if women gained power, this did not have to mean that men lost an equivalent amount of it. Rather, we should think about processes of empowerment in more complex ways, though this is often framed within the terms of prevailing discourses.

Since both genders come to be constituted through discourse, attention switches to the ways particular gendered identities are articulated and disarticulated. We learn to think about how identities are fragmented as they exist across diverse discourses, so that we no longer think of them in homogenised terms, as a single thing. This has the effect of displacing any 'psychological' concerns with self-worth, self-esteem and personal empowerment, as if these processes have to be envisaged as taking place within a discrete inner psychological space of their own. This means that early feminist insights into the ways that women are reduced to things and made to feel they do not exist for themselves, but only in relation to their partners and husbands, cease to be persuasive for they seem to rely upon an 'essentialist' conception of self. Against this it is argued that it is only through the articulation of discourse that we gain any notion of 'experience' at all. We are assured that there is no 'experience' that exists prior to discourse.

But this post-structuralist assumption goes against an insight familiar in early feminist work concerning the tension between language and experience. Within consciousness-raising practices, as we have already mentioned, there was a recognition that women were reduced to silence and rendered unable to speak 'in the company of men' who were ready to ridicule and devalue their words. This was an insight that both Wittgenstein and Simone Weil, in different ways, also appreciated. They questioned the autonomy of language and recognised that language only comes into play within discrete contexts of use. Often women experience a suffering that they cannot name. Sometimes they prefer to remain silent rather than betray their experience, through framing it in terms of a rationalist culture that already assumes that emotions and feelings are irrational. They choose not to show their feelings, knowing that what they say will probably be discounted because of them.[7]

Against a theoretical post-structuralism, radical feminism has insisted upon a traditional analysis of male power and violence. It has resisted the temptation to think of power in gender-neutral terms, fearing that this will take attention away from the violence that is daily perpetrated by men in relation to women. It also wants to keep the focus on the transformation of relationships, rather than the rearticulation of discourses, and so keep faith with earlier impulses of the feminist project that was centrally concerned with empowering women and resisting male power. It was feared that feminism as a political movement for change was giving way as power was being refigured. Feminist writings and interventions, particularly in relation to issues of domestic violence and rape, remain crucial reminders of the destructive power of unaccountable male power.

Rationalist masculinities

Is it possible for men to take up a radical feminist analysis of men and masculinities? A number of motivations led diverse groups of men to accept that masculinities could not be redefined because they were defined exclusively as relationships of power. Men tended to accept a radical feminist analysis that masculinities so defined were the problem so they could be no part of the solution. This produced its own forms of self-rejection that encouraged men to identify with women but to feel paradoxically estranged from their experiences as men. At best they thought they could support the women's movement in whatever goals it set, but saw little possibility of working with men to transform their inherited masculinities. Of course it was vital that men learnt to recognise their positions of power within patriarchal cultures and accept responsibility for how institutions had been traditionally shaped within the terms of dominant masculinities. But it proved difficult within a rationalist modernity to recognise both the sufferings of women and the possibilities for transforming masculinities.

Although Connell refuses to take a post-structuralist path, his form of structural Marxism leads him to an analysis that shares many features with a radical feminist analysis. There is some sympathy with certain elements of socialist feminism. Somewhat paradoxically this meant that while women could learn from their practice of consciousness-raising that 'the personal is political', these insights were not possible for men. Rather, the idea that men could learn to 'name' their experience as masculine was framed within 'personal' and 'subjective' terms and came to be reduced to their realisation of their power in relation to women. Connell's analysis allowed for some understandings of emotional lives within his larger framework of analysis, but these tended to be framed as 'therapeutic'. There might be particular difficulties that men face in making connections between the personal and the political, but these need to be explored in personal terms alone.

But when Connell draws a sharp distinction between the 'therapeutic' and the 'political' he is trying to exclude the explorations of men's emotional lives that were a feature of the sexual politics of the 1970s. While there is a need to question the moralism that often prevailed, as it did with much feminism and sexual politics, it is unhelpful to characterise the work that Achilles Heel in Britain and other groups around the world were doing as 'therapeutic', since Achilles Heel was directly concerned with exploring connections between men's emotional lives and the structures of male power. For many, 'therapeutic' was not a negative term to be defined in contrast to 'real politics'; within Achilles Heel people appreciated the need to revision individualistic modes of psychotherapy while recognising the need for men to work on their lives emotionally. We were attempting to explore the complex interrelation between power and emotional life and how to revision relations between 'the psychic' and 'the social' that did not reduce men to the masculinities they represented.[8]

Also, many men, even then, could not recognise themselves in descriptions of men as bearers of power, since they often did not experience themselves as powerful in their own lives. This was not simply a misperception that needed to be corrected in the light of a modernist reason, but had to do with a need to engage theoretically with the lived contradictions in men's lives and tensions experienced between different spheres of life. A man might feel quite effective and able to set boundaries at work, but in his personal life he might find it hard to express his emotional needs and set boundaries that can help establish a clear sense of emotional identity. As we recognise the various gender experiences of different generations, so we have to theorise different patterns of relationships between men and women.

We need to be aware that for many younger people, especially in the West, gender equality is often thought of as something realised in the past: feminism is seen as a movement relating to an earlier generation. This has a different effect on the genders and for young men it can sustain a rationalist notion that they *should be able to* exercise control over their emotions. We cannot illuminate these complex shifts in gender relations by affirming the fluidity and flux of gender and sexual identities. We also need to appreciate how discourses have sometimes narrowed, leaving people bereft of emotional languages in which to explore the dynamics of gay and straight relationships. Where women have grown up to think of themselves as equal to men, able to compete on whatever terms men set within the labour market, they can feel disappointed and shocked when they are left literally 'holding the baby' after the birth of a child. Because they cannot understand the dependencies that shape relationships of pregnancy and birth, having learnt to shun them, like men, as a sign of weakness within a post-feminist culture, their relationships often break down as a consequence.[9]

In thinking about the relationships between diverse masculinities in terms of power alone, Connell shares certain features with a radical feminist analysis. He leaves little space for men to explore emotionally the tensions between their experience as men in various settings and socially defined masculinities. Rather, his theoretical framework can unwittingly reinforce a rationalist modernity that devalues the consciousness and emotional work men need to do. Theoretically splitting the 'therapeutic' from the 'political' can have the consequence of separating the 'personal' from the 'political' in men's lives. This can also make it difficult to theorise diverse cultural masculinities and to explain how these have developed historically and culturally to shape men's diverse gender and sexed experiences. Unless we are careful, we find ourselves returning to a traditional conception of the 'political' that echoes shared assumptions of liberalism and orthodox Marxisms that injustices and oppressions are only 'real' when they take place within the public realm of politics.

Connell's language of social practices cuts across traditional distinctions between the public and the private, work and intimate relations, so that we may fail to appreciate the devaluation of emotional life. We end up with a universal theorisation of masculinities that expresses a dominant masculinity. While we recognise the workings of power between men and women and also between diverse masculinities as a material process embodied in social practices, we lose insight into the relations between power and emotions, sexuality and desire. We can paradoxically be left with a universal and gender-blind conception of power, as with Foucault, but within a patriarchal analysis of male power.

Connell's theory unwittingly reproduces assumptions of a dominant masculinity that needs questioning. He develops a universal 'theory of masculinities' which people think can be applied, with a few local amendments, to different cultural settings, rather than encourage people to theorise from 'the ground up'. Taking for granted a rationalist modernity, Connell's analysis, for all its strengths in shifting the theoretical focus towards global masculinities, threatens to forget men's complex relationships with their emotions. His theorisation of power also tends to disavow issues of culture, memory and traumatic histories of displacement. These aspects of men's lives need to be related to material relations of power, but they cannot be reduced to them.

Postmodern masculinities

A universal theory can appear to claim authority, even if this is very far from its intention, especially if it tacitly works to devalue the cultural, personal and emotional. Within the West, universal theoretical traditions have often been framed in dominant masculine terms. A rationalist modernity has often given a secular form to a dominant Christian tradition in which the body comes to be identified with sexuality and the 'sins of the flesh'.

It is only by refiguring 'the human' so that it is no longer set in radical opposition to 'the animal' that we can imagine transforming masculinities. Enlightenment conceptions of nature and culture have played a part here. They also justified colonial relations of power as European masculinities were framed as representing a culture and modernity that colonised 'others' could only hope to realise and so make a transition from 'nature' to 'culture' through accepting subordination.

Simone Weil questioned France's colonial relations of power in the 1930s. Her reading of *The Iliad* inspired a different vision of power that allowed her to illuminate how it works to reduce people to matter. Her materialist analysis of power insists upon sustaining connections between ethics and politics. Although she gives priority to non-distributive conceptions of justice, so that we think of it in terms of the humane treatment of others, she rejects a sense of 'psychological' injury that would separate the therapeutic from the ethical and political. Weil grasps how power works to attack a person's sense of self-worth, confidence and esteem. While she questions a psychological discourse that is framed individualistically, so separating the 'psyche' from the 'social', she insists on the importance of bodily integrity and the harm that is done, say in rape, as a violation that is also moral, political and spiritual.

When Weil talks about violation as injustice she is framing a different relationship between ethics and politics and questioning a tradition of liberal humanism that sees injustice as adequately framed as an infringement of rights. She insists that we understand the harm done to others as a violation that challenges a rationalist tradition. Within a postmodern culture that is sceptical about the validity of universal moral judgements, Weil can be a very challenging thinker. Wary of moral relativism, she wants to insist, against the liberal common sense of her time, that slavery is morally wrong in every society and that the fact that Aristotle was prepared to justify it showed both a personal and theoretical failing that needs to be understood. She can help us to appreciate that feminism's recognition of how identities are framed by the body remains a vital challenge to a rationalist modernity. Not only did feminism challenge a prevailing distinction between reason and emotion, and insist that bodies and emotions can be sources of knowledge, but it opened up a space to revision 'the human'.

Weil offers a different vision of 'the human' as she acknowledges rape as a gendered violation of the soul, although she did not think of herself as a feminist. But if she rejects the autonomy of the psychological, insisting on connecting it with social and moral relations of power, she does not reject the psychological as reflecting a liberal humanist essentialism, as post-structuralist feminisms can be tempted to do. She questions a humanist tradition where this is conceived in disembodied and rationalist terms, as if we can identify 'being human' with 'being rational'. Paradoxically a post-structuralist tradition challenges 'humanism' by assuming that it involves a 'given' conception of human nature while at the same time sustaining its rationalism through its emphasis upon the discursive character of experience, too often conceived in rationalist terms.

When Weil in her essay 'Human Personality' talks about a young girl being dragged into a brothel against her will, she is drawing attention to how someone can be made to suffer without realising what is happening to them. The fact that a young woman has no language in which to communicate her suffering can leave her even more alone and isolated. Weil recognises that traumatic experiences cannot be healed, even if people can learn to live with them in different ways. She knows that talking to others can help, but that it will not take the pain away. She also rejects the notion that rape is a matter of 'psychological damage' – an idea that has taken hold within a postmodern therapeutic culture. As she says, everything about the person has been harmed when a person is violated, not just their 'personality'.[10]

Weil also insists on the importance of bodily integrity, and thus a sense of human vulnerability, as part of how we revision 'the human' as we break from an Enlightenment rationalism. Again she echoes a later feminist insight that bodies cannot be separated off as part of a disenchanted nature, but have to be grasped as part of a human identity. Although she does not think in gendered terms, and in many respects remains caught within a Christian tradition of self-denial, she explores an ethics of bodily vulnerabilities that points the way to a potential revisioning of 'the human'. She discovered within Christianity a moral language to illuminate the moral indignities and harms that are so often rendered invisible within traditions of liberal humanism. She also has the intellectual resources to grasp the violation of male rape and the vulnerability of male bodies that might otherwise present themselves as hard machines. Possibly she would have refused to accept that if women perpetrate violence and abuse towards their partners or children, this has to be explained as an indirect consequence of male power and violence.

Weil refused to accept that the powerless always have virtue on their side, though she insisted through her own experience of factory work on the power of social relations to reduce a sense of self-worth. She recalled how she had status in the university but none when she was working on an assembly line.

As gender relations of power are transformed, we can no longer assume that in the end it is men who have to be held responsible and women who need to be excused. We have to think differently about relations between virtue and power so that we do not deny women their own active subjectivity, as if they cannot be held responsible for their own actions. Of course there is violence that is justifiable resistance to male power, but we need a moral language of gender relations of power that also allows for the transformations of those relations. Sometimes women are responding to their own painful and traumatic histories with their own mothers.

Wittgenstein, Gramsci and Weil in different ways offer us resources for rethinking 'the human' and enable us to rethink relations between the 'psyche' and the 'social'.[11] But we also need to engage critically with their inheritances because they remain unable to think about the fluidity and uncertainties of postmodern identities. It was a strength of post-structuralist traditions that they could help restore a sense of women as active subjects, so questioning notions of 'woman' that were framed within hetero-normative frameworks. Recognising the fluidity of identities generally has helped us to question gendered identities as fixed and foreclosing. But this has tended to foster constructivist theories that disorient people, who find themselves paradoxically positioned as observers of their own experience. Shut out from their lived experience, they experience disjunction and contradictions. Constructivist theories foster their own suspicions of identity politics and tend to produce their own rationalist accounts. Unable to recognise their own displacements and able to accept psychoanalysis as a theory of subjectivities but not as a clinical practice, postmodern gender theories no longer recognise the difficulties that people can have in *grounding* their own experience. This explains a shift towards more neutral languages of bodies, affect and technologies of the self that can produce their own distancing procedures.

Although Weil learns from Eastern traditions and seeks resonances between different religious and spiritual traditions, she is less open to issues of difference and the transnational migrations that shape contemporary societies. She is sensitive to issues of embodiment and vulnerability, but she can feel too constrained by Catholic traditions of sexual denial to help us think our way towards bodily self-nourishment and sexual freedom. If she is aware of the ease with which people can hurt each other in sexual relationships, she remains sceptical about what can be learnt from psychoanalysis and embodied psychotherapies. But the vision of justice as respect for others can open up considerations of class, 'race', gender and sexualities. She can also help us to think across boundaries of the personal and institutional, recognising the need to transform institutions and social practices if respect for others is to be realised.

Gramsci recognised a need to rethink the relationship between Marx and the Catholic religious traditions of Southern Italy. He helpfully questioned a modern distinction between secular and religious, and provides us with resources to question the easy dismissal of religious traditions as 'backward' or 'superstitious' and so bound to disappear when they come up against the 'truths' of scientific progress. This forced Gramsci to rethink his inherited readings of Marx and to appreciate the diverse sources within Hegel and Marx that could be drawn upon to think differently about culture, history and ethics. Questioning the implicit universalism that had traditionally informed the rationalist modernity of Marxism, he sought for ways of thinking about the relations of power, ethics and emotional life.[12] If we are to give up the search for universal theories that can be applied to particular cultural settings, we need to be able to think differently about diverse cultures of masculinity so that we can open up dialogues between different cultural, religious and spiritual traditions. In a post-9/11 world these forms of cultural dialogue have become more urgent.

If we are to engage with the newly globalised sources of United States power in its 'war against terror', then we need to open up spaces within which different traditions can communicate with each other. As I argued in *Man Enough*, we also need to engage critically with different theoretical traditions in relation to men and masculinities as well as the different practices that have developed to work with different generations of men. Rejecting choices between anti-Sexist and mythopoetic traditions, we need to shape a new direction of theory and practice that can engage with diverse cultural, ethnic and sexed masculinities. In a period when AIDS has fostered such devastation in different regions of the world it is important to shape models of intervention that can engage with gender relations within specific histories, cultures and traditions. We need to explore ways of talking about sex, intimacy and desire within cultural traditions that have historically shunned such concerns. Through art, drama and performance we need to find ways of reaching different generations of men, rather than assume that a discourse of power will allow us to communicate across cultural traditions.

I hope I have raised helpful questions about prevailing ways of thinking about masculinities and opened up new spaces for thinking and engaging the complex relations between men's lived experiences and the masculinities they can feel obliged to conform to. This involves learning how to question inherited assumptions of a rationalist modernity, recognising with Wittgenstein how necessary it is to appreciate how experience, bodies, thoughts and emotions have been shaped through Cartesian traditions within a European modernity. Rather than assuming that universal theories can be translated across different cultures, we need to appreciate within a globalised world that we must engage with cultural, religious and spiritual traditions. As we learn from our own experiences of change, so we can share these experiences with others and recognise differences of culture, religion, history, sexuality and spiritual tradition.

Learning to listen to ourselves and deepening the contact we have with ourselves can also make us more open in listening to others.

Rather than fixing identities, we can appreciate how different needs and desires gradually shape themselves at different moments in our lives. As we appreciate the significance of generation, so we also learn about the difficulties of translation across time and space, for we recognise how hard it can be for one generation to share insights with another that has grown up in very different circumstances. Rather than accepting globalised visions of a hegemonic masculinity, we need to create spaces for reflection in which diverse cultural masculinities can be recognised. Men also need to be encouraged to engage in processes of transforming masculinities to help sustain more equal, loving and open relationships with partners and children as they struggle to realise new visions of gender and sexual justice.

Notes

Preface and acknowledgements

1 For a helpful social and political context to the emergence of second-wave feminism and for the centrality of the notion that 'the personal is political', see Sheila Rowbotham, *Woman's Consciousness, Man's World* (1972) and *Dreams and Dilemmas* (1983). For a more general account of the theoretical movements see Allison Jagger, *Feminist Politics and Human Nature* (1988).

2 For a sense of the emergence of heterosexual men's responses to the challenges of feminism and how this emerged in relation to different women's movements in the West, see Victor J. Seidler, *Rediscovering Masculinity: Reason, language and sexuality* (1989).

3 For an early account that seeks to explore issues around sexual harassment, see C. MacKinnon *The Sexual Harassment of Working Women* (1979).

4 For some helpful discussion on the relative pressures of work and family, see, for instance, Susan Moller Okin, *Justice, Gender and the Family* (1989) and J. Williams, *Unbending Gender: Why family and work conflict and what to do about it* (2000).

5 The notion of 'emotional labour' was introduced by Jean Baker Miller, *Towards a New Psychology of Women* (1976).

6 For a sense of the diversity of different feminisms and the need to explore diverse cultural and religious traditions in their relationships to issues of gender, 'race', ethnicities and sexualities, see, for example, C.T. Mohanty, *Third World Women and the Politics of Feminism* (1991); U. Narayan, *Dislocating Cultures: Identities, traditions and the third world* (1997), and M. Nussbaum and J. Glover (eds) *Women, Culture and Development: A study of human capabilities* (1995).

Chapter 1

1 For a sense of the development of Bob Connell's work, see *Gender and Power: Society, the person and sexual politics* (1987) and his later *Masculinities* (1995).

2 Connell's use of Gramsci's notion of hegemony when referring to 'hegemonic masculinities' also needs to be questioned. Gramsci tended to think of hegemony in *Selections from the Prison Notebooks* (1971) in relation to a process of critical self-awareness that gets lost in Connell's structural reading. He is thinking about

encouraging the development of a counter-hegemony towards capitalist social relations through questioning their moral and political legitimacy.

3 The ease with which modernity allows a dominant masculinity to legislate what is good for others because it can assume a rationality that does not depend upon listening to others was a theme I initially explored in *Rediscovering Masculinity: Reason, language and sexuality* (1989).

4 Caroline Merchant, *The Death of Nature* (1980) explores the relationship between changing historical conceptions of nature in science and the status of women. This is also a theme in D. Ehrenreich and D. English, *For Her Own Good* (1970).

5 B. Farrington, *The Philosophy of Francis Bacon* (1964) shows how masculinity was a critical term through which the scientific revolution came to conceive itself. See also related discussion in Brian Easlea, *Science and Sexual Oppression* (1981).

6 Daniel Boyarin, *Carnal Israel: Reading sex in Talmudic Judaism* (1993) has shown how Judaism came to be identified with 'Carnal Israel' in the dominant Christian discourses. This helps to explain the disavowal of the body and sexuality and how this disavowal was rendered invisible within secular modernities that often remained silent in relation to its theological groundings.

7 Susan Moller Okin, *Women in Western Political Thought* (1980) explores how gender frames Rousseau's social and political thinking. It helps reveal the contingent and historical nature of distinctions we often learn to take as 'natural'.

8 How 'others' come to be represented within traditions of social theory that have been framed around a dominant masculinity is a central concern in Victor J. Seidler, *Unreasonable Men: Masculinity and social theory* (1994).

9 Susan Griffin, *Pornography and Silence* (1980) makes crucial connections between the denigration of nature through the disavowal of bodies and sexualities within modernity and implicit structures of sexism, racism and anti-Semitism.

10 Chris Hedges, *War is a Force that Gives us Meaning* (2003) provides helpful discussions of his involvement in recent ethnic conflicts which reflect upon relationships between masculinities and war and the particular dangers of the 'war against terror'.

11 Victor J. Seidler (ed.), *The Achilles Heel Reader: Men, sexual politics and socialism* (1991) and the later *Men, Sex and Relationships: Writings from Achilles Heel* (1992) that I edited for the collective gathered many early materials and show how the emotional and the political were being related.

12 Victor J. Seidler, *Man Enough: Embodying masculinities* (2000) attempts to set out and clarify assumptions around different traditions that have emerged in relation to men and masculinities. It explores both anti-sexism and the mythopoetic work of Robert Bly.

13 'The formation of a diasporic intellectual: An interview with Stuart Hall', by Kuan-Hsing Chen, where he says: 'I learnt about culture, first as something which is deeply subjective and personal, and at the same time, as a structure you live' (p. 488) in *Stuart Hall: Critical dialogues in cultural studies* (ed.) David Morley and Kuan-Hsing Chen (1996).

14 Janet Sayers, *Divine Therapy: Love, mysticism and psychoanalysis* (2003) helps to relate psychoanalysis to its own history and makes visible its relationship to diverse spiritual traditions.

Chapter 2

1 Sven Lindqvist's *Exterminate All the Brutes* (2002) explores connections between colonialism framed as the 'white man's burden' and prevailing forms of social theory. He illustrates relationships between a dominant white European masculinity and the superiorities it assumed in its colonial dominations and the ways it continues to echo within a common-sense framework in post-imperial times.

2 Simone Weil in *The Need for Roots* (1972) talks about a scientific modernity that becomes the inheritance of working-class men in relationships with colonised 'others'. She shows the connections between a taken-for-granted superiority and the split within Western culture between the sciences and the humanities that has had profound implications for the way we think about relationships between ethics and power.

3 For some helpful introductions to the ways Levinas frames an ethics in relation to the obligations of hospitality towards 'the other', see Adriaan T. Peperzak (ed.), *Ethics as First Philosophy: The significance of Emanuel Levinas* (1995); Robert Bernasconi and Simon Critchley, *Re-reading Levinas* (1991) and Howard Caygill, *Levinas and the Political* (2002).

4 J.-P. Sartre, *Anti-Semite and Jew* (1960) proved to be a seminal text in showing how the project of emancipation that was offered with an Enlightenment modernity had its dark side that demanded that Jewish consciousness, like other forms of collective consciousness to do with class, gender, 'race' and ethnicities, should be dissolved as people learnt to identify themselves as free and equal citizens within a liberal democratic state. For a helpful setting which shows that although Sartre does not refer to the Holocaust directly, this is a text that is written in its early shadows and the shifts over time in Sartre's own thinking about Jewishness, see J.H. Friedlander, *Vilna on the Sein* (1990).

5 For some helpful discussion of some of the sources of Christian anti-Semitism see Franklin Littel, *The Crucifixion of the Jews* (1975). See also Richard Libowitz (ed.), *Faith and Freedom: A tribute to Franklin H. Little* (1987).

6 The classic account of the Spanish Inquisition that set the terms for scholarship for generations was Henry Charles Lea, *A History of the Inquisition in Spain*, 4 vols (1906). See also Benzion Netanyahu, *The Marranos of Spain* (1966; reprint 1973) and Angel Alcala (ed.), *The Spanish Inquisition and the Inquisitorial Mind* (1987).

7 For an illuminating discussion for the shaming of bodies within Christian theologies see Peter Brown, *The Body and Society: Men, women and sexual renunciation in early Christianity* (1990). To explore how this has shaped traditions of Christian anti-Semitism and to grasp Jewish traditions in relation to bodies and sexualities see Daniel Boyarin, *Carnal Israel: Reading sex in Talmudic Judaism* (1993).

8 The implications of Kantian moral rationalism and the implications of the radical split Kant makes between reason and nature for the ways he conceives gender relations is explored in Victor J. Seidler, *Kant, Respect and Injustice: The limits of liberal moral theory* (1986). Kant's discussions of gender, sexuality and the family are also referred to in Hans Fink, *Social Philosophy* (1981).

9 Susan Griffin, *Pornography and Silence* (1980) explores how men's identification with culture and disavowal of their connections with bodies and sexualities deemed to be part of nature can work to project onto others emotions and desires they are not willing to acknowledge. In this way she suggests valuable connections

between misogyny, 'racism' and anti-Semitism, so bringing together discussions that are often left separate.

10 A distinction between the 'therapeutic' and the 'political' informs R.W. Connell's work from *Gender and Power* (1987) to his later *Masculinities* (1995). It is a distinction that makes it difficult to appreciate the particular strengths and weaknesses of the sexual politics that emerged in the 1970s since these diverse movements come to be framed as pre-political.

11 Although the focus in *Rediscovering Masculinity: Reason, language and sexuality* is mainly upon exploring the relationships of language to masculinities within a largely Northern European Protestant modernity, it opens up the specificities of a particular relationship to language that is often presented in universal terms. The ways in which men come into language within particular historical and cultural settings still needs to be carefully investigated.

12 For some interesting discussions on how cultural masculinities help to shape men's friendships and relationships see S. Miller, *Men and Friendship* (1983); D.H.J. Morgan, *Family Connections* (1996); G.L. Mosse, *The Image of Man: The creation of modern masculinity* (1996); P.M. Nardi (ed.), *Men's Friendships* (1992) and P.M. Nardi, *Gay Men's Friendships: Invisible communities* (1999).

13 For an interesting discussion of how Western conceptions of modernity have shaped discourses of race and difference, see for instance Mary Louise Pratt, *Imperial Eyes* (1992); Sander Gilman, *On Blackness without Blacks* (1982); Leon Poliakov, *The Aryan Myth* (1974); Patricia Hill Collins, *Black Feminist Thought: Knowledge, consciousness and the politics of empowerment* (1991) and Paul Gilroy, *The Black Atlantic: Modernity and double consciousness* (1993).

14 Robert Bly's *Iron John* (1990) had a widespread influence in helping a generation of men rethink their relationships with their fathers. Its influence was partly guaranteed through its analysis of the difficulties many men had experienced through their relationship with feminism, as well as the assurance he seemed to provide that if men explored their inherited masculinities they would not have to deal with their homophobic feelings. In *Man Enough: Embodying masculinities* (2000) I explored the strengths and weaknesses of Bly's mythopoetic work and the movement that emerged around him.

15 In *Recreating Sexual Politics: Men, feminism and politics* (1991) I traced the moral traditions that informed diverse traditions within sexual politics. I showed how modernity had been shaped through the secularisation of a dominant Protestant tradition in Northern Europe and the United States and how this influenced how a dominant masculinity was identified with a notion of reason radically separated from nature.

Chapter 3

1 For an illuminating discussion of the myths around war and the powers of nationalism that helps us to think about ethnic conflicts and wars that emerged in the wake of the ending of the Cold War, so providing a background to the present 'war on terror', see Chris Hedges, *War is a Force that Gives us Meaning* (2003). See also J. Glenn Gray, *The Warriors: Reflections on men in battle* (1998).

2 For some helpful attempts to relate issues of globalisation to those of feminism and concerns with masculinity, see, for example, Maria Mies and Vandana

Shiva, *Ecofeminism* (1993) and Vandana Shiva, *Staying Alive: Women, ecology and survival* (1988). This work builds on the pioneering studies of Carolyn Merchant, *The Death of Nature: Women, ecology and the scientific revolution* (1982) and Brian Easlea, *Science and Sexual Oppression* (1981).

3 I experienced some of these tensions first hand through work that I was doing with academics and activists in Mexico from the mid-1990s, and the difficulties of sustaining a dialogue that could appreciate the strengths of both the theoretical work on men and masculinities as well as the work different activist groups were engaging in. The appeal of a universal theory related to masculinities was difficult to resist, especially for the academics concerned to establish a theory that could later be applied to Mexican realities.

4 In *Unreasonable Men: Masculinity and social theory* (1994) I sought to trace some of the connections that could make visible how a rationalist modernity was tied in with a dominant white European heterosexual masculinity. I was concerned to investigate how men, able to take their reason for granted, could work to silence women, who were defined as 'emotional' and therefore as 'unreasonable'.

5 For discussion on themes related to fathering that were opened up by Robert Bly's *Iron John* and which became a central theme, particularly in the United States, see, for instance, D. Blankenhorn, *Fatherless America: Confronting our most urgent social problem* (1995); A. Burgess, *Fatherhood Reclaimed: The making of the modern father* (1997); B. Cohen (ed.) *Fatherhood Today: Men's changing roles in the family* (1988); C.R. Daniels (ed.) *Lost Fathers: The politics of fatherlessness in America* (1998).

6 For a sense of the early movements that emerged in relation to men and masculinities in response to the women's movement see, for example, Victor J. Seidler, *Rediscovering Masculinity: Reason, language and sexuality* (1987); Jeff Hearn, *The Gender of Oppression: Men, masculinity and the critique of Marxism* (1987); H. Brod, *The Making of Masculinities* (1987); Victor J. Seidler, *The Achilles Heel Reader: Men, sexual politics and socialism* (1991); Michael M. Kimmel (ed.), *Changing Men: New directions in research on men and masculinity* (1987).

7 For some helpful background to Spain in the period of Reconquista and the Inquisition, see, for instance, Edward Peters, *Heresy and Authority in Medieval Europe* (1980); Henry Kamen, *The Spanish Inquisition* (1965).

8 To explore the implications of a radical distinction between reason and nature for the shaping of Kantian ethical theory, see Victor J. Seidler, *Kant, Respect and Injustice: The limits of liberal moral theory* (1986). For some of the gender implications see G. Lloyd, *The Man of Reason: 'Male' and 'female' in Western philosophy* (1984) and S. Ruddick, *Maternal Thinking: Towards a politics of peace* (1989).

9 For a sense of the complexity of different positions taken up in relation to gender equality in Scandinavian countries, see, for instance, Mari Teigen, 'The universe of gender quotas' in *NIKK – Nordic Institute for Women's Studies and Gender Research*, No. 3, 2002, pp. 4–8. See also H. Hernes, *Welfare State and Woman Power: Essays in state feminism* (1987) and Christina Bergquist et al., *Equal Democracies* (1999).

10 For the widespread discussions that have taken place in Scandinavia around issues of men and masculinities, see the work collected in two volumes by

S. Ervo and T. Johansson (eds), *Among Men: Moulding masculinities*, vols 1 and 2 (2002).

11 Kant's essay 'What is Enlightenment?' has proved to be a seminal statement about the aspirations towards an Enlightenment modernity, though it was barely recognised how this set out a programme for a dominant European masculinity. David Goldberg, *Racist Culture* (1998) quotes Kant as saying elsewhere that 'so fundamental is the difference between [the Negro and the white] races of man, and it appears to be as great in regard to natural capacities as in colour'. Kant is also quoted as saying 'the fellow was quite black from head to foot, a clear proof that what he said was stupid'.

Chapter 4

1 For some helpful discussion exploring issues around male violence see, for instance, Jeff Hearn, *The Violences of Men* (1998); J.L. Bowker (ed.), *Masculinities and Violence* (1998); D. Green, *Gender Violence in Africa* (1999); M.S. Kimmel and M.A. Messner (eds), *Men's Lives* (1995); K. Barry, *Female Sexual Slavery* (1979); Susan Faludi, *Backlash : The undeclared war against women* (1991); R.E. Dobash, R.P. Dobash, K. Cavanagh and R. Lewis, *Changing Violent Men* (2000); H. Stecopoulos and M. Uebel (eds), *Race and the Subject of Masculinities* (1997).

2 For a sense of the theoretical positions that Kaufman has been developing, see M. Kaufman, *Beyond Patriarchy* (1987) and his more recent *Cracking the Armor: Power, pain and the lives of men* (1993).

3 The television programme that was shown on BBC in Britain under the title *Macho* describes itself as 'A documentary with a surprising story about *macho* Latin America: meet Nicaragua's Men Against Violence Group tackling violence and sexual abuse. Fresh solutions to the universal problem of men behaving badly, from the last place on earth you'd expect'. Directed and produced by Lucinda Broadbent and available from Broadbent Productions, 345 Renfrew St, Glasgow G3 6UW, Scotland, e-mail Lucinda@cqm.co.uk

4 For a discussion of different readings of Genesis and ways they have been shaped through different religious traditions, see Elaine Pagels, *Adam, Eve and the Serpent* (1988) and her *The Origins of Satan* (1996).

5 A helpful overview of the work in relation to men and masculinities in Nicaragua that sets the group Cantera in a wider setting is given in Patrick Welsh, *Men Aren't from Mars: Unlearning machismo in Nicaragua* (2001). See also Cantera, *Hombre, Violencia y Crisis Social* (Managua, Nicaragua, May 1995) and Cantera, *Genero, Podery Violencia* (Managua, Nicaragua, May 1996).

6 For some helpful reflections about working with adolescent men in different Latin American contexts see José A. Olavarria, *Varones Adolescentes: Genero, identidades y sexualidades en América Latina* (2003). To contrast with work that has been done in relation to boys in Europe and the United States see, for instance, S. Askew and C. Ross, *Boys Don't Cry: Boys and sexism in education* (1988); R.W. Connell, *The Men and the Boys* (2000); D. Epstein, J. Elwood, V. Hey and J. Maw (eds), *Failing Boys? Issues in gender and achievement* (1998); S. Frosh, A. Phoenix and R. Pattman, *Young Masculinities* (2002).

7 For an illuminating discussion of how men can be shaped by childhood experiences of violence and the ways this can affect their relationships as adults, see Jim Gilligan, *Violence: Reflections on our deadliest epidemic* (1997).

8 For a helpful background to the development of gender politics in Africa see, for instance, Ifi Amadiume, *Male Daughters, Female Husbands: Gender and sex in an African society* (1974) and her more recent *Re-Inventing Africa: Matriarchy, religion and culture* (1987); A. Mama, *Beyond the Masks: Race, gender and subjectivity* (1995); O. Oyewumi, *The Invention of Women: Making an African sense of Western gender discourses* (1997); Robert Morell (ed.), *Changing Men in Southern Africa* (2001).

Chapter 5

1 For helpful discussion on the transformation of intimacy and sexual relationships within contemporary Western societies, see, for instance, P. Middleton, *The Inward Gaze: Masculinity and subjectivity in modern culture* (1992); S. Miller, *Men and Friendship* (1983); A. Giddens, *The Transformation of Intimacy* (1992); S. Faludi, *Stiffed: The betrayal of the modern man* (1999); P. Nardi (ed.), *Men's Friendships* (1992); U. Beck and E. Beck-Gersheim, *The Normal Chaos of Love* (1995).

2 For a sense of how feminisms have transformed women's expectations in hetero-sexual relationships, see, for instance, L. Segal, *Is the Future Female?* (1989), and her more recent *Why Feminism?* (1999); C. Vance (ed.) *Pleasure and Danger: Exploring female sexuality* (1984); N. Walter, *The New Feminism* (1998).

3 For discussions of the changing balance between spaces of work and intimacy, see, for instance, J. Williams, *Unbending Gender: Why family and work conflict and what to do about it* (2000); M. Kimmell, *The Gendered Society* (2000); Arlie Hochschild, *The Second Shift* (1989) and her more recent *The Time Bind* (1997).

4 For discussion on the experiences of South Asian women in the diaspora see Nirmal Puwar (co-editor), *South Asian Women in the Diaspora* (2003) and her more recent *Space Invaders: Race, gender and bodies out of place* (2004).

5 I have explored the relationships between authority, fathering and masculinity in 'Fathering, authority and masculinity', in R. Chapman and J. Rutherford (eds), *Male Order: Unwrapping masculinity* (1988) and also in 'Fathering, masculinity and parental relationships', in S. Ervo and T. Johansson (eds), *Among Men: Moulding masculinities* (2002). It is also a theme historically explored in J.R. Gillis, *A World of Their own Making: Myth, ritual and the quest for family values* (1996).

6 It is partly the identification of a dominant masculinity with reason that works to produce its disavowals of emotions that are traditionally identified as 'feminine'. We need to explore how diverse cultural masculinities learn to experience certain emotions as signs of weakness and so as threat to male identities. The significance of exploring issues of emotional life and a realisation of how they are tied up with relations of power was a theme in Victor J. Seidler (ed.), *Men, Sex and Relationships: Writings from Achilles Heel* (1992).

7 In *Recovering the Self: Morality and social theory* (1994) I tried to show how different readings of Marx shaped the reception that was given to Gramsci in the Anglo-American world. Often we remain marked by the generation through which we learn social theory, and it can be difficult to appreciate how certain structural and post-structuralist traditions worked against thinking emotional life and embodied memories.

8 For a sense of the Althusserian influence on the readings of Gramsci, see, for instance, Stuart Hall, B. Lumley and G. McLennan (eds), *On Ideology* (reproduction of Working Papers in Cultural Studies, 10) (1978) and S. Hall, 'Rethinking the "base and superstructure" metaphor', in J. Bloomfield et al. (eds), *Class, Hegemony and Party* (1977). There are some illuminating reflections on Hall's period at the Birmingham Centre for Cultural Studies and the diverse challenges that were made to intellectual orthodoxies of the time in David Morley and Kuan-Hsing Chen, *Stuart Hall: Critical dialogues in cultural studies* (1996). See also Chantal Mouffe, *Gramsci and Marxist Theory* (1979) and the more recent Chantal Mouffe and Ernesto Laclau, *Hegemony and Social Strategy: Towards a radical democratic politics* (1985).

9 Gramsci shares his reflections on the importance of developing a critical consciousness in the footnotes to his 'The study of philosophy: Problems of philosophy and history', in the *Prison Notebooks* (1971), pp. 323–77. For some useful introductions to Gramsci's writings see Carl Boggs, *Gramsci's Marxism* (1976); A. Davidson, *Antonio Gramsci: Towards an intellectual biography* (1977) and G. Fiori, *Antonio Gramsci: Life of a revolutionary* (1980).

10 Gramsci's *Letters from Prison* (trans. L. Lawner) (1975) show him rethinking the kind of Leninist traditions that had influenced his earlier work. Not only is he challenging its moralism but also how it taught him to relate to personal and emotional life.

11 For some helpful reflections on a postmodern turn within social theory, see Zygmunt Bauman, *Intimations of Postmodernity* (1994) and his later *Postmodernity and its Discontents* (1997). For a sense of how Bauman came to rethink some of his earlier formulations in relation to the postmodern, see Zygmunt Bauman, *Liquid Modernity* (2000).

12 I have explored some of the implications of Marx's 'On the Jewish question' for the forms of rationalist humanisms that shaped traditions of social theory within the West in *Recovering the Self: Morality and social theory* (1994). This is also a theme that has been explored in Norman Geras, *Marx and Human Nature: Refutation of a legend* (1983).

13 Feminist political theory has helped to question how modernity has been figured within the terms of a dominant European masculinity, but these insights have sometimes been lost when feminism has been construed as a discourse of modernity that is organised around the emancipation of a unified conception of 'woman'. See, for instance, Carol Pateman, *The Sexual Contract* (1988); Alice Jardine, *Gynesis: Configurations of women and modernity* (1985); J. Butler, *Gender Trouble: Feminism and the subversion of identity* (1990); Margaret Whitford, *Luce Irigaray: Philosophy in the feminine* (1991); Jeffrey Weeks, *Invented Moralities* (1995); S. Benhabib, *Situating the Self* (1991); A. Jaggar, *Feminist Politics and Human Nature* (1988).

14 Though Foucault's discussion of relationships between power and knowledge has proved vital within social theory, he tended to focus upon how power worked to articulate cultural notions of 'femininity' and 'masculinity' in ways that drew attention away from how personal and institutional power is exercised by men within patriarchal cultures to reduce women to silence. It is a strength of Simone Weil's understanding of the workings of power that she grasps how power works to reduce people to matter. This is a theme I explored in Lawrence Blum and Victor J. Seidler, *A Truer Liberty: Simone Weil and Marxism* (1991), chs 8 and 9.

Chapter 6

1 To think about the relationships between fatherhood, masculinity and cultural traditions of authority see, for example, F. Bozett and S. Hanson (eds), *Fatherhood and Families in Cultural Context* (1991); N. Chodorow, *The Reproduction of Mothering: Psychoanalysis and the sociology of gender* (1978); B. Cohen (ed.), *Fatherhood Today: Men's changing roles in the family* (1988); P. Bourdieu, *Masculine Domination* (2001); N.E. Dowd, *Redefining Fatherhood* (2000).

2 For an appreciation of differences between dominant masculinities shaped through Protestant and Catholic traditions, see the work that has developed in relation to Latin American masculinities, for instance Mathew Gutmann's work in Mexico, *The Meanings of Macho: Being a man in Mexico City* (1996) and the interesting collections, *Masculinidades y Equidad de Genero en América Latina*, eds Terésa Valdes and José Olavarria (1998) and the more recent work on young men, *Varones Adolscentes: Genero, identidades y sexualidades en América Latina*, ed. José Olavarria (2003). See also Norma Fuller, *Masculinades, Cambios y Permancencias* (2001); M.V. Viveros, 'Identidades masculinas. Diversidades regionales y cambios generacionales', in M. Viveros, J. Olavarria and N. Fuller, *Hombres e Identidades de Genero. Investigaciones desde América Latina* (2001); S. Chant and M. Gutmann, *Mainstreaming Men in Gender and Development* (2000).

3 For investigations into young Asian women growing up in Britain, see, for instance, Amrit Wilson, *Finding a Voice: Asian women in Britain* (1976).

4 For helpful reflections on the ways Rousseau framed women's sexuality as a threat to male reason, see Susan Moller Okin, *Women in Western Political Thought* (1980); Susan Mendes, *Tolerance and the Limits of Liberalism* (1989); C. Pateman, *The Sexual Contract* (1988); Elizabeth Grosz, *Sexual Subversions* (1989).

5 Some of the implications of Kant's radical separation of reason from nature are explored in my *Kant, Respect and Injustice: The limits of liberal moral theory* (1986), in Z. Bauman, *Postmodern Ethics* (1993) and B. Williams, *Ethics and the Limits of Philosophy* (1985).

6 The connections between honour, shame and women's bodies are well explored in Ana Amuchástegui, *Virginidad e Iniciacion Sexual en Mexico: Experiencias y significados* (2001).

7 The significance of the symbolism that surrounds the Virgin Mary has been explored by Marina Warner, *Alone of All Her Sex* (1983).

8 The Inquisition, though rarely engaged with in its complexities and regional differences, became a significant source for totalitarian thinking that was to play a crucial role in the particular forms of Spanish colonial conquest of Central and Latin America. For a sense of the different ways that the Inquisition shaped thinking about totalitarianism see, for instance, Kamen, *The Spanish Inquisition* (1965) and H. Arendt, *The Origins of Totalitarianism* (1968).

9 If we are to revision a conception of 'the human' that allow us to question how a dominant Western tradition has defined it through a radical split from 'the animal' and so from nature, then we have to recognise how ecological thinking has provided a challenge to a rationalist modernity set within masculinist terms. See, for instance, my *Unreasonable Men: Masculinity and social theory* (1994); Val Plumwood, *Feminism and the Mastery of Nature*

(1996); *Ecological Feminism*, ed. Karen J. Warren (1994); A. Naess, *Ecology, Community and Lifestyle*, trans. and ed. David Rothenberg (1989); P. McAllister, (ed.), *Reweaving the Web of Life: Feminisn and non-violence* (1982); J. Plant, (ed.), *Healing the Wounds: The promise of ecofeminism* (1989) and V. Shiva, *Staying Alive: Women, ecology and development* (1988).

10 For an interesting exploration in the history of ideas that allows us to think differently about the relationship of virtue to nature and the images of growth that continue to shape visions of identity, see M.C. Horowitz *Seeds of Virtue and Knowledge* (1997).

11 For an appreciation of Gnostic traditions within the West and the ways their silencing has been related to shaping dominant Christian traditions in masculine terms, see Elaine Pagels, *The Gnostic Gospels* (1982). To appreciate connections with the ways bodies and sexualities came to be shamed, see Peter Brown, *The Body and Society: Men, women and sexual renunciation in early Christianity* (1990).

12 For an interesting exploration of the ways in which gendered bodies have been imagined at different moments in Western history and culture, see Tom Lacquer, *Making Sex* (1990).

13 The ways in which men within diverse cultures are encouraged to define their male identities through affirming superiority in relation to others is a theme I have explored in *Man Enough: Embodying masculinities* (2000).

14 The challenges created by diasporas and migrations across national boundaries for the ways social theory has traditionally conceived of the nation-state and the different ways we imagine forms of assimilation, integration and community so that diverse cultures can live together was explored in Britain in the Parekh Report and the discussions it provoked. See for instance, *Bhikhu Parekh, Rethinking Multiculturalism: Cultural diversity and political theory* (2000).

Chapter 7

1 Some of the complex processes involved in 'coming out' in different class and cultural settings have been explored both historically and in terms of changing contemporary cultures in Jeffrey Weeks, *Coming Out: Homosexual politics in Britain* (1977) and *Invented Moralities* (1995); Ken Plummer, *Telling Sexual Stories: Power, change and social worlds* (1995); A. Nayak and M. Kehily, 'Playing it straight: Masculinities, homophobias and schooling', *Journal of Gender Studies* 5(2)(1996): 211–30; M. Mac an Ghail, *The Making of Men: Masculinities, sexualities and schooling* (1994).

2 Issues around bullying were made increasingly visible in British schools in the late 1990s and they are the theme in Stephen Frosh, Ann Phoenix and Rob Pattman, *Young Masculinities* (2002). See also Les Back, *New Ethnicities and Urban Culture* (1996); D. Epstein, J. Elwood, V. Hey and J. Maw (eds), *Failing Boys? Issues in gender and achievement* (1998) and B. Thorne, *Gender Play: Girls and boys in school* (1993).

3 Some helpful attempts to explore the emotional lives of young men at school are provided in Stephen Frosh, Ann Phoenix and Rob Pattman, *Young Masculinities* (2002); R. Hewitt, *White Talk Black Talk: Inter-racial friendships and communication amongst adolescents* (1986); N. Duncan, *Sexual Bullying* (1999).

4 Some of the issues surrounding the shootings at Colombine were explored by Michael Moore in the documentary he made and also in the book *Stupid White Men* (2004).

5 The increasingly globalised circulation of Western images of thin bodies through the Internet and global media have had an enormous impact in shaping young women and increasingly young men's relationships to their bodies, sexualities and senses of self-worth. It has also fostered an increase in surgical interventions to shape bodies according to prevailing cultural images. See, for instance, Susan Bordo, *Unbearable Weight: Feminism, Western culture and the body* (1993); R. Weitz (ed.), *The Politics of Women's Bodies: Sexuality, appearance and behaviour* (1998); O. Edut (ed.), *Body Outlaws: Young women write about body image and identity* (2000); I.M. Young, *Throwing Like a Girl and Other Essays in Feminist Philosophy and Social Theory* (1990) and K. Davis, *Reshaping the Female Body: The dilemmas of cosmetic surgery* (1995).

6 For some exploration of men's relationships to their bodies, see, for instance, Susan Bordo, *The Male Body: A new look at men in public and private* (1999); L.A. Hall, *Hidden Anxieties: Male sexuality 1900–1950* (1991); S. Heath, *The Sexual Fix* (1982); K. Plummer (ed.), *The Making of the Modern Homosexual* (1981); F. Mort, *Dangerous Sexualities: Medico-moral politics in England since 1830* (1987); V.J. Seidler (ed.), *Men, Sex and Relationships* (1991).

7 Issues around emotional literacy and the importance of communication within relationships have been a theme in Carol Gilligan, *In a Different Voice: Psychological theory and women's development* (1982); C. Gilligan, J.V. Ward and J.M. Taylor (eds), *Mapping the Moral Domain* (1988); Daniel Goleman, *Emotional Intelligence* (1996).

8 A recognition that new forms of individualism and a fragmentation of collective identities have tended to shape late modernity is a theme explored by Z. Bauman, *Liquid Modernity* (2000), *The Individualized Society* (2001); Ulrich Beck, *Ecological Enlightenment: Essays on the politics of a risk society*, trans. Mark Ritter (1995); Anthony Giddens, *The Transformation of Intimacy: Sexuality, love and eroticism in modern societies* (1992).

9 For some helpful discussion on the ways in which the Internet and virtual reality have opened up spaces for exploration, performance and discovery see V.J. Seidler, 'Embodied knowledge and virtual space' in J. Wood (ed.), *The Virtual Embodied: Presence, practice, technology* (1998).

10 To help revision conceptions of identity and question traditions of identity politics that have been implicitly shaped around somewhat 'given' and 'fixed' identities, see, for instance, Stuart Hall, 'Who needs "identity"?' in Stuart Hall and Paul du Gay (eds), *Questions of Cultural Identity* (1996); Christopher Lash, *The Minimal Self: Psychic survival in troubled times* (1984); Jonathan Rutherford, *I Am No Longer Myself Without You: An anatomy of love* (1999) and *Stuart Hall: Critical dialogues in cultural studies*, ed. David Morley and Kuan-Hsing Chen (1996).

11 For a sense of the development of Jung's work see Andrew Samuels, *Jung and the Post-Jungians* (1974). This work has influenced the mythopoetic work on men and masculinities through the work of Robert Bly's *Iron John* (1990).

12 For a helpful exploration of the relationship between gay men and psychoanalysis, see Jack Drescher, *Psychoanalytic Therapy and Gay Men* (1998); J. Dresher, A. D'Ercole and E. Schoenberg, *Psychotherapy with Gay Men*

and Lesbians: Contemporary dynamic approaches (2003); T. Domenici and R.C. Lesser (eds), *Disorienting Sexuality: Psychoanalytic reappraisals of sexual identities* (1995); K. Lewes, *Psychoanalysis and Male Homosexuality* (1995); N. O'Connor and J. Ryan, *Wild Desires and Mistaken Identities: Lesbianism and psychoanalysis* (1993).

Chapter 8

1 For a sense of how masculinities were figured as relations of power in the early reflections on men and feminism, see, for instance, H. Brod, *The Making of Masculinities: The new men's studies* (1987); R.W. Connell, *Gender and Power* (1987); Jeff Hearn, *The Gender of Oppression: Men, masculinity and the critique of Marxism* (1987) and *Men in the Public Eye* (1992), D.H.J. Morgan, *Discovering Men* (1992); Arthur Brittan, *Masculinity and Power* (1989); Victor J. Seidler, *Rediscovering Masculinity: Reason, language and male sexuality* (1987) and Victor J. Seidler (ed.), *The Achilles Heel Reader: Men, sexual politics and socialism* (1990).

2 For helpful reflections upon the ways in which public and private spheres have been gendered differently in diverse cultural settings, see, for example, Susan Moller Okin, *Women in Western Political Thought* (1979, new edn 1992); M. Kimmel, *The Gendered Society* (2000); A. Jaggar, *Feminist Politics and Human Nature* (1988); C.T. Mohanty, *Third World Women and the Politics of Feminism* (1991); U. Narayan, *Dislocating Cultures: Identities, traditions and third world feminism* (1997); M. Nussbaum, *Sex and Social Justice* (1999).

3 See Mary Wollstonecraft, *A Vindication of the Rights of Women* (1970). The enormous contribution that Mary Wollstonecraft made to early feminist thinking is explored in Barbara Taylor, *Eve and New Jerusalem* (1983) and more fully in her later *Mary Wollstonecraft and the Feminist Imagination* (2002) and also in Sheila Rowbotham, *Hidden from History* (1973). This theme in Kant's writing was explored in Victor J. Seidler, *Kant, Respect and Injustice: The Limits of liberal moral theory* (1986).

4 Mary Wollstonecraft, quoted in Virginia Sapiro, *A Vindication of Political Virtue,* (1992), p. 179.

5 For some interesting explorations of fatherhood as a relationship of authority, see J.R. Gillis, *A World of their Own Making: Myth, ritual, and the quest for family values* (1996); R.L. Griswold, *Fatherhood in America: A history* (1993); P. Aries, *Centuries of Childhood: A social history of family life* (1962); P. Bourdieu, *Masculine Domination* (2001); V.J. Seidler, 'Fathering, authority and masculinity' in R. Chapman and J. Rutherford (eds), *Male Order: Unwrapping masculinity* (1996).

6 Alice Miller explores the predicaments of father and child relationships that emerge from historical and contemporary pedagogies in *For Your Own Good: Hidden cruelty in child-rearing and the roots of violence* (1983); *Thou Shalt Not Be Aware: Society's betrayal of the child* (1984) and *Breaking the Veil of Silence* (1998).

7 The fear of intimacy, which can take different forms in different class, cultural and ethnic settings, is a theme I explored in an essay 'Fear and intimacy,' in A. Metcalf and M. Humphries, *The Sexuality of Men* (1987). It was a theme

further developed in my *Rediscovering Masculinity: Reason, language and male sexuality* (1989).

8 Papers from the gender flux conference where I originally heard Fatima Adimo's paper have been collected in Anne Boran and Bernadette Murphy's *Gender in Flux* (2004).

9 Some of these insights were gathered through participating in a training programme on Masculinities and Drug Use at Orexis, a drugs centre in southeast London where the director is Dean Whittington. I thank all the participants for their openness and willingness to engage with issues around men and masculinities. During this period I was supervising Dean Whittington's PhD 'Men, violence and substance abuse: A study of white working class masculinities in Deptford,' Goldsmiths College, University of London, 2004.

10 For some interesting reflections upon the role of Black Churches in the United States and the cultures of resistance they were able to sustain through a recognition of love, see bell hooks, *Sisters of the Yam: Black women and self-recovery* (1994) and *Salvation: Black people and love* (2001).

11 For discussion about the experience of different generations of Afro-Caribbean migration into Britain see Paul Gilroy, *There Aint no Black in the Union Jack* (1987); J. Rex, *Ethnic Minorities in the Modern Nation State* (1996); P. Werbner and T. Mahood (eds), *Debating Cultural Hybridity: Multicultural identities and the politics of anti-racism* (1997).

12 Some of the predicaments of racialised male identities are explored in different contexts in W.E.B. Du Bois, *The Souls of Black Folk* (1969), *Black Atlantic* (1993); Cornell West, *Race Matters* (1993); Philip Brian Harper, *Are We Not Men? Masculine identity and the problem of African American identity* (1996); Gail Bederman, *Manliness and Civilisation: A cultural history of gender and race in the United States 1880–1917* (1995); Andrew Hacker *Two Nations: Black, white, separate, hostile and unequal* (1992); Hazel V. Carby, *Race Men* (1998).

13 Otto Weininger, *Sex and Character* (Heinemann, 1906) had an important influence on both Freud and Wittgenstein, and was critical in shaping of Nazi racist ideologies. It established a framework of thought that allowed connections to be made between sexism, racism anti-Semitism and homophobia. Unable to aspire to live the ethical life that Kant seemingly defined as civilised the young philosophy student Weininger committed suicide. Hitler was to say later that he was the only Jew in Europe who deserved to survive.

Chapter 9

1 I have explored Jewish migrant aspirations towards becoming 'English' within an assimilationist culture in Britain in the 1950s and how these were framed within a post-Holocaust world in which the Holocaust could not yet be widely spoken about in *Shadows of the Shoah: Jewish identity and belonging* (2001).

2 For an interesting exploration of Jewish masculinities and the different ways they have been figured, see, for instance, Sander Gillman, *Jewish Self-hatred* (1989) and Daniel Boyarin, *Unheroic Conduct: Rise of heterosexuality and the invention of the Jewish man* (1997).

3 A helpful study that both shares a personal history and introduces research done in relation to second-generation experience in the United States, Europe and Britain is Ann Karpf's *The War After* (1997).

4 For a sense of pre-war Vienna and the sudden transformations that took place in Jewish life there as Hitler's army marched into the city to be given an overwhelming welcome by the population, see George Clare, *Last Waltz in Vienna* (1982).

5 For an interesting exploration of the theme of whiteness, see Vron Ware, *Beyond the Pale* (1992) and Les Back and Vron Ware's *Out of Whiteness: Color, politics, and culture* (2001).

6 For some helpful writings on Black masculinities see Franz Fanon, *Black Skin, White Mask* (1986); David Marriott, 'Reading Black masculinities', in *Understanding Masculinities*, ed. M. Mac an Ghaill (1996), pp. 185–201; bell hooks in M. Berger, B. Wallis and S. Watson (eds), *Constructing Masculinity* (1995) and *Yearning: Race, gender and cultural politics* (1991) and the discussions provoked by Robert Staples *Black Masculinity: The Black man's role in American society* (1982); see also K. Mercer and I. Julien, 'Race, sexual politics and Black masculinity: a dossier', in R. Chapman and J. Rutherford (eds), *Male Order: Unwrapping masculinity* (1988).

7 This is an experience that bell hooks explores in *Sisters of the Yam* (1993). It can also be illuminating to read the dialogue between bell hooks and Cornell West which touches in different ways on issues of black masculinities in *Breaking Bread* (1994).

8 Some of the connections between Black and Jewish histories of catastrophe have been suggested in the concluding chapter of Paul Gilroy's *The Black Atlantic: Modernity and double consciousness* (1993). Connections between the traumatic histories of slavery and the Holocaust have also been suggestively explored by Laurence M. Thomas in *Vessels of Evil: American Slavery and the Holocaust* (1993).

Chapter 10

1 Pat Barker has written in an illuminating way about the impact of the First World War on both the generation that fought and on their families when they returned. She explores the difficulties for families produced through the silences soldiers often felt a stoic duty to sustain. See her trilogy, *Regeneration* (1991), *The Eye in the Door* (1993) and *The Ghost Road* (1995).

2 Walter Benjamin recognised that the First World War was a vital watershed in European history and culture that helped to shape the silences produced between generations. In his essay 'The Storyteller' in *Illuminations* (1973) he explores the difficulties that men had in offering guidance and counsel to their children given that so much they had lived through and witnessed in war remained unspoken.

3 Links between dominant white, heterosexual masculinities and empire have been explored by Robert Aldrich in *Colonialism and Homosexuality* (2002).

4 For introductions to Reich's work see Myron Sharaf, *Fury on Earth: A biography of Wilhelm Reich* (1983); David Boadella, *In the Wake of Reich* (1976).

5 Simone Weil explores how relations of power can work so that those who have more power within a hierarchy can 'pass on' the pain they have endured to those who are weaker or less powerful. Often those who are unable to 'pass on' the pain have to somehow deal with it themselves. How power can work to reduce people to matter was a central concern in Weil's essay on the Iliad.

This is a theme I have explored in *A Truer Liberty: Simone Weil and Marxism* (with Lawrence Blum) (1991), ch. 8 'Power'.

6 Some of these examples have been developed through discussions with Dean Whittington as I was supervising his thesis.

Chapter 11

1 For studies that explore the impact of drug use on community life, see for example Howard Parker, *Living with Heroin: The impact of a drug epidemic on an English community* (1985); A. Banks and T. Waller, *Drug Misuse* (1988); Felicity de Zulueta, *From Pain to Violence: the traumatic roots of destructiveness* (1993); J. Gilligan, *Violence: Reflections on our deadliest epidemic* (2000); T. Newburn and E. Stanko (eds), *Just Boys Doing Business* (1994); J. Wild, *Working with Men for Change* (1999).

2 Dean Whittington's work was established through in-depth counselling work with white working-class men in Deptford, southeast London. He explores the complex relationships across generations between violence and substance misuse. See his PhD thesis submitted through the Sociology Department, University of London 'Men, violence and substance misuse: A Study of white working-class masculinities in Deptford' (University of London, 2004).

3 Richard Sennett and Jonathan Cobb, *The Hidden Injuries of Class* (1972) was an early inspiration for me when it was first published in the 1970s because it seemed to be exploring an emotional language of class that was adequate to an appreciation of the workings of class power and subordination. It recognised the need for a moral language of respect and self-worth that could enrich the political languages of Marxism that were available at the time. Sennett has returned to some of these themes and explores a narrative that can illuminate the changed experience of a different generation brought up within very different work cultures in *The Corrosion of Character: The personal consequences of work in the new capitalism* (1998). Though he does not engage explicitly with themes of masculinity, his work opens up issues of narrative that can help to explore new ways of thinking about the relation between the 'psyche' and the 'social' for men and masculinities.

4 Zymunt Bauman reflects upon the processes of individualization that have taken place within late modernity in *Liquid Modernity* (2000) and in the collection of essays brought together under the title, *The Individualised Society* (2001). This is also a theme in his more recent *Liquid Love* (2003). See also Richard Sennett, *The Uses of Disorder: Personal identity and city life* (1996) and Ulrick Beck, *The Risk Society: Towards a new modernity* (1992).

5 A refusal to erase tensions between 'language' and 'experience' shows connections between Wittgenstein's later work in *Philosophical Investigations* and some of the early feminist insights into what cannot easily be spoken of. Recognition of the problematic nature of the category of experience, especially when it is identified with what is given and the centrality of language in the articulation of experience, does not have to deny continuing tensions between language and experience. For discussion of a continental philosophical tradition, see Sonia Kruks, *Retrieving Experience: Subjectivity and recognition in feminist politics* (2001). See also Joan Scott, 'Experience,' in *Feminists Theorize the Political*, ed. Judith Butler and Joan Scott (1992) pp. 22–40; Denise Rily, '*Am I that Name?*'

Feminism and the category of 'women' in history (1988); Shane Phelan, *Getting Specific: Postmodern lesbian politics* (1994); Chandra Talpade Mohanty, 'Feminist Encounters: Locating the politics of experience', in *Destabilising Theory: Contemporary feminist debates*, ed. Michele Barrett and Anne Philips (1992), pp. 74–92; Victor J. Seidler, *Unreasonable Men: Masculinity and social theory* (1994).

6 For some helpful explorations reflections on the impact of domestic violence, see, for instance, Felicity de Zulueta, *From Pain to Violence: The traumatic roots of destructiveness* (1993); D.W. Winnicott, *Through Paediatrics to Psychoanalysis* (1958); M.B. Straus (ed.), *Abuse and Victimisation across the Life Span* (1988); D. Cicchetti and V. Carlson (eds), *Child Maltreatment: Theory and research on the causes and consequences of child abuse and neglect* (1989); J.E. Korbin (ed.), *Child Abuse and Neglect: Cross cultural perspectives* (1989); E. Fromm, *The Anatomy of Human Destructiveness* (1974).

7 The ways in which a Protestant ethic works to shape a relation between work cultures and masculinities has often been an implicit theme in theoretical work relating to men and masculinities in the Anglophone world. It was a theme that I attempted to make explicit, Victor J. Seidler, *Recreating Sexual Politics: Men, feminism and politics* (1991).

8 Exploring male violence and how it works to shape different generations of men from different class, 'race' and ethnic backgrounds was a theme in T. Newburn and E. Stanko, *Just Boys Doing Business* (1994); J. Gilligan, *Violence: Reflections on our deadliest epidemic* (2000); R. Coombs, *The Family Context of Adolescent Drug Use* (1988); K. Thewelait, *Male Fantasies*, vol. 1 (1977), vol. 2 (1978).

9 The language of 'arrows' and 'stings' emerges from Elias Cannetti, who explores how relationships of power allow people to take out their anger and rage on those who are weaker and less powerful than themselves. Wanting to move beyond a sociological language of values and attitudes and a Freudian psychoanalytic account of emotional projection, Cannetti in *Crowds and Power* (1960, repr. 1973) shows the effects of power on the bodies and psyches of others. In this way he explores the materiality of power and how it works to disfigure and disorganise bodies and emotional lives.

Chapter 12

1 Sheila Rowbotham, *Dreams and Dilemmas* (1983) bring together writings from this period showing the ways that different political streams within socialist and left libertarian politics made themselves felt in the women's movement and gay liberation. It is useful to read this next to her early work *Women's Consciousness, Man's World* (1973). See also Micheline Wandor, *The Body Politic* (1972), which brought together feminist writings of the period. For similarly influential work in the United States, see Robin Morgan, *Sisterhood is Powerful* (1970) and her more recent attempt at a global collection, *Sisterhood is Global* (1984). For more recent assessments, see Maggie Humm (ed.), *Feminisms* (1992); Caroline Ramazanoglu, *Feminism and the Contradictions of Oppression* (1989) and Caroline Ramazanoglu (ed.), *Up Against Foucault* (1993); Henrietta Moore, *A Passion for Difference* (1994) and Mary Evans, *The Woman Question* (1994).

2 The difficulties of generations of men in thinking of themselves in gendered terms is a theme that has continued from the early writings on men and masculinities. More recently it has taken on new forms, as there has been a wider currency of discourses in relation of men and masculinities and a tendency to create a parallelism theoretically with feminisms. See, for example, Victor J. Seidler, *Rediscovering Masculinity: Reason, language and sexuality* (1989); W. Connell, *Gender and Power* (1987); Arthur Brittan, *Masculinity and Power* (1989); Jeff Hearn, *The Gender of Oppression: Men, masculinity and the critique of Marxism* (1987); H. Brod (ed.), *The Making of Masculinities: The new men's studies* (1987); Lynne Segal, *Slow Motion: Changing masculinities, changing men* (1997).

3 A crucial difference in conceptualisation of masculinities and male power relates to whether men can change and so around visions of transformation. A 'hegemonic' vision has tended to think that if men have power, then their sufferings can only be recognised as 'personal' and psychological and so not as 'structural' and political. With power, men supposedly have all the opportunities denied to others so that masculinities have to be deconstructed and opportunities more equally shared. If men have power, they supposedly cannot have hurts and since masculinities can be theorised as relations of power, we do not have to engage with diverse cultures of masculinity and visions of transformation.

4 Helpful texts that relate issues of gender to classical traditions of social theory are K.A. Sydie, *Natural Woman, Cultured Men* (1987); R. Braidotti, *Patterns of Dissonance* (1991); R.W. Bologh, *Love or Greatness: Max Weber and masculine thinking* (1990); H. Brod and M. Kaufman, *Theorizing Masculinities* (1994); S. Hall (ed.), *Representations: Cultural representations and signifying practices* (1997); Louis McNay, *Foucault and Feminism* (1992); Linda Nicholson (ed.), *Feminism/Postmodernism* (1990); Evelyn Fox Keller, *Reflections on Gender and Science* (1985).

5 As categories of class, 'race' and gender were recognised as unstable and so no longer shaping identities as they might have for previous generations, there were moves to think about the relations between these different 'sectors' within forms of intersectional analysis that wanted to trace the influence of these structural categories as they worked in relation to each other. Others recognised that theoretical issues remained and that intersectional analyses failed to appreciate the need to move away from thinking in terms of identities at all. But moves to think 'beyond gender' and 'beyond race' tended to assume a misleading duality between a 'fixity' that needed to be overcome and the fluidity of identifications that were to be welcomed. But too easy celebrations of hybridity and flux could also forget the pain and sufferings that need also to be recognised as aspects of traumatic histories and cultural displacements. Transnational migrations take very different forms, but we can only learn to think beyond dualities when we have appreciated how rationalist traditions of modernity easily transmute into postmodern rationalism.

6 Judith Butler, *Gender Trouble: Feminism and the subversion of identity* (1990) was followed later by her *Bodies that Matter: The discursive limits of 'sex'* (1993). See also her 'Revisiting bodies and pleasures', *Theory, Culture and Society* (special issue on Performativity and Belonging, ed. Vikki Bell (1999), 16:2, pp. 11–20).

7 To think about the complexity of emotional lives and appreciate how they are shaped through social and cultural relations of power see, for instance, Elizabeth Spellman, *Inessential Woman: Problems of exclusion in feminist thought* (1988); Vron Ware, *Beyond the Pale: White women, racism and history* (1992); Sara Ruddick, *Maternal Thinking: Towards a New Politics of Peace* (1990); Vered Amit-Talai and Caroline Knowles, *Re-situating Identities: The politics of race, ethnicity, culture* (1996).

8 Some of the early work of Achilles Heel in Britain has been collected in two volumes that show the different tendencies at work in responses of men to feminisms. See Victor J. Seidler (ed.), *The Achilles Heel Reader: Men, sexual politics and socialism* (1991) and *Men, Sex and Relationships: Writings from Achilles Heel* (1992). For an account of the critical engagements with therapeutic practices at the time and an introduction to Red Therapy (a collective initiated in east London to bring therapy and politics into relation with each other) see Sheila Ernst and Lucy Goodison, *In Our Own Hands* (1981).

9 For a sense of how a newer generation of women in the 1990s have questioned some of the feminist assumptions they seemed to have inherited from an earlier generation, see Natasha Walter, *The New Feminism* (1998).

10 Simone Weil's essay 'Human personality' appears in the *Selected Essays 1934–43*, ed. R. Rees (1962). See also the discussion of this essay in Lawrence Blum and Victor J. Seidler, *A Truer Liberty: Simone Weil and Marxism* (1991) and in Peter Winch, *A Just Balance: Reflections on the philosophy of Simone Weil* (1989). For a helpful biography of Weil that also explores her later spiritual engagements with Eastern traditions, see David McLellan, *Utopian Pessimist: The life and thought of Simone Weil* (1990).

11 For an illuminating biography of Wittgenstein that helps explore the critical relationship he develops with a rationalist modernity, see Ray Monk, *Ludwig Wittgenstein* (1986). See also Stanley Cavell, *The Claims of Reason* (Clarendon 1979) and essays on Wittgenstein in his *Must We Mean What We Say?* (1969).

12 For a discussion of critical self-consciousness, at least as it relates to issues of social, cultural and ethnic difference/s, see A. Gramsci, *The Prison Notebooks* (1971). For a sense of his more personal reflections see his *Letters from Prison*, ed. L. Lawner (1975). Issues relating to Gramsci's Marxism and the ways it resisted the structuralist readings that were dominant in the 1980s are explored in Victor J. Seidler's *Recovering the Self: Morality and social theory* (1994).

Bibliography

Adam, B. (1990) *Time and Social Theory*, Cambridge: Polity Press.

Adorno, T.H. (1974) *Aspects of Sociology*, London: Heinemann.

Adorno, T.H. and Horkheimer, M. (1973) *Dialectic of Enlightenment* (trans. J. Cumming), London: Allen Lane.

Alcala, A. (ed.) (1987) *The Spanish Inquisition and the Inquisitorial Mind*, Boulder, CO: Social Science Monographs.

Aldrich, R. (2002) *Colonialism and Homosexuality*, London: Routledge.

Althusser, L. (1970) *For Marx*, London: Verso.

Altman, D. (1982) *The Homosexualisation of America*, Boston, MA: Beacon.

Amadiume, I. (1974) *Male Daughters, Female Husbands: Gender and sex in an African society*, London: Zed Books.

Amadiume, I. (1987) *Re-inventing Africa: Matriarchy, religion and culture*, London: Zed Books.

Amit-Talai, V. and Knowles, C. (1996) *Re-situating Identities: The politics of race, ethnicity, culture*, Ontario, Canada: Broadview Press.

Amuchástegui, A. (2001) *Virginidad e Iniciacion Sexual en Mexico: Experiencias y significados*, Mexico City: EDAMEX/ The Population Council.

Anderson, B. (1991) *Imagined Communities*, London: Verso.

Archer, J. and Lloyd, B.B. (1985) *Sex and Gender*, Cambridge: Cambridge University Press.

Arendt, H. (1958) *The Human Condition*, Chicago, IL: University of Chicago Press.

Arendt, H. (1968) *The Origins of Totalitarianism*, New York: Harcourt, Brace, Jovanovich.

Aries, P. (1962) *Centuries of Childhood: A social history of family life*, London: Jonathan Cape.

Askew, S. and Ross, C. (1988) *Boys Don't Cry: Boys and sexism in education*, Milton Keynes: Open University Press.

Assiter, A. (1996) *Enlightenment Women: Modernist feminism in a postmodern age*, London: Routledge.

Back, L. (1996) *New Ethnicities and Urban Culture*, London: UCL Press.

Back, L. and Ware, V. (2001) *Out of Whiteness: Color, politics, and culture*, Chicago, IL: University of Chicago Press.

Baker Miller, J. (1976) *Towards a New Psychology of Women*, Harmondsworth: Penguin.

Banks, A. and Waller, T. (1988) *Drug Misuse*, Oxford: Blackwells.

Barker, P. *The Regeneration Trilogy:* (1991) *Regeneration;* (1993) *The Eye in the Door;* (1995) *The Ghost Road,* London: Penguin.
Barry, K. (1979) *Female Sexual Slavery,* Princeton, NJ: Prentice Hall.
Battersby, C. (1998) *The Phenomenal Woman: Feminist metaphysics and the patterns of identity,* Cambridge: Polity Press.
Bauman, Z. (1990) *Modernity and the Holocaust,* Cambridge: Polity Press.
Bauman, Z. (1993) *Postmodern Ethics,* Cambridge: Polity Press.
Bauman, Z. (1994) *Intimations of Postmodernity,* London: Routledge.
Bauman, Z. (1997) *Postmodernity and its Discontents,* Cambridge: Polity Press.
Bauman, Z. (2000) *Liquid Modernity,* Cambridge: Polity Press.
Bauman, Z. (2001) *The Individualized Society,* Cambridge: Polity Press.
Bauman, Z. (2003) *Liquid Love,* Cambridge: Polity Press.
Beail, N. and McGuire, J. (eds) *Fathers: Psychological perspectives,* London: Junction Books.
Beauvoir, S. de (1973) *The Second Sex,* New York: Vintage.
Beck, U. (1992) *The Risk Society: Towards a new modernity,* London: Sage.
Beck, U. (1995) *Ecological Enlightenment: Essays on the politics of a risk society,* trans. M. Ritter, Atlantic Highlands, NJ: Humanities Press.
Beck, U. (2000) *The Brave New World of Work,* Cambridge: Polity Press.
Beck, U. and Beck-Gersheim, E. (1995) *The Normal Chaos of Love,* Cambridge: Polity Press.
Beck, U. Giddens, A. and Lash, S. (1995) *Reflexive Modernization,* Cambridge: Polity Press.
Bederman, G. (1995) *Manliness and Civilisation: A cultural history of gender and race in the United States 1880–1917,* Chicago, IL: University of Chicago Press.
Bell, V. (ed.) (1999) *Performativity and Belonging,* London: Sage.
Benhabib, S. (1997) *Situating the Self,* Cambridge: Polity Press.
Benjamin, J. (1990) *Bonds of Love,* London: Virago.
Benjamin, J. (1998) *Shadow of the Other: Intersubjectivity and gender in psychoanalysis,* New York: Routledge.
Benjamin, W. (1973) *Illuminations* (trans. H. Zohn), London: Collins/Fontana.
Berger, M., Wallis, B. and Watson, S. (eds) (1995) *Constructing Masculinity,* New York: Routledge.
Bergquist, C. et al. (1999) *Equal Democracies,* Oslo: Scandinavian University Press.
Berlin, I. (1981) *Against the Current,* Oxford: Oxford University Press.
Bernasconi, R. and Critchley, S. (1991) *Re-reading Levinas,* Bloomington, IN: Indiana University Press.
Bettleheim, B. (1991) *Freud and Man's Soul,* London: Fontana Books.
Biddulph, S. (1994) *Manhood: A book about setting men free,* Sydney: Finch.
Blankenhorn, D. (1995) *Fatherless America: Confronting our most urgent social problem,* New York: Basic Books.
Blum, L. and Seidler, V.J. (1991) *A Truer Liberty: Simone Weil and Marxism,* New York: Routledge.
Bly, R. (1990) *Iron John,* New York: Addison-Wesley.
Boadella, D. (1976) *In the Wake of Reich,* London: Coventure.
Bock, G. and James, S. (eds) *Beyond Equality and Difference: Citizenship, feminist politics and female subjectivity,* London: Routledge.
Boggs, C. (1976) *Gramsci's Marxism,* London: Pluto Press.

Bologh, R.W. (1990) *Love or Greatness: Max Weber and masculine thinking*, London: Unwin Hyman.

Boran, A. and Murphy, B. (eds) (2004) *Gender in Flux*, Chester: Chester Academic Press.

Bordo, S. (1993) *Unbearable Weight: Feminism, Western culture, and the body*, Berkeley, CA: University of California Press.

Bordo, S. (1999) *The Male Body: A new look at men in public and in private*, New York: Farrar, Straus and Giroux.

Bourdieu, P. (2001) *Masculine Domination*, Stanford, CA: Stanford University Press.

Bowker, J.L. (ed.) (1998) *Masculinities and Violence*, Thousand Oaks, CA: Sage.

Boyarin, D. (1993) *Carnal Israel: Reading sex in Talmudic Judaism*, Berkeley, CA: University of California Press.

Boyarin, D. (1994) *A Radical Jew: Paul and the politics of identity*, Berkeley, CA: University of California Press.

Boyarin, D. (1997) *Unheroic Conduct: The rise of heterosexuality and the invention of the Jewish man*, Berkeley, CA: University of California Press.

Bozett, F. and Hanson, S. (eds) (1991) *Fatherhood and Families in Cultural Context*, New York: Springer.

Braidotti, R. (1991) *Patterns of Dissonance*, Cambridge: Polity Press.

Brennan, T. (ed.) (1989) *Between Feminism and Psychoanalysis*, London: Routledge.

Brittan, A. (1989) *Masculinity and Power*, Oxford: Basil Blackwell.

Brod, H. (ed.) (1987) *The Making of Masculinities*, Boston, MA: Allen and Unwin.

Brod, H. and Kaufman, M. (eds) *Theorizing Masculinities*, Thousand Oaks, CA: Sage.

Brown, P. (1990) *The Body and Society: Men, women and sexual renunciation in early Christianity*, London: Faber.

Buhle, M.J. (1998) *Feminism and its Discontents*, Cambridge, MA: Harvard University Press.

Burgess, A. (1997) *Fatherhood Reclaimed: The making of the modern father*, London: Vermillion.

Butler, J. (1990) *Gender Trouble: Feminism and the subversion of identity*, New York: Routledge.

Butler, J. (1993) *Bodies that Matter: The discursive limits of 'sex'*, New York: Routledge.

Butler, J. and Scott, J.W. (eds) (1992) *Feminists Theorize the Political*, New York: Routledge.

Cannetti, E. (1960, repr. 1973) *Crowds and Power*, Harmondsworth: Penguin.

Cantera (May, 1995) *Hombre, Violencia y Crisis Social*, Managua, Nicaragua.

Cantera (May, 1996) *Genero, Podery Violencia*, Managua, Nicaragua.

Carby, H.V. (1998) *Race Men*, Cambridge, MA: Harvard University Press.

Cavell, S. (1969) *Must We Mean What We Say?*, New York: Scribners.

Cavell, S. (1979) *The Claims of Reason*, Oxford: Clarendon Press.

Caygill, H. (2002) *Levinas and the Political*, London: Routledge.

Chant, S. and Gutmann, M. (2000) *Mainstreaming Men in Gender and Development*, Oxford: Oxfam, GB.

Chapman, R. and Rutherford, J. (eds) (1988) *Male Order: Unwrapping masculinity*, London: Lawrence and Wishart.

Chodorow, N. (1978) *The Reproduction of Mothering: Psychoanalysis and the sociology of gender*, London: University of California Press.

Chodorow, N. (1994) *Femininities, Masculinities, Sexualities: Freud and beyond*, London: Free Association Books.

Cicchetti, D. and Carlson, V. (eds) (1989) *Child Maltreatment: Theory and research on the causes and consequences of child abuse and neglect*, Cambridge: Cambridge University Press.

Clare, A. (2000) *On Men: Masculinity in crisis*, London: Chatto and Windus.

Clare, G. (1982) *Last Waltz in Vienna*, London: Macmillan.

Clatterbaugh, K. (1990) *Contemporary Perspectives on Masculinity: Men, women and politics in modern society*, Boulder, CO: Westview Press.

Cockburn, C. (1983) *Brothers: Male dominance and technological change*, London: Pluto Press.

Cockburn, C. (1991) *In the Way of Women: Men's resistance to sex equality in the organizations*, Basingstoke: Macmillan.

Cohen, B. (ed.) (1988) *Fatherhood Today: Men's changing roles in the family*, New York: Wiley.

Cohen, P. (1997) *Rethinking the Youth Question*, Basingstoke: Palgrave.

Collier, R. (1998) *Masculinities, Crime and Criminology*, London: Sage.

Connell, R.W. (1983) *Which Way is Up? Essays on sex, class and culture*, London: Allen and Unwin.

Connell, R.W. (1987) *Gender and Power: Society, the person and sexual politics*, Cambridge: Polity Press.

Connell, R.W. (1995) *Masculinities*, Cambridge: Polity Press.

Connell, R.W. (2000) *The Men and the Boys*, Cambridge: Polity Press.

Connolly, P. (1998) *Racism, Gender Identities and Young Children*, London: Routledge.

Coombs, R. (1988) *The Family Context of Adolescent Drug Use*, Binghamton, NY: Haworth Press.

Cornwall, A. and Lindisfarne, N. (eds) *Dislocating Masculinity: Comparative ethnographies*, London: Routledge.

Craib, I. (1989) *Psychoanalysis and Social Theory: The limits of sociology*, London: Harvester Wheatsheaf.

Craib, I. (1994) *The Importance of Disappointment*, London: Routledge.

Craig, S. (ed.) (1992) *Men, Masculinity and the Media*, Thousand Oaks, CA: Sage.

Daniels, C.R. (ed.) (1998) *Lost Fathers: The politics of fatherlessness in America*, New York: St Martin's Press.

Davidhoff, L. (1995) *Worlds Between: Historical perspectives on gender and class*, Cambridge: Polity Press.

Davidhoff, L. and Hall, C. (1987) *Family Fortunes: Women and men of the English middle class 1780–1850*, London: Routledge.

Davidson, A. (1977) *Antonio Gramsci: Towards an intellectual biography*, London: Merlin Books.

Davis, K. (1995) *Reshaping the Female Body: The dilemmas of cosmetic surgery*, New York: Routledge.

Dawson, G. (1986) *Soldier Heroes: British adventure, empire and the imagining of masculinities*, London: Routledge.

Deleuze, G. (1990) *Expressionism in Philosophy: Spinoza*, tr. M. Joughin, New York: Zone.

Deleuze, G. (1993) *Nietzsche and Philosophy*, tr. H. Tomlinson, Minneapolis, MN: University of Minnesota Press.

Deleuze, G. and Guattari, F. (1997) *Anti-Oedipus*, Minneapolis, MN: University of Minnesota Press.

De Zulueta, F. (1993) *From Pain to Violence: The traumatic roots of destructiveness*, London: Whurr Publishers.

Dinnerstein, D. (1987) *The Mermaid and the Minotaur: The rocking of the cradle and the ruling of the world*, London: The Women's Press.

Dobash, R.E., Dobash, R.P., Cavanagh, K. and Lewis, R. (2000) *Changing Violent Men*, London: Sage.

Dollimore, J. (1998) *Death, Desire and Loss in Western Culture*, London: Penguin.

Domenici, T. and Lesser, R.C. (eds) (1995) *Disorienting Sexuality: Psychoanalytic reappraisals of sexual identities*, New York: Routledge.

Donzelot, J. (1979) *The Policing of Families*, London: Hutchinson.

Dowd, N.E. (2000) *Redefining Fatherhood*, New York: New York University Press.

Drescher, J. (1998) *Psychoanalytic Therapy and Gay Men*, Hillsdale, NJ: The Analytic Press.

Dresher, J., D'Ercole, A. and Schoenberg, E. (2003) *Psychotherapy with Gay Men and Lesbians: Contemporary dynamic approaches*, New York: Harrington Park Press.

Dreyfus, H. and Rabinow, P. (1983) *Michel Foucault: Beyond structuralism and hermeneutics*, Chicago, IL: University of Chicago Press.

Du Bois, W.E.B. (1969) *The Souls of Black Folk*, rpt. New York: New American Library.

Du Bois, W.E.B. (1993) *Black Atlantic*, Cambridge, MA: Harvard University Press.

Duncan, N. (1999) *Sexual Bullying*, London: Routledge.

Easlea, B. (1981) *Science and Sexual Oppression: Patriarchy's confrontation with women and nature*, London: Weidenfeld and Nicolson.

Easlea, B. (1983) *Fathering the Unthinkable: Masculinity, scientists and the nuclear arms race*, London: Pluto Press.

Edley, N. and Wetherell, M. (1995) *Men in Perspective – Practice, power and identity*, London: Harvester Wheatsheaf.

Edut, O. (ed.) (2000) *Body Outlaws: Young women write about body image and identity*, Seattle, WA: Seal Press.

Edwards, T. (1994) *Erotics and Politics: Gay male sexuality, masculinity and feminism*, London: Routledge.

Ehrenreich, B. (1983) *The Hearts of Men: American dreams and the flight from commitment*, London: Pluto Press.

Ehrenreich, D. and English, D. (1970) *For Her Own Good*, London: Pluto Press.

Eisenstein, H. (1985) *Contemporary Feminist Thought*, London: Unwin.

Elam, D. (1994) *Feminism and Deconstruction*, London: Routledge.

Elliot, A. and Frosh, S. (eds) *Psychoanalysis in Context: Paths between theory and modern culture*, London and New York: Routledge.

Elshtain, J.B. (1981) *Public Man, Private Woman*, Princeton, NJ: Princeton University Press.

Epstein, D., Elwood, J., Hey, V. and Maw, J. (eds) (1998) *Failing Boys? Issues in gender and achievement*, Buckingham: Open University Press.

Ernst, S. and Goodison, L. (1981) *In Our Own Hands*, London: The Women's Press.

Ervo, S. and Johansson, T. (eds) (2002) *Among Men: Moulding masculinities*, vols 1 and 2, Aldershot: Ashgate.

Evans, M. (1994) *The Woman Question*, London: Sage.

Faludi, S. (1991) *Backlash: The undeclared war against women*, London: Vintage Books.

Faludi, S. (1999) *Stiffed: The betrayal of the modern man*, London: Chatto and Windus.

Fanon, F. (1986) *Black Skin, White Mask*, London: Pluto Press.

Farrington, B. (1964) *The Philosophy of Francis Bacon*, Liverpool: Liverpool University Press.

Fasteau, M.F. (1974) *The Male Machine*, New York: McGraw-Hill.

Featherstone, M., Hepworth, M. and Turner, B.S. (eds) *The Body: Social process and cultural theory*, London: Sage.

Ferree, M. Lorber, J. and Hess, B. (eds) (1999) *Revisioning Gender*, London: Sage.

Figlio, K. (2000) *Psychoanalysis, Science and Masculinity*, London: Whurr Publishers.

Fink, H. (1981) *Social Philosophy*, London: Methuen.

Fiori, G. (1980) *Antonio Gramsci: Life of a revolutionary*, London: New Left Books.

Flax, J. (1990) *Thinking Fragments: Psychoanalysis, feminism and postmodern in the contemporary West*, Berkeley, CA: University of California Press.

Flax, J. (1993) *Disputed Subjects: Essays on pscyhoanalysis, politics and philosophy*, New York and London: Routledge.

Foucault, M. (1975) *Discipline and Punish: The birth of the prison*, Harmondsworth: Penguin.

Foucault, M. (1976) *The History of Sexuality*, vol. 1, London: Penguin.

Foucault, M. (1980) *Power/Knowledge: Selected interviews and other writings, 1972–1977*, New York: Pantheon.

Fox Keller, E. (1985) *Reflections on Gender and Science*, New Haven, CT: Yale University Press.

Fox Keller, E. (1992) *Secrets of Life, Secrets of Death: Essays on language, gender and science*, New York and London: Routledge.

Freud, S. (1960) *Totem and Taboo*, London: Ark Paperbacks.

Freud, S. (1977) *On Sexuality*, Penguin Freud Library, vol. 7, London: Penguin.

Freud, S. (1994) (1930) *Civilisation and its Discontents*, New York: Dover.

Friedlander, J.H. (1990) *Vilna on the Sein*, New Haven, CT: Yale University Press.

Fromm, E. (1974) *The Anatomy of Human Destructiveness*, Harmondsworth: Penguin.

Frosh, S. (1994) *Sexual Difference: Masculinity and psychoanalysis*, London and New York: Routledge.

Frosh, S., Phoenix, A. and Pattman, R. (2002) *Young Masculinities*, Basingstoke: Palgrave.

Fuller, N. (2001) *Masculinades, Cambios y Permancencias*, Lima, Peru: Fondo Editorial de la Universidad Catolica del Peru.

Gallager, C. and Laqueur, T. (eds) *The Making of the Modern Body: Sexuality and society in the nineteenth century*, Berkeley, CA: University of California Press.

Gallop, J. (1982) *Feminism and Psychoanalysis: The daughter's seduction*, London: Macmillan.

Gallop, J. (1988) *Thinking Through the Body*, New York: Columbia University Press.

Game, A. and Pringle, R. (1984) *Gender at Work*, London: Pluto Press.

Gay, P. (1988) *Freud: A life of our time*, London: Macmillan.

Gay, P. du (1996) *Consumption and Identity at Work*, London: Sage.

Geras, N. (1983) *Marx and Human Nature: Refutation of a legend*, London: Verso.

Giddens, A. (1991) *Modernity and Self-Identity: Self and society in the late modern age.* Cambridge: Pluto Press.

Giddens, A. (1992) *The Transformation of Intimacy: Sexuality, love and eroticism in modern societies*, Cambridge: Polity Press.

Gilligan, C. (1982) *In a Different Voice: Psychological theory and women's development*, Cambridge, MA: Harvard University Press.

Gilligan, C., Ward, J.V. and Taylor, J.M. (eds) (1988) *Mapping the Moral Domain*, Cambridge, MA: Harvard University Press.

Gilligan, J. (1997) *Violence: Reflections on our deadliest epidemic*, New York: Vintage.

Gilligan, J. (2000) *Violence: Reflections on our deadliest epidemic*, London: JKP.

Gillis, J.R. (1996) *A World of Their Own Making: Myth, ritual and the quest for family values*, New York: Basic Books.

Gillman, S. (1989) *Jewish Self-hatred*, Baltimore, MD: Johns Hopkins University Press.

Gilman, S. (1982) *On Blackness Without Blacks*, Boston, MA: G.K. Hall.

Gilmore, D.G. (1990) *Manhood in the Making: Cultural concepts of masculinity*, New Haven, CT: Yale University Press.

Gilroy, P. (1987) *There Ain't no Black in the Union Jack*, London: Unwin Hyman.

Gilroy, P. (1993) *The Black Atlantic: Modernity and double consciousness*, Cambridge, MA: Harvard University Press.

Goldberg, D. (1998) *Racist Culture*, Oxford: Blackwell.

Goleman, D. (1996) *Emotional Intelligence*, London: Bloomsbury.

Gorz, A. (1985) *Paths to Paradise*, London, Pluto.

Gramsci, A. (1971) *Selections from the Prison Notebooks*, London: Lawrence and Wishart.

Gramsci, A. (1975) *Letters from Prison* (trans. L. Lawner), London: Jonathan Cape.

Gray, J. (1999) *Men are from Mars, Women are from Venus*, London: Vintage/Ebury.

Gray, J.G. (1998) *The Warriors: Reflections on men in battle*, Lincoln, NE: University of Nebraska Press.

Green, D. (1999) *Gender Violence in Africa*, Basingstoke: Macmillan.

Griffin, S. (1980) *Pornography and Silence*, London: The Women's Press.

Griffin, S. (1982) *Women and Nature*, London: The Women's Press.

Griswold, R.L. (1993) *Fatherhood in America: A history*, New York: Basic Books.

Grosz, E. (1989) *Sexual Subversions*, London: Allen and Unwin.

Grosz, E. (1994) *Volatile Bodies: Towards a corporeal feminism*, Bloomington, IN: Indiana University Press.

Gutmann, M. (1996) *The Meanings of Macho: Being a man in Mexico City*, Berkeley, CA: University of California Press.

Hacker, A. (1992) *Two Nations: Black, white, separate, hostile and unequal*, New York: Macmillan.

Hall, C. (2002) *Civilising Subjects: Metropole and colony in the English imagination 1830–1867*, Cambridge: Polity Press.

Hall, L.A. (1991) *Hidden Anxieties: Male sexuality 1900–1950*, Cambridge: Polity Press.

Hall, S. (1977) 'Rethinking the "base and superstructure" metaphor' in J. Bloomfield et al. (eds), *Class, Hegemony and Party*, London: Lawrence and Wishart.

Hall, S. (1996) in D. Morley and K.-H. Chen (eds), *Critical Dialogues in Cultural Studies*, London: Routledge.

Hall, S. (ed.) (1997) *Representations: Cultural representations and signifying practices*, London: Sage.

Hall, S. and du Gay, P. (eds) (1996) *Questions of Cultural Identity*, London: Sage.

Hall, S. and Jefferson, T. (eds) *Resistance through Rituals*, London: Hutchinson.

Hall, S., Lumley, V. and McLennan, G. (eds) (1978) *On Ideology* (reproduction of Working Papers in Cultural Studies 10), London: Hutchinson/CCS.

Harper, P.B. (1996) *Are We Not Men? Masculine identity and the problem of African American identity*, New York: Oxford University Press.

Hearn, J. (1987) *The Gender of Oppression: Men, masculinity and the critique of Marxism*, Brighton: Harvester Press.

Hearn, J. (1992) *Men in the Public Eye*, London: Routledge.

Hearn, J. (1998) *The Violences of Men*, London: Sage.

Hearn, J. and Morgan, D. (eds) (1990) *Men, Masculinities and Social Theory*, London: Unwin Hyman.

Heath, S. (1982) *The Sexual Fix*, London: Macmillan.

Heckman, S.J. (1990) *Gender and Knowledge: Elements of a postmodern feminism*, Oxford: Polity Press.

Hedges, C. (2003) *War Is a Force that Gives Us Meaning*, New York: Anchor Books.

Held, D. (1986) *Models of Democracy*, Cambridge: Polity Press.

Held, V. (1993) *Feminist Morality: Transforming culture, society and politics*, Chicago, IL: University of Chicago Press.

Hernes, H. (1987) *Welfare State and Woman Power: Essays in state feminism*, Oslo: Norwegian University Press.

Hewitt, R. (1986) *White Talk Black Talk: Inter-racial friendships and communication amongst adolescents*. Cambridge: Cambridge University Press.

Hill Collins, P. (1991) *Black Feminist Thought: Knowledge, consciousness and the politics of empowerment*, London and New York: Routledge.

Hochschild, A.R. (1989) *The Second Shift*, New York: Avon Books.

Hochschild, A.R. (1997) *The Time Bind*, New York: Metropolitan Books.

Hodson, P. (1984) *Men: An investigation into the emotional male*, London: BBC Books.

Holland, J., Ramazanoglu, C. and Sharpe, S. (1993) *Wimp or Gladiator: Contradictions in acquiring male sexuality*, London: Tufnell Press.

Holland, J., Ramazanoglu, C., Sharpe, S and Thomson, R. (1998) *The Male in the Head: Young people, heterosexuality and power*, London: Tufnell Press.

hooks, b. (1991) *Yearning: Race, gender and cultural politics*, London: Turnabout.

hooks, b. (1994) *Sisters of the Yam: Black women and self-recovery*, Boston, MA: South End Press.

hooks, b. (2000) *All About Love*, New York: HarperCollins.

hooks, b. (2001) *Salvation: Black people and love*, New York: HarperCollins.

Horowitz, M.C. (1997) *Seeds of Virtue and Knowledge*, Princeton, NJ: Princeton University Press.

Humm, M. (ed.) (1992) *Feminisms*, Hemel Hempstead: Harvester.

Irigaray, L. (1985) *Speculum of the Other Woman*, Ithaca, NY: Cornell University Press.

Irigaray, L. (1985) *The Sex which is not One*, Ithaca, NY: Cornell University Press.

Jackson, D. (1990) *Unmasking Masculinity: A critical autobiography*, London: Unwin Hyman.

Jackson, S. (1999) *Heterosexuality in Question*, London: Sage.

Jagger, A. (1988) *Feminist Politics and Human Nature*, Savage, MD: Rowman and Littlefield.

Jagger, G. and Wright, C. (eds) (1999) *Changing Family Values*, London: Routledge.

Jameson, F. (1972) *The Prison-House of Language: A critical account of structuralism and Russian formalism*, Princeton, NJ: Princeton University Press.

Jamieson, L. (1998) *Intimacy: Personal relationships in modern societies*, Cambridge: Polity Press.

Jardine, A. (1985) *Gynesis: Configurations of women and modernity*, Ithaca, NY: Cornell University Press.

Jardine, A. and Smith, P. (eds) (1987) *Men in Feminism*, London: Methuen.

Johnson, S. and Meinhof, U.H. (eds) *Language and Masculinity*, Oxford: Blackwell.

Jukes, A. (1993) *Why Men Hate Women*, London: Free Association Books.

Kamen, H. (1965) *The Spanish Inquisition*, New York: New American Library.

Karpf, A. (1997) *The War After*, London: Minerva.

Kaufman, M. (1987) *Beyond Patriarchy*, Toronto: Oxford University Press.

Kaufman, M. (1993) *Cracking the Armor: Power, pain and the lives of men*, Toronto: Penguin/Viking.

Kimmel, M.S. (ed.) (1987) *Changing Men: New directions in research on men and masculinity*, Newbury Park, CA: Sage.

Kimmel, M.S. (ed.) (1995) *The Politics of Manhood*, Philadelphia, PA: Temple University Press.

Kimmel, M.S. (1996) *Manhood in America: A cultural history*, New York: Free Press.

Kimmel, M.S. (2000) *The Gendered Society*, New York: Oxford University Press.

Kimmel, M.S. and Messner, M.A. (eds) (1989) *Men's Lives*, Boston, MA: Allyn and Bacon.

Korbin, J.E. (ed.) (1989) *Child Abuse and Neglect: Cross cultural perspectives*, Berkeley, CA: University of California Press.

Kruks, S. (2001) *Retrieving Experience: Subjectivity and recognition in feminist politics*, Ithaca, NY: Cornell University Press.

Lacquer, T. (1990) *Making Sex: Body and gender from the Greeks to Freud*, Cambridge, MA: Harvard University Press.

Lasch, C. (1977) *Haven in a Heartless World: The family besieged*, New York: Basic Books.

Lasch, C. (1984) *The Minimal Self: Psychic survival in troubled times*, London: Pan Books.

Lasch, C. (1991) *The Culture of Narcissism: American life in an age of diminishing expectations*, New York: Norton and Co.

Lash, S. and Urry, J. (1987) *The End of Organised Capitalism*, Cambridge: Polity Press.

Lea, H.C. (1906) *A History of the Inquisition in Spain*, 4 vols, New York: Macmillan.

Lees, S. (1986) *Losing Out: Sexuality and adolescent girls*, London: Hutchinson.

Lennon, K. and Whitford, M. (eds) *Knowing the Difference: Feminist perspectives on epistemology*, London: Routledge.

Lewes, K. (1995) *Psychoanalysis and Male Homosexuality*, Northvale, NJ: Aronson.

Lewis, C. and O'Brian, M. (eds) *Reassessing Fatherhood: New observations on fathers and the modern family*, Newbury Park, CA: Sage.

Libowitz, R. (ed.) (1987) *Faith and Freedom: A tribute to Franklin H. Littel*, Oxford: Pergamon Press.

Lindqvist, S. (2002) *Exterminate All the Brutes*, London: Granta Books.

Lingard, B. and Douglas, P. (1999) *Men Engaging Feminisms: Pro-feminism, backlashes and schooling*, Buckingham: Open University Press.

Littel, F. (1975) *The Crucifixion of the Jews*, New York: Harper and Row.

Lloyd, G. (1984) *Man of Reason: 'Male' and 'female' in Western philosophy*, London: Methuen.

Lloyd, T. (1990) *Work with Boys*, Leicester: National Youth Bureau.

Lyotard, J.-F. (1994) *The Postmodern Condition: A report on knowledge*, Manchester: Manchester University Press.

McAllister, P. (ed.) (1982) *Reweaving the Web of Life: Feminism and non-violence*, Philadelphia, PA: New Society Publishers.

Mac an Ghail, M. (1994) *The Making of Men: Masculinities, sexualities and schooling*, Buckingham: Open University Press.

Mac an Ghail, M. (ed.) (1996) *Understanding Masculinities*, Buckingham: Open University Press.

MacInnes, J. (1998) *The End of Masculinity*, Buckingham: Open University Press.

MacKinnon, C. (1979) *The Sexual Harassment of Working Women*, New Haven, CT: Yale University Press.

McLellan, D. (1989) *Utopian Pessimist: The life and thought of Simone Weil*, Basingstoke: Macmillan.

McNay, L. (1992) *Foucault and Feminism*, Cambridge: Polity Press.

McNay, L. (1994) *Gender and Agency*, Cambridge: Polity Press.

McRobbie, A. and Nava, M. (eds) (1984) *Gender and Generation*, Basingstoke: Palgrave.

Maguire, M. (1995) *Men, Women, Passion and Power*, London: Routledge.

Mahony, P. (1985) *Schools for Boys? Co-Education Reassessed*, London: Hutchinson.

Majors, R. and Billson, J. (1992) *Cool Pose: The dilemmas of black manhood in America*, New York: Lexington.

Mama, A. (1995) *Beyond the Masks: Race, gender and subjectivity*, London: Routledge.

Mangan, J.A. and Walvin, J. (1987) *Manliness and Morality: Middle class masculinity in Britain and America*, Manchester: Manchester University Press.

Martin, E. (1991) *The Woman in the Body: A cultural analysis of reproduction*, Milton Keynes: Open University Press.

May, L. (1998) *Masculinity and Morality*, New York: Cornell University Press.

Mendes, S. (1989) *Tolerance and the Limits of Liberalism*, London: Macmillan.

Mercer, K. (ed.) *Welcome to the Jungle*, London: Routledge.

Merchant, C. (1980) *The Death of Nature: Women, ecology and the scientific revolution*, London: Wildwood House.

Messner, M.A. (1992) *Power at Play: Sports and the problem of masculinity*, Boston, MA: Beacon Press.

Messner, M.A. (1997) *Politics of Masculinities: Men in movements*, Thousand Oaks, CA: Sage.

Metcalf, A. and Humphries, M. (1987) *The Sexuality of Men*, London: Pluto Press.

Middleton, P. (1992) *The Inward Gaze: Masculinity and subjectivity in modern culture*, London: Routledge.

Mies, M. and Shiva, V. (1993) *Ecofeminism*, London: Zed Books.

Miller, A. (1983) *For Your Own Good: Hidden cruelty in child-rearing and the roots of violence*, London: Faber and Faber.

Miller, A. (1984) *Thou Shalt Not Be Aware: Society's betrayal of the child*, New York: Farrar, Straus and Giroux.

Miller, A. (1998) *Breaking the Veil of Silence*, London: Virago.

Miller, S. (1983) *Men and Friendship*, London: Gateway Books.

Minsky, R. (1996) *Psychoanalysis and Culture: Contemporary states of mind*, Cambridge: Polity Press.

Mirande, A. (1997) *Hombres Machos: Masculinity and Latino culture*, Boulder, CO: Westview Press.

Mitscherlich, A. (1993) *Society without Father: A contribution to social psychology*, New York: HarperCollins.

Mohanty, C.T. (1991) *Third World Women and the Politics of Feminism*, Indiana, IN: Indiana University Press.

Mohanty, C.T. (1992) 'Feminist encounters: Locating the politics of experience', in M. Barrett and A. Philips (eds) *Destabilising Theory: Contemporary feminist debates*, Stanford, CA: Stanford University Press, pp. 74–92.

Moller Okin, S. (1980) *Women in Western Political Thought*, London: Virago.

Moller Okin, S. (1989) *Justice, Gender and the Family*, New York: Basic Books.

Monk, R. (1986) *Ludwig Wittgenstein*, London: Vintage.

Moore, H. (1994) *A Passion for Difference*, Cambridge: Polity Press.

Moore, M. (2004) *Stupid White Men*, London: Penguin.

Morell, R. (ed.) (2001) *Changing Men in Southern Africa*, London: Zed Press.

Morgan, D. (1992) *Discovering Men*, London: Routledge.

Morgan, D.H.J. (1996) *Family Connections*, Cambridge: Polity Press.

Morgan, R. (1970) *Sisterhood is Powerful*, New York: Vintage Books.

Morgan, R. (1984) *Sisterhood is Global*, Harmondsworth: Penguin.

Morrison, B. (1993) *And When Did You Last See Your Father?*, London: Granta Books.

Mort, F. (1987) *Dangerous Sexualities: Medico-moral politics in England since 1830*, London: Routledge.

Mort, F. (1996) *Cultures of Consumption: Masculinities and social space in late twentieth century Britain*, London: Routledge.

Mosse, G.L. (1996) *The Image of Man: The creation of modern masculinity*, New York: Oxford University Press.

Mouffe, C. (1979) *Gramsci and Marxist Theory*, London: Routledge.

Mouffe, C. and Laclau, E. (1985) *Hegemony and Social Strategy: Towards a radical democratic politics*, London: Verso Books.

Naess, A. (1989) *Ecology, Community and Lifestyle*, trans. and ed. D. Rothenberg, Cambridge: Cambridge University Press.

Narayan, U. (1997) *Dislocating Cultures: Identities, traditions and the third world*, New York: Routledge.

Nardi, P.M. (ed) (1992) *Men's Friendships*, Thousand Oaks, CA: Sage.

Nardi, P.M. (1999) *Gay Men's Friendship: Invisible communities*, Chicago, IL: University of Chicago Press.

Nardi, P.M. (ed.) (2000) *Gay Masculinities*, Thousand Oaks, CA: Sage.

Nayak, A. and Kehily, M. (1996) 'Playing it straight: Masculinities, homophobias and schooling', *Journal of Gender Studies* 5(2): 211–30.

Netanyahu, B. (1966) *The Marranos of Spain*, New York: American Academy for Jewish Research. 1966. Kraus Reprint, Millwood, New York, 1973.

Newburn, T. and Stanko, E. (eds) (1994) *Just Boys Doing Business? Men, masculinities and crime*, London: Routledge.

Nicholson, L. and Seidman, S. (eds) (1996) *Social Postmodernism: Beyond identity politics*, Cambridge: Cambridge University Press.

Nicholson, L.J. (ed.) (1990) *Feminism/Postmodernism*, New York: Routledge.

Nixon, S. (1996) *Hard Looks: Masculinities, spectatorship and contemporary consumption*, London: UCL Press.

Nussbaum, M. and Glover, J. (eds) (1995) *Women, Culture and Development: A study of human capabilities*, Oxford: Clarendon Press.

O'Connor, N. and Ryan, J. (1993) *Wild Desires and Mistaken Identities: Lesbianism and psychoanalysis*, London: Virago.

Olavarria, J.A. (2003) *Varones Adolescentes: Genero, identidades y sexualidades en América Latina*, Santiago, Chile: FLACSO-Chile.

Oliver, K. (1997) *Family Values: Subjects between nature and culture*, New York: Routledge.

Olsen, R. (1980) *Silences*, London: Virago.

Oyewumi, O. (1997) *The Invention of Women: Making an African sense of Western gender discourses*, Minneapolis, MN: University of Minnesota Press.

Pagels, E. (1982) *The Gnostic Gospels*, Harmondsworth: Penguin.

Pagels, E. (1988) *Adam, Eve and the Serpent*, London: Vintage Books.

Pagels, E. (1996) *The Origins of Satan*, New York: Vintage Books.

Parekh, Bhikhu (2002) *Rethinking Multiculturalism: Cultural diversity and political theory*, London: Macmillan.

Parker, H. (1985) *Living with Heroin: The impact of a drug epidemic on an English community*, Liverpool: Liverpool University Press.

Pateman, C. (1988) *The Sexual Contract*, Stanford, CA: Stanford University Press.

Peperzak A.T. (ed.) (1995) *Ethics as First Philosophy: The significance of Emanuel Levinas*, London: Routledge.

Peters, E. (1980) *Heresy and Authority in Medieval Europe*, London: Scolar Press.

Phelan, S. (1994) *Getting Specific: Postmodern lesbian politics*, Minneapolis, MN: University of Minnesota Press.

Plant, J. (ed.) (1989) *Healing the Wounds: The promise of ecofeminism*, Philadelphia, PA: New Society Publishers.

Plummer, K. (1995) *Telling Sexual Stories: Power, change and social worlds*, London: Routledge.

Plummer, K. (ed.) (1981) *The Making of the Modern Homosexual*, London: Hutchinson.

Plumwood, V. (1996) *Feminism and the Mastery of Nature*, London: Routledge.

Poliakov, L. (1974) *The Aryan Myth*, London: Sussex University Press.

Poster, M. (1998) *Critical Theory of the Family*, London: Pluto Press.

Pratt, M.L. (1992) *Imperial Eyes*, London: Routledge.

Puwar, N. (2004) *Space Invaders: Race, gender and bodies out of place*, Oxford: Berg.

Puwar, N. and Raghuram, P. (eds) (2003) *South Asian Women in the Diaspora*, Oxford: Berg.

Ramazanoglu, C. (1989) *Feminism and the Contradictions of Oppression*, London: Routledge.

Ramazanoglu, C. (ed.) (1993) *Up Against Foucault*, London: Routledge.
Rex, J. (1996) *Ethnic Minorities in the Modern Nation State*, London: Macmillan.
Ricoeur, P. (1992) *Oneself as Another*, Chicago, IL: Chicago University Press.
Rifkin, J. (1996) *The End of Work*, New York: Putnam.
Rily, D. (1988) *'Am I That Name?' Feminism and the category of 'women' in history*, Minneapolis, MN: University of Minnesota Press.
Robinson, S. (2000) *Marked Men: White masculinity in crisis*, New York: Columbia University Press.
Roper, M. and Tosh, J. (1991) *Manful Assertions: Masculinities in Britain since 1800*, London: Routledge.
Rose, N. (1989) *Governing the Soul: The shaping of the private self*, London: Routledge.
Rowbotham, S. (1972) *Woman's Consciousness, Man's World*, Harmondsworth: Penguin.
Rowbotham, S. (1973) *Hidden from History*, London: Pluto Press.
Rowbotham, S. (1983) *Dreams and Dilemmas*, London: Virago.
Ruddick, S. (1989) *Maternal Thinking: Towards a politics of peace*, London: The Women's Press.
Rutherford, J. (1992) *Men's Silences: Predicaments in masculinity*, London: Routledge.
Rutherford, J. (1999) *I am no Longer Myself Without You: An anatomy of love*, London: Flamingo.
Ruxton S. (ed.) (2004) *Gender Equality and Men: Learning from practice*, Oxford: Oxfam, UK.
Sabo, D. and Gordon, D.F. (eds) *Men's Health and Illness*, Thousand Oaks, CA: Sage.
Samuels, A. (1974) *Jung and the Post-Jungians*, London: Routledge.
Samuels, A. (1993) *The Political Psyche*, London: Routledge.
Sapiro, V. (1992) *A Vindication of Political Virtue*, Chicago, IL: University of Chicago Press.
Sartre, J.-P. (1960) *Anti-Semite and Jew*, New York: Shocken Books.
Sawicki, J. (1991) *Disciplining Foucault: Feminism, power and the body*, New York: Routledge.
Sayers, J. (2003) *Divine Therapy: Love, mysticism and psychoanalysis*, Oxford: Oxford University Press.
Scott, S. and Morgan, D. (eds) *Body Matters*, London: Falmer Press.
Segal, L. (1989) *Is the Future Female?*, London: Virago.
Segal, L. (1990) *Slow Motion: Changing masculinities, changing men*, London: Virago.
Segal, L. (1999) *Why Feminism? Gender, psychology, politics*, Cambridge: Polity Press.
Segal, L. (1999) *Why Feminism?*, Cambridge: Polity Press.
Seidler, V.J.J. (1986) *Kant, Respect and Injustice: The limits of liberal moral theory*, London: Routledge.
Seidler, V.J.J. (1989) *Rediscovering Masculinity: Reason, language and sexuality*, London and New York: Routledge.
Seidler, V.J.J. (1991) *A Truer Liberty: Simone Weil and Marxism*, chs 8 and 9, New York: Routledge.
Seidler, V.J.J. (1991) *Recreating Sexual Politics: Men, feminism and politics*, London and New York: Routledge.

Seidler, V.J.J. (1991) *The Moral Limits of Modernity: Love, inequality and oppression*, Basingstoke: Macmillan.

Seidler, V.J.J. (1994) *Recovering the Self: Morality and social theory*, London and New York: Routledge.

Seidler, V.J.J. (1994) *Unreasonable Men: Masculinity and social theory*, London and New York: Routledge.

Seidler, V.J.J. (1996) 'Fathering, authority and masculinity' in R. Chapman and J. Rutherford (eds), *Male Order: Unwrapping masculinity*, London: Lawrence and Wishart.

Seidler, V.J.J. (2000) *Man Enough: Embodying masculinities*, London: Sage.

Seidler, V.J.J. (2001) *Shadows of the Shoah: Jewish identity and belonging*, Oxford: Berg.

Seidler, V.J.J. (ed.) (1991) *The Achilles Heel Reader: Men, sexual politics and socialism*, London: Routledge.

Seidler, V.J.J. (ed.) (1992) *Men, Sex and Relationships: Writings from Achilles Heel*, London: Routledge.

Seidman, S. (1996) *Contested Knowledge: Social theory in the postmodern era*, Cambridge, MA: Blackwell.

Sennett, R. (1996) *The Uses of Disorder: Personal identity and city life*, London: Faber.

Sennett, R. (1998) *The Corrosion of Character: The personal consequences of work in the new capitalism*, New York: W.W. Norton.

Sennett, R. and Cobb, J. (1972) *The Hidden Injuries of Class*, New York: Vintage Books.

Sharaf, M. (1983) *Fury on Earth: A Biography of Wilhelm Reich*, New York: St Martin's Press.

Shilling, C. (1983) *The Body and Social Theory*, London: Sage.

Shiva, V. (1988) *Staying Alive: Women, ecology and development*, London: Zed Books.

Snodgrass, J. (ed.) (1977) *A Book of Readings for Men Against Sexism*, Albion, CA: Times Change Press.

Spellman, E. (1988) *Inessential Woman: Problems of exclusion in feminist thought*, Boston, MA: Beacon Press.

Squires, J. (1999) *Gender in Political Theory*, Cambridge: Polity Press.

Stanley, L. and Wise, S. (1993) *Breaking Out Again: Feminist ontology and epistemology*, London: Routledge.

Staples, R. (1982) *Black Masculinity: The black man's role in American society*, San Francisco, CA: Black Scholar Press.

Stecopoulos, H. and Uebel, M. (eds) *Race and the Subject of Masculinities*, Durham NC: Duke University Press.

Steinberg, L. Epstein, D. and Johnson, R. (eds) (1997) *Border Patrols: Policing the boundaries of heterosexuality*, London: Cassell.

Stoltenberg, J. (2000) *The End of Manhood: Parables on sex and selfhood*, London: UCL Press.

Straus, M.B. (ed.) (1988) *Abuse and Victimisation Across the Life Span*, Baltimore, MD: Johns Hopkins University Press.

Sweetman, C. (ed.) *Men and Masculinity*, Oxford: Oxfam, UK.

Sydie, R.A. (1987) *Natural Woman, Cultured Men: A feminist perspective on sociological theory*, Milton Keynes: Open University Press.

Taylor, B. (1983) *Eve and New Jerusalem*, London: Virago.

Taylor, B. (2002) *Mary Wollstonecraft and the Feminist Imagination*, Cambridge: Cambridge University Press.

Thewelait, K. (1977) *Male Fantasies*, vol. 1; (1978) vol. 2, Cambridge: Polity Press.

Thomas, L.M. (1993) *Vessels of Evil: American slavery and the Holocaust*, Philadelphia, PA: Temple University Press.

Thorne, B. (1993) *Gender Play: Girls and boys in school*, Buckingham: Open University Press.

Turner, B. (1984) *The Body and Society: Explorations in social theory*, Oxford: Basil Blackwell.

Turner, B. (1992) *Regulating Bodies: Essays in medical sociology*, London: Routledge.

Vance, C. (ed.) (1984) *Pleasure and Danger: Exploring female sexuality*, London: Routledge.

Viveros, M.V. (2001) 'Identidades Masculinas. Diversidades regionales y cambios generacionales,' in M. Viveros, J. Olavarria and N. Fuller (eds), *Hombres e Identidades de Genero, Investigaciones desde América Latina*, Bogota, Columbia: CES, Universidad Nacional de Columbia.

Walby, S. (1990) *Theorizing Patriarchy*, Oxford: Blackwell.

Walkerdine, V. (1990) *Schoolgirl Fictions*, London: Verso.

Walkerdine, V. (1997) *Daddy's Girl: Young girls and popular culture*, Basingstoke: Palgrave.

Wallace, M. (1979) *Black Macho*, London: Calder.

Walter, N. (1998) *The New Feminism*, London: Little Brown.

Wandor, M. (1972) *The Body Politic*, London: Stage 1.

Ware, V. (1992) *Beyond the Pale: White women, racism and history*, London: Verso Books.

Warner, M. (1983) *Alone of All Her Sex,* London: Vintage Books.

Warren, K.J. (ed.) (1994) *Ecological Feminism*, London: Routledge.

Weber, M. (1970), *The Protestant Ethic and the Spirit of Capitalism*, London: Allen and Unwin.

Weeks, J. (1977) *Coming out: Homosexual politics in Britain*, London: Quartet.

Weeks, J. (1989) *Sex, Politics and Society*, Harlow: Longman.

Weeks, J. (1991) *Sexuality and its Discontents: Meanings, myths and modern sexualities*, London: Routledge.

Weeks, J. (1995) *Invented Moralities: Sexual values in an age of uncertainty*, Cambridge: Polity Press.

Weeks, J. (2000) *Making Sexual History*, Cambridge: Polity Press.

Weeks, J. and Porter, K. (eds) (1998) *Between the Acts: Lives of homosexual men 1885–1967*, London: Rivers Oram Press.

Weil, S. (1962) 'Human Personality' in R. Rees (ed.) *Selected Essays 1934–43*, Oxford: Oxford University Press.

Weil, S. (1972) *The Need for Roots*, London: Routledge.

Weininger, O. (1906) *Sex and Character*, London: Heinemann.

Weitz, R. (ed.) (1998) *The Politics of Women's Bodies: Sexuality, appearance and behaviour*, Oxford: Oxford University Press.

Welsh, P. (2001) *Men Aren't from Mars: Unlearning machismo in Nicaragua*, London: CIIR, Catholic Institute of International Relations.

Werbner, P. and Mahood, T. (eds) (1997) *Debating Cultural Hybridity: Multicultural identities and the politics of anti-racism*, London: Zed Books.

West, C. (1993) *Race Matters*, Boston, MA: Beacon Press.

West, C. (1994) *Breaking Bread*, New York: Vintage.

Whitehead, S.M. (2004) *Men and Masculinities*, Cambridge: Polity Press.

Whitford, M. (1991) *Luce Irigaray: Philosophy in the feminine*, London: Routledge.

Wild, J. (1999) *Working with Men for Change*, London: UCL Press.

Williams, B. (1985) *Ethics and the Limits of Philosophy*, London: Fontana.

Williams, J. (2000) *Unbending Gender: Why family and work conflict and what to do about it*, Oxford: Oxford University Press.

Willis, P. (1977) *Learning to Labour*, Aldershot: Gower.

Wilson, A. (1976) *Finding a Voice: Asian women in Britain*, London: Virago Press.

Winch, P. (1989) *A Just Balance: Reflections on the philosophy of Simone Weil*, Cambridge: Cambridge University Press.

Winnicott, D.W. (1958) *Through Paediatrics to Psychoanalysis*, New York: International Universities Press.

Winnicott, D.W. (1974) *Playing and Reality*, Harmondsworth: Penguin.

Wittgenstein, L. (1958) *Philosophical Investigations*, Oxford: Blackwell.

Wittgenstein, L. (1980) *Culture and Value*, Oxford: Blackwell.

Wollstonecraft, M. (1970) *A Vindication of the Rights of Women*, London: Dent.

Woodward, K. (ed.) (1997) *Identity and Difference*, London: Sage.

Young, I.M. (1990) *Justice and the Politics of Difference*, Princeton, NJ: Princeton University Press.

Young, I.M. (1990) *Throwing Like a Girl and Other Essays in Feminist Philosophy and Social Theory*, Bloomington, IN: Indiana University Press.

Young, R. (1990) *White Mythologies*, London: Routledge.

Index

Lightning Source UK Ltd.
Milton Keynes UK
24 February 2010

150557UK00003B/22/P